CHINA'S STOCKMARKET

OTHER ECONOMIST BOOKS

Guide to Analysing Companies
Guide to Business Modelling
Guide to Economic Indicators
Guide to the European Union
Guide to Financial Markets
Guide to Management Ideas
Numbers Guide
Style Guide

Business Ethics
Economics
E-Commerce
E-Trends
Globalisation
Measuring Business Performance
Successful Innovation
Successful Mergers
Wall Street

Dictionary of Business
Dictionary of Economics
International Dictionary of Finance

Essential Director
Essential Finance
Essential Internet
Essential Investment

Pocket Asia
Pocket Europe in Figures
Pocket World in Figures

CHINA'S STOCKMARKET

A Guide to its Progress, Players and Prospects

Stephen Green

To my family and friends

THE ECONOMIST IN ASSOCIATION WITH
PROFILE BOOKS LTD

Published by Profile Books Ltd
58A Hatton Garden, London EC1N 8LX

Typeset in EcoType by MacGuru
info@macguru.org.uk

Printed in Great Britain by
St Edmundsbury Press, Bury St Edmunds

A CIP catalogue record for this book is available
from the British Library

ISBN 1 86197 665 8

Contents

List of figures

List of tables

Acknowledgements

To build a stockmarket worth over $200bn in the space of some 12 years is a remarkable achievement. It has been a privilege during the course of my research to meet some of the people involved. Their experience and expertise has shaped my understanding of the development of the market's institutions and problems. My hope is that this book reflects both the good and bad aspects of development so far.

This book relies heavily on research done during my extended stays in Shanghai, Beijing, Shenzhen and Hong Kong during 1999–2001 for my PhD thesis. Subsequent trips to Shenzhen in July 2001 and to Shanghai and Beijing in July and August 2002 were crucial in bringing the story up-to-date. I am particularly grateful to the management of the Shenzhen Stock Exchange for their generous welcome and help in collecting materials, as well as to staff at the Shanghai exchange and China Securities Regulatory Commission for their help. The Economic and Social Research Council generously supported my PhD research (Award no. R00429824432).

Other sections grew out of work I have done over the past couple of years for *Business China*, a magazine published by the Economist Intelligence Unit. I am indebted to its former and current editors, Laura Burt and Margaret Dooley, for allowing me the freedom to report on most of the things that sparked my interest, and for allowing me to use parts of that research in this book. A paper I wrote as a background briefing for the Organisation of Economic Co-operation and Development and which was subsequently largely absorbed into their *China in the World Economy* report, as well as pieces I have written for *CFO China*, China Online and Oxford Analytica were useful in developing ideas and funding the research. Among the many English and Chinese sources from which I have benefited *Caijing* (Finance and Economics) magazine deserves special mention. Many of the stories of corruption related here could not have been told without the investigations of its journalists; they, like many of the young professionals I met at the stock exchanges and China Securities Regulatory Commission, are the market's brightest hope.

Writing about any aspect of China's rapidly evolving economy is a huge challenge: statistical sources, if they exist, rarely agree; much that is true is reported via rumour and over dinner; and much that is untrue finds its way into official media sources. That said, the researcher faces far fewer problems than he or she would have done, say, ten years ago, and if there is one thing that people in China generally do love talking about, it is the stock market. I have interviewed over sixty Chinese officials and those working in the industry, read widely, in both Chinese and English (and a few of the sources are listed in the selected bibliography) and tried as far as possible to cross-check information. Despite all this, there will inevitably be some inaccuracies, for which I apologise. I am enormously grateful to all those who chatted with me, allowed me into their libraries and pointed out where I was being, by turns, too cynical and hopelessly naïve. Some of them did so on the basis of anonymity. Among those I can name, I would like to express my thanks for benefit of the experience, expertise, and help of Pieter Bottelier, Nick Bridge, Tom Canalakiss, Chen Jian, Chen Yixin, Charles Cheung, Tim Clissold, Dai Wenhua, Kenneth DeWoskin, Jane Duckett, Peter Ferdinand, Dudley Fishburn, Gao Peiji, Ge Jun, Brian Goldstein, Guo Yan, Ken Ho, Christopher Howe, Hu Ruyin, Jiang Jiang, Jin Xiaobin, Tom Kass, Li Dapeng, Lin Chun, Andrew Lin, Min Yoo, Nathan Midler, Tom Mitchell, Anthony Neoh, Jaime Andreas Nino, Qu Qiang, Ren Jin, Andy Rothman, Stuart Schonberger, Sandy Sha, Situ Danian, Dan Slater, Hoi-yin Siu, Tu Guangshao, Xia Youli, Carl Walter, Anthony Wu, Wu Xiaoping, Steven Xiong, Yuan Guoliang, Zhang Jun, Zhang Xin, Zhao Xijun, Zhou Xiao, Zhou Xingguo, James Zhan and Dominic Ziegler. Thanks to David Wall for his long-standing interest in and support of my research; to Martin Liu and Stephen Brough at Profile Books for their faith in the project; and to Penny Williams for her sharp-eyed editing of the text. This book is dedicated to them, my family and those other friends without whose support it would not have been possible. Thanks. I alone am responsible for the views expressed here.

I am now happily employed at the Royal Institute of International Affairs in London. E-mail me at sgreen@riia.org or visit the website, www.riia.org/asia, to find out how the research is going.

Stephen Green
March 2003

As for securities and the stockmarket, are they finally good or bad?
Are they dangerous? Are they things that only capitalism has or
can socialism also make use of them? To decide whether they can
be used we must experiment first.
Deng Xiaoping, 1992

The stock exchange serves the construction of a socialist economy.
Li Peng, Shanghai, 1991

China's stockmarket is worse than a casino.
At least in a casino there are rules.
Wu Jinglian, 2001

GENERAL NOTES

Exchange rate
Since 1994: Remnibi (Rmb) 8.3 = US$1

Data
– means no data

Accounting year
People's Republic of China (PRC) January–December
Hong Kong Special Administrative Region (HKSAR) No formal accounting
year. Companies can choose their year-end. Most opt for either December
(in line with the Mainland) or March (in line with their parent companies).
Taiwan January–December

Abbreviations
This book uses many abbreviations. A list is given on page 217.

Preface

Few other aspects of reform in China fascinate more than the stockmarket. Since the first haphazard trading in shares took place in Shanghai and Shenyang in 1986, when prices were marked up in chalk on blackboards, the market has grown unrecognisably. Its story has all the makings of a dynastic epic. The market has been at the centre of huge, era-defining policy battles between economic reformers pushing for capitalism and conservatives wanting to preserve socialist controls. As well as the ideological clashes, other disputes erupted in the 1990s as the stockmarket, with its tremendous capacity for generating funds, attracted the envious attention of officials from dozens of government departments. Bureaucrats from local government, the central bank, the industrial planning apparatus and the securities regulator fought continuous turf wars for the authority to regulate the market. In the market itself, hundreds of fortunes have been made, some legally, and many thousands of small investors have had their savings wiped out by ill-judged efforts at "stir-frying" shares (*chao gupiao*). Regular scandals, several of which have fundamentally shaken the market, have torn back the veil that normally hides the extensive corruption.

For those with an eye on the future, the capital market is one of the most exciting ways in which China can reintegrate with the modern world. This is a world where international portfolio capital flows easily in and out of stocks from Australia to Zambia, where governments are withdrawing from ownership on a scale unprecedented in history and where banks are being disintermediated as firms find their investors directly through the capital market. Hong Kong, which returned to mainland control in 1997, provides an enviable example of how best to integrate into the global economy. For those with an eye on history, reform China's stockmarket represents a return to Shanghai's pre-revolutionary days when the city's exchange was the largest in Asia. By all accounts, it was then a byword for speculative excess and foreign exploitation. So far, at least, only the former has returned.

And herein lies, of course, the paradox that most puzzles observers of China's experiment with equities. The old stockmarket was the apotheosis of the speculative capitalism that Mao Zedong vowed to destroy. Indeed, it was on his personal orders that the old Shanghai exchange was closed by the Red Army on June 10th 1949. But it was on the orders of his successor, Deng Xiaoping, that it opened again on December 19th 1990. A stockmarket seems, at least on the surface, to be completely at odds with market socialism, the present government's template for an economy where the state remains the dominant owner of industrial assets, retains strategic control of the economy and attempts to enforce some semblance of socialist equality. It is this paradox – a stockmarket, that most capitalist of institutions – being nurtured in a country run by a communist party, that most fascinates observers.

This guide to China's stockmarket attempts to explain that paradox. It deals with all its institutions, players and policy issues, as well as its likely trajectory in the future.

After an intoductory chapter, the book breaks down as follows:

- Chapter 2 presents a history of the market, from the first share issues in the mid-1980s to the development of on-line trading in recent years. It describes the major institutions, many of which, like the shareholding company structure and non-tradable shares, are particular to China, as well as the political struggles that have taken place over the market's policies and institutions. Comparisons are made with other markets round the world to provide perspective on the Chinese experience. Finally, the nascent Treasury and corporate bond markets are introduced and continuing reforms in this area are examined.
- Chapter 3 tackles the B- and H-share markets that have allowed foreigners access to People's Republic of China (PRC) equities, the former in China, the latter overseas. It explains why the B-share market has failed, the ups and downs of investors' love-hate relationship with H-shares, and why other forms of equity, including private companies' – the so-called p-chips – are becoming more popular. The final part of the chapter considers the government's strategy for domestic and overseas issuance.
- Chapter 4's focus is on the investors, both individual and institutional. Media accounts commonly portray this share market as being dominated by the former. This chapter explains why this view is mistaken. After looking at the trading habits of small investors, it turns to examine in detail the businesses of securities companies, investment funds and other institutional investors, many of which are not formally recognised. It assesses the vulnerability of securities companies to market falls, the impact investment funds have had on volatility and the

importance that *simu jijin* (privately-raised funds) have for the market.

◪ Chapter 5 turns to the listed companies and points to the extensive problems caused by continued government ownership. It examines their performance, their rights issue and dividend policies, and problems such as administrative interference, false disclosures and asset-stripping. The chapter concludes by discussing the gradual privatisation of listed state-owned enterprises (SOEs) via off-market M&A deals, and the sale of state-owned shares as the only means by which corporate governance, and thus profitability, can be improved.

◪ Chapter 6 introduces the regulatory framework and explains how it has developed since 1984. Particular attention is paid to the initial dominance of local governments in regulation and the rise of the China Securities Regulatory Commission (CSRC), the central government's regulatory bureau, since its foundation in 1992. Reviews of current primary- and secondary-market regulation follow, as well as a discussion of why implementation of the rules has been poor.

◪ Chapter 7 considers the future, and outlines likely developments. The most important challenge is to create a market in property rights, something that will not be realisable within five years but towards which progress can be made given a willingness to engage in institutional reform. Three new priorities in economic policy – privatisation, resolving the government's debt problem and pension reform – will help. Each will increase the incentives for the government to improve both regulation and the quality of companies that are listed. The chapter also reviews recent improvements involving the activities of the CSRC, the media, the courts and parliament, as well as moves to make boards of directors more independent, to increase the severity of punishments for crimes and to improve the delisting mechanism. Finally, the matter of reducing the government's stake in listed companies is considered, and, following an examination of two previous attempts at selling off state shares, some suggestions are made about the future direction of policy.

◪ Chapter 8 looks at the prospects for foreign investors. There are opportunities and dangers, many in unexpected places, involving such things as equity purchases through the Qualified Foreign Institutional Investor scheme and direct purchases of B-shares.

The impact of China's accession to the World Trade Organisation on the sector is seen as limited, but that does not limit the possibilities of further liberalisation. Indeed, as economic reform progresses, the imperative will be for China to join the rest of the world in terms of both trade and finance. There is an internal logic to opening up this sector.

1 Introduction

In August 1986 the mayor of Shanghai, Jiang Zemin, called a meeting on industrial reform that was to change the face of China's economy. At the meeting, two managers who worked at a local branch of the Industrial and Commercial Bank of China, Huang Guixian and Hu Ruiquan, proposed setting up an over-the-counter (OTC) market for company shares. Already by this time around 20 companies wholly or partly owned by the government in the cities of Shanghai and Shenzhen, as well as Sichuan province and Shenyang in Liaoning province, had structured themselves into companies limited by shares. Motivated by the extra capital that could be raised through such a restructuring, they chose to issue shares, mostly to their own employees. However, the employees had nowhere to sell the shares and so were reluctant to buy them (or more often, accept them in lieu of wages). Kerb markets on the streets outside these factories sprang up. Being somewhat entrepreneurial in nature, Hu bravely argued that "the life of shares is in their trading": only by allowing people to buy and sell their shares legitimately, he claimed, would enough demand be created for equity. Only then could China make a success of corporate restructuring. Impressed, Mayor Jiang gave his personal assent and an OTC market for shares was opened on September 26th 1986 at a Jing'an branch of the Industrial and Commercial Bank of China at 1,806 West Nanjing Road. Along with a similar OTC in Shenyang in Liaoning province, China's current stockmarket was born.

Less than 20 years later, China has what is undoubtedly the developing world's most important stockmarket. Since the establishment of the two stock exchanges in Shanghai and Shenzhen in December 1990, the market has evolved rapidly to assume an important role in the national economy. By December 2002 the two exchanges together listed 1,224 firms, and boasted a tradable capitalisation of some Rmb1.25trn ($150bn), about 12% of China's gross domestic product (GDP). The market had become an important source of financing for SOEs and an important contributor to the state's fiscal revenues. In 2000, a bumper year, companies raised an enormous Rmb152.7bn through all types of A-share issues, some 1.7% of China's GDP. In comparison, companies listing on the New York Stock Exchange (NYSE) and NASDAQ during 2000 raised Rmb930bn, around 1% of America's GDP. The stamp tax on share trading brought Rmb48.6bn into China's state coffers in 2000, some 3.6% of the government's total financial revenues that year. As the stockmarket grew in size during the 1990s, ideological opposition weakened. After much debate within the Chinese Communist Party (CCP) the market was recognised in 1997 "as an important component of the national economy" at its 15th Congress. According to Jiang Zemin, general secretary of the CCP between 1989 and 2002, it has since become "an essential part of socialist market economy". Already Asia's third largest, China's stockmarket is on course to overtake Hong Kong's before the end of the 1990s, even despite its poor performance during 2001–2.

Economic reform in China

In the late 1970s, with the return to power of Deng Xiaoping, China turned away from Communism and set its face towards the market. The country has changed unrecognisably since. "Reform China" has witnessed the rapid emergence of private business, the withering of state-owned industry, huge inflows of foreign investment and radical reductions on tariffs on imports. According to official statistics, the national economy has grown above 7% in every year since – and the economy of the coastal area has grown even quicker. The average income per head is now above $1,000 (at current exchange rates) nationwide, above $3,000 in many of the richer coastal urban centres (including Shanghai), and well above $5,000 in the southern cities of Shenzhen and Guangzhou. If present trends continue, China will become the largest manufacturing country in terms of gross output by 2012, and will have an economy worth some $5trn (again, at market exchange rates) by 2025.

Changes in the rules governing farming provided the foundation for economic growth. By quietly dismantling the commune system, allowing farmers to lease their land for extended periods and sell their produce in local towns, the government engineered a rapid rise in agricultural output in the early 1980s. Farming households accumulated funds to invest in small-scale industry and buy the consumer goods that these new factories produced. Local governments, suddenly able to keep a portion of the tax revenues they levied on business (instead of giving it all up to Beijing), became interested in investing in and generally supporting these new firms. Tens of thousands of government and party officials jumped into business, rejecting Maoist dogmas even if they still espoused them in public. According to official statistics, over 2m private firms have been established – the real number is certainly higher.

Of course, the one area of life where competition was still banned was in politics. Deng introduced the concept of the "socialist market economy" to explain his vision for the future. This was an economy in which private property and prices had important roles to play, but it was also an economy that would grow within the bounds of a one-party state – at least for as long as the Communist Party could hold together the contradictions evinced by freer markets and an undemocratic political system. Perhaps no other new institution better represents these contradictions than the stockmarket.

Why is a stockmarket important?

A stockmarket can benefit the economy of a developing country in a number of ways. As long as prices fairly accurately reflect supply and demand, it can help improve the efficiency with which capital is allocated. Companies that offer exciting growth prospects will be able to raise equity capital, forcing banks to compete to supply the same financing. The public issuance of shares can provide precious investment resources for enterprises that do not have enough retained earnings or which are unable, or unwilling, to go to the banks. In addition to acting as a source of finance, the stockmarket also offers firms the opportunity of varying the costs and risks of their financing structures, potentially insulating them from higher interest rates and a credit crunch. Finally, the market can also play a role in facilitating long-term asset management. As governments round the world withdraw from providing welfare, individuals must increasingly rely upon private insurance and pension funds to manage their own health and retirement needs over the long term. A stockmarket is one crucial way for such assets to be effectively managed.

However, a stockmarket does not automatically provide any of these benefits. For a developing economy, or for one undergoing transition from a socialist plan, an efficient banking system is a far greater priority to get right than a stockmarket. This is because the latter relies on an elaborate array of institutions for its benefits to be realised. These institutions, such as a free press, an efficient and independent legal system, lawyers and accountants, professional underwriters and a group of mature institutional investors are difficult to establish at an early stage of economic development. In such circumstances, banks are better equipped at valuing businesses and monitoring their use of capital.

Without an investigative press and in the absence of adequate (and enforced) laws, companies will cheat and lie. Because of the lack of

3

reliable corporate disclosures, trading in immature stockmarkets often takes place on the basis of rumour. If, in addition, a government lacks the ability, or the will, to create or enforce laws that protect small investors, then insider dealing and price manipulation is likely to be common. And when everyone is speculating and playing for short-term gains a stockmarket has little economic benefit. It does not channel capital towards good-quality firms or productive investments; it does not discipline managers; it wastes people's time. If public funds are involved too, then it can have damaging consequences for the government's finances. In short, a stockmarket can have a deleterious impact on a country's economy and its corporate development. No less an economist than John Maynard Keynes compared it with a casino (after a short and successful career as a trader himself). A number of economists in China have echoed his comments when talking about their own market. But very few have asked the basic question of whether China actually needed a stockmarket at such an early stage of development.

China's stockmarket

At a press conference at the end of the plenary session of the National People's Congress (NPC) in spring 2000, Premier Zhu Rongji remarked that China's stockmarket had developed quickly, achieved much, but was still not well-ordered (*bu guifan*). Zhu, a man long suspicious about the benefits of the market he helped create, was using a much-used euphemism to refer to the rampant speculation, poor-quality listed firms, defective regulation and widespread corruption that characterised the market. Some of these problems can be explained by things that many developing countries suffer from: limited government capacity, a lack of regulatory expertise and weak rule of law. Others, however, can be traced back to something that is very particular to China's experience: the political logic that has shaped the market's development.

In the West, when share prices rise, it is a bull market; when it falls, the market is a bear. China, so the joke goes, does not have bulls and bears: rather, it has pig markets. Throughout the 1990s, Zhu is widely believed to have used editorials in the *People's Daily*, an official newspaper, to sing the praises of share investment or to condemn rampant speculation. These comments would set the market's course for months. In December 1996, for example, an editorial compared the market with that of the United States on the eve of the October 1929 crash. Unsurprisingly investors panicked and prices collapsed. The joke is that Zhu's surname is a homonym for the Chinese word for "pig". The government's intervention is, however, far more widespread and serious than the occasional op-ed. The market has been used to support the loss-making SOE sector on a huge scale, to raise fiscal revenues and even, in May 1999, as part of a government attempt to reflate the economy by encouraging consumers to spend more. Public ownership of almost every entity involved in the market allows the government and the CCP plenty of mechanisms of indirect influence and direct interference. The vast majority of firms that are listed are state-owned. The firms that broke, trade and underwrite shares, and the ones that manage the 50-plus formal investment funds, are state-owned. Huge amounts of public money are invested in stocks, and even the two stock exchanges and industry association are directly administered by the CSRC, the government regulator. While this is hardly surprising given the current political system, it largely prevents the stockmarket providing the positive benefits that it could and should provide.

While the market represents, in many important ways, the resurgence of capitalism in China, it is a compromised form of capitalism in which prices and private property, the basic principles of the capitalist system, are not yet properly established. It currently operates more or less as an appendage of the state, and it now needs to escape. Many reformers working within the CSRC are acutely aware of the need for institutional reform rather than simply increasing the size of the market and the number of instruments traded there. They understand that successful development depends on the stockmarket becoming a viable market in ownership rights.

Ownership implies three things: that the owner has the de facto rights to control the asset, to transfer it and to profit from it. In other words, an owner of a listed firm has a say in its running, usually through appointing the board of directors (control); he has the ability to sell his ownership stake, that is, his shares (transfer) and the right to receive a share of any money the firm might make (profit) in the form of a dividend. However, these rights do not yet properly exist in China. Minority shareholders are ignored at shareholders' meetings, and frequently abused outside them. Company disclosures are so unreliable as to make real supervision of corporate activities impossible. In terms of the transfer of ownership, there are also important limits: individuals face huge obstacles in gaining influence over listed firms, state shareholders do not yet have the right to sell their shareholdings and changes of ownership are usually negotiated through, and approved by, government bodies.

Few dividends are paid and company funds are often siphoned off by majority shareholders. Because of these deficiencies, no true market in corporate ownership yet exists.

Major institutional change is required. Ultimately, this means creating a market in which public and private firms compete on a level playing field, it means regulation that is carried out independently of government and of the CCP, and it probably also means that most of the players in the market are privatised. Adding new instruments and increasing trading volume may impress on a superficial level, but unless fundamental reforms, affecting the clarity and enforceability of property rights, are undertaken, China's stockmarket will remain an inefficient distributor of capital and a corrupt place to trade. Foreign investors will participate on a significant scale only when they are assured that their rights as owners of corporate assets are guaranteed, that they can rely on corporate disclosures and accounts, and that their rights as minority owners are respected. China's small investors would also benefit enormously from such moves and would then commit more capital to the market. Severing the ties that bind the market to the state has to be the main thrust of policy over the next decade if it is to mature. What remains to be seen is how far China's political elite will allow such reforms to go.

Opening up to the world

One huge step forward was taken in December 2001 when China joined the World Trade Organisation (WTO). After years of hesitation and false promise, China's leadership appears committed to applying the *gaige kaifang* (reform and opening up) policy to the capital market. Foreign financial institutions are now permitted, subject to approval by the CSRC, to take minority stakes in joint-venture fund management firms (JVFMFs) and joint-venture securities firms (JVSFs). The demand for JVFMFs has been significant, and some 20 agreements between prospective partners had been signed by June 2002. A handful of prospective agreements for JVSFs had also been signed.

However, this opening-up will be gradual. The currency, the renminbi, remains unconvertible on the capital account and cannot be exchanged freely for buying financial instruments; it can only be exchanged for trade-related transactions. Foreign investment in domestic-currency A-shares has not been permitted and no foreign companies have yet been allowed to do securities business on their own in China. But this will change. And it will change not because of WTO membership, but because a growing number of the policy elite realises that their country would benefit from such a liberalisation. In late 2001 the former chairman of the CSRC, Zhou Xiaochuan, promised that China would "increase the speed at which it is opening its capital markets to the outside world. It will not only do so to comply with its WTO commitments," he continued, "but because this is a necessary requirement of the domestic economy."

Indeed, allowing foreign institutions into China's capital markets would be beneficial in a number of ways. Their participation in the A-share market would increase the capital available to domestic issuers, as well as introduce international expertise and experience into the market. Foreign firms in the financial market would transfer the technology required to manage more complex financial instruments, such as index futures and open-ended mutual funds, as well as other skills, such as portfolio management. Many of these transfers are already taking place. JP Morgan Fleming Asset Management, a subsidiary of JP Morgan Chase, has been training staff at Hua'an Fund Management since 1999 and the two have agreed to set up a JVFMF. Morgan Stanley was responsible for providing the training that helped make China International Capital Corporation (CICC) China's leading securities house. Another advantage of allowing foreign firms greater access to the stockmarket is that the expertise and capital resources of the international investment banks would greatly improve the chances of Chinese companies waiting to expand abroad and build world-class businesses achieving their ambitions. And allowing the subsidiaries of foreign corporations to list in Shanghai would provide new standards of governance in the market.

Careful liberalisation would undoubtedly deepen and improve the efficiency of China's stockmarket, although there are risks involved too, notably those involving the currency. Allowing unrestricted international investment in shares would necessitate opening up China's capital account and making the renminbi freely exchangeable. This, say some, would make share prices, listed companies and the renminbi itself vulnerable to the whims of a small number of fund managers based in New York, London and Hong Kong. There is something to this argument. The Asian financial crisis of 1997–98 had many causes, but one of the most immediate was that investors sold shares and then converted out of the domestic currency into the safety of American dollars. Most of these investors were domestic, rather than foreign, though it was politically convenient for foreigners and fund managers to be blamed. Although an economy can sometimes absorb sudden and large falls in share prices without too much economic turmoil, a sudden sharp fall in the exchange rate can have more dangerous repercussions. In order to avoid this, the leadership is likely to keep China's capital controls firmly in place for the foreseeable future.

Even so there will still be opportunities for foreign firms. A number of investment banks are already dealing with small portions of bad bank loans; Morgan Stanley and Goldman Sachs are leading the restructuring – and listing abroad – of major Chinese SOEs; a large number of firms are currently setting up JVFMFs and are hoping to manage China's new pension pool. In November 2002 the CSRC announced that it would follow Taiwan's lead and allow foreign institutions to invest directly in A-shares via a qualified foreign institutional investor framework. It appears likely that the acquisition of majority stakes in listed companies by foreign investors will soon be possible and it is also possible that a number of foreign subsidiaries operating in China, such as those of Unilever, HSBC, Kodak and Michelin, will be allowed to list on the Shanghai Stock Exchange (SHGSE). The opportunities over the medium term are certainly not boundless, but they are significant. The rest of this book is an attempt to identify and evaluate these opportunities, as well as the many dangers, that reside in China's stockmarket.

2 A brief history of China's stockmarket

Informal markets in company stocks first appeared in Shanghai, Shenzhen, Chengdu and several other cities in the early 1980s. As part of their experiments in turning their companies into shareholding firms, a number of urban enterprises issued securities to the public, employees and corporate friends. These securities were usually debentures: capital was returned at a set date and a mixture of interest and dividend payments were made. Ownership did not change hands. The early issuers were most often collective firms owned by a small group of people, usually including a local government organ. At the time, SOE managers still had access to bank credit and were unwilling to experiment with such a radical thing as equity. In contrast, collective firms found securing bank loans much harder and, since they were run on a profit basis, some of their managers were prepared to run risks when raising investment. In January 1985, Shanghai Yanzhong Industrial made the first public offering of standardised equity in reform China. Feile Acoustics had issued shares a few days earlier, but all of them were placed with corporate investors. Black markets in these securities, as well as in Treasury and local government bonds, soon developed in cities across the country. Small OTC markets were established in Shanghai and Shenyang in late 1986, but they did little to restrain speculation or to contain kerb trading.

The shareholding reforms, 1984–89

Jiang Zemin, then mayor of Shanghai, supported the OTC set up by the Industrial and Commercial Bank of China. On the national level, the shareholding reforms were strongly supported by officials within the State Commission for Restructuring the Economic Structure (SCORES), the think-tank of Zhao Ziyang, China's premier between 1980 and 1987 and then party general secretary until 1989. Zhao himself was also a keen supporter of the experiment. Liu Hongru, the first head of the CSRC in 1992, was a deputy minister at the SCORES in the mid- and late 1980s and also pushed hard for shareholding reform as a means of raising finance and improving corporate governance in SOEs. Young policy turks at the People's Bank of China (PBOC) went one step further and supported the creation of a share market, although a market in which only institutions, mostly SOEs, could trade. Even in the mid-1980s, few envisioned a share market open to the masses.

Previous efforts to instil more efficiency into the SOEs had largely failed. In the early 1980s the government had tried profit retention schemes, which allowed firms to retain a small proportion of their earnings. This increased overall investment, but distortions created by price controls and the fact that firms did not pay interest on borrowed capital meant that there were limited efficiency gains. In the mid-1980s, reformers attempted to expand the autonomy of firm managers and rolled out the contract responsibility system (CRS). Hiring and firing authority, as well as a slew of other powers, were devolved down to enterprise managers, and a level of tax remittance to the government was determined. Because firms could retain funds earned above this tax quota, an incentive to engage in profit-making activities was created. However, under the CRS prices for resources and products were still fixed and funds from the budget and banks were still free – there were no interest charges on borrowings, so in effect they did not have to be repaid. And so managers did not have to worry about the cost of capital or the threat of bankruptcy. The limits of the CRS were soon recognised. By the third plenum of the 14th Congress in 1993, the party had decided to go one step further: a modern enterprise system, with shareholding reforms at its heart, was announced as the new strategy. Government-owned enterprises were to be restructured into modern corporations with boards of directors and shareholders. They were to be given full legal and financial autonomy, even if ownership remained in government hands via majority shareholdings, and they were to be forced to borrow capital from banks rather than free ride on state funds.

Much ideological brow-beating went into justifying this new thinking. Party theoreticians crafted sophisticated arguments aimed at showing that shareholding did not represent a break with socialism but was simply a means of improving economic efficiency while retaining socialist principles. In April 1990, an economist, Huang Shao'an, explained the new orthodoxy in a leading journal, *Economic Research*. Privatisation, Huang asserted, was not workable in China since, as every good Marxist knows, public ownership was "the key to productive forces". Public ownership is good: the only problem with the planned economy, Huang claimed, was that the state interferes in company management too much. What needs to happen, he argued, is for SOEs to be run independently of the government. A modern corporation, limited by shares, Huang argued, fitted the bill while "not negating the original nature of ownership". This was revolutionary stuff: it presaged a countrywide conversion to shareholding and opened the door to the prospect of real privatisation to begin in the early 2000s.

Local political support for this new agenda was strong: officials at provincial and city levels were the chief beneficiaries since SOEs that raised funds through shares would rely less on local government for funds. In addition, the hope was that with these new funds firms could expand their operations, increase revenues, pay more tax and out of profits pay dividends to their local government shareholders. During 1986–88 the pent-up demand among firms for investment, the ease with which securities could be issued and the fact that local governments were supportive, led to shares being issued by thousands of SOEs across the country. Informal markets sprang up in many places. Centres set up for trading Treasury bonds earlier in the decade often provided convenient facilities for trading in shares. In Beijing, however, officials worried about their loss of control and the inflation such investment was unleashing, and attempted to crack down on both share issuance and trading. During 1988–89 it attempted to curb the credit explosion by warning local PBOC directors of the dangers of authorising loans in excess of their loan "quota", by drawing non-bank financial institutions such as the trust and investment companies (TICs) set up by local government into the national credit plan, thus limiting their autonomy in credit issuance, and it also instructed local governments to consult the PBOC in Beijing before authorising any share issuance.

Setting up the stock exchanges, 1989–90

Given the official backlash against share reforms, it was no surprise that by the time of the Tiananmen Square protests in May and June 1989 only nine companies had been listed on the OTCs in Shanghai and Shenzhen. But these OTCs were inconvenient to use, deeply corrupt and difficult for local authorities to regulate. Black markets in shares continued to flourish. It was clear that stock exchanges, with their central registration of stocks and competitive pricing systems, were required if the market was to grow. But what hope was there of movement on such a radical agenda in the aftermath of the massacre of several hundred civilians on the streets of Beijing in June 1989, the resurgence of conservative politics in Beijing and a re-emphasis on planning controls for the economy? In such an atmosphere, one would have expected proposals to establish stock exchanges to have been put on hold, and perhaps even "rectification" (that is, closure) of the whole market. The fact that the opposite occurred is due to a few members of the Beijing elite, a group of senior officials in Shanghai and Shenzhen and Deng Xiaoping.

In Beijing a group of reformists working at the SCORES, MOF, PBOC and the TICS had been preparing plans for a stock exchange since September 1988. Gao Xiqing (later to become CSRC deputy chairman) and a number of others who had recently returned from Wall Street, as well as some Beijing-based bureaucrats, including Zhou Xiaochuan (then at the SCORES), prepared a report for the party's Finance and Economics Leading Group, the top authority on economic issues. In November 1988 its representatives heard the report and Yao Yilin, a senior neo-conservative leader, provisionally authorised setting up a stock exchange. In Shanghai Zhu Rongji, then party secretary and mayor of Shanghai, having realised the potential of the OTC, saw that the stock exchange would be useful in his attempts to develop Pudong, Shanghai's new investment zone in the east of the city.

Zhu put the idea to Deng shortly after the Tiananmen Square events and the paramount leader offered his support: the stockmarket was a useful symbol of Deng's own reform agenda, and, at this delicate stage in China's transition, Deng did not wish to give in completely to the hard-liners. Early in 1990 the official press began talking up the share market's future and when Chen Yun, another senior conservative, visited Shanghai in mid-1990, Zhu inserted the exchange proposal in the Pudong brief and the whole package received Chen's authorisation. The story in Shenzhen was rather different. Instead of carefully nurturing support in Beijing, Shenzhen's leaders ignored the capital and went ahead with opening their stockmarket when nothing was heard concerning their application to the PBOC in Beijing. The Shanghai and Shenzhen exchanges both began operations in December 1990. Shenzhen started a few days earlier, although it was only four months later that the PBOC gave it grudging approval. This is the basis of both exchanges claiming to be reform China's first stock exchange.

Stockmarket fever, 1992–93

After all this excitement, few companies actually issued shares in 1991, share prices moved little and the public remained largely suspicious of this new commodity known as *gupiao* (shares). Neither did Premier Li Peng's visit to the SHGSE in November 1991 provoke much excitement. After asking if the brokers there worked for SOEs, and receiving a satisfactory reply, Li wrote an inscription to commemorate his visit: "The stock exchange serves socialist economic construction." While this was perhaps not the most obvious use of the stockmarket, the statement was curiously prescient of how the market was to be used for much of the next decade.

But despite receiving this stamp of approval from a senior conservative (admittedly one who needed to stay on the right side of Deng), an intense struggle over the direction of economic reform and the role of shares in it was still being fought in Beijing. Investors knew better than to invest without clearer signals from the leadership about the market's future.

That signal came in January 1992. Deng, while supposedly on holiday in the south of China, made a series of high-profile calls for rapid economic growth, increased investment and experiments with shares. "What about our stockmarket?" he asked. "Is it socialist or capitalist? To decide, we must experiment first. If the experiment is a success, it can be popularised. If problems arise, we can close it." Deng's modest words had enormous implications. As news of his call to reform leaked out – and conservative newspapers in Beijing tried their best to restrict coverage – people ran to buy shares. Stockmarket fever (*gupiao re*) broke out and thousands discovered that fortunes could be made (and lost) through share trading. In June 1992 the *People's Daily* noted that the Shenzhen Stock Exchange (SHZSE) had become a major tourist attraction.

The sudden exuberance caught the regulatory authorities by surprise. The problem was not so much the rapid price rises at the two exchanges, although this did cause concern. Rather, Deng's call triggered another round of mass issuance of shares throughout the country and by late 1992 this was throwing the macro economy out of balance again. Officially, all applications for share issuance had to be authorised by the central headquarters of the PBOC. Local leaders, however, were eager to maximise their investment funds and instructed local PBOC staff to authorise share issuance themselves. The result was that companies issued as many shares as they wanted. There are various, mostly contradictory, statistics about the scale of the problem. One source claims that 865 enterprises in 34 cities and provinces issued shares worth Rmb27.7bn ($12.0bn) during 1992. Simultaneously, bank lending also increased rapidly, again sponsored by local leaders anxious to reap quick returns in the wake of Deng's call to reform. In Beijing the economists at the PBOC watched the sudden increase in money supply with alarm as the national credit plan was thrown into chaos. Inflation, they knew, was not far behind. Party leaders also worried that the share experiment would quickly lead to the mass privatisation of Chinese industry. In August 1992, however, their attention turned to a far more pressing problem.

The 8.10 riot, August 1992
The Shenzhen government badly mishandled an initial public offering

(IPO) in August 1992 and a riot on the city's streets resulted. On August 9th 1992, an estimated 1m people, half of them from outside Shenzhen, waited in line on the city's streets to buy 5m IPO application forms (*rengouzheng*) at 303 sales points around the city. According to the original PBOC and municipal government plan, 10% of these forms were to be chosen by lottery and their "owners" allowed to subscribe to IPO shares. It would have normally required three days for all the forms to sell out, but at 9pm, after delays in sales throughout the day, officials announced that all the forms had been sold. The crowds suspected, correctly as it transpired, that most had been sold on to the black market or stolen by police, bank staff and the other government officials involved in the sale. Anyone who got hold of a few application forms had a good chance of being able to subscribe to the shares, and since the share price was expected to multiply several times on the first day of trading there were substantial profits to be made. On the following day, August 10th (thus the signifier "8.10"), this dissatisfaction spilled over into rioting, the most serious social disturbance in China since the 1989 Tiananmen Square protests. Police met people carrying placards reading "Fight corruption" with tear gas and the army was called in. Five men were arrested for causing the riots and castigated in the official press as "hooligans". In the days following, the central government sent its own team of investigators and found rather that extensive corruption on the part of government officials was to blame. The local authorities were forced to apologise and the city's mayor was transferred to a backwater.

In Beijing, the riot presented the conservatives with the perfect opportunity to undermine the new vice-premier, Zhu Rongji. Earlier, in February 1992, Chen Yun had criticised Deng's reforms as overly ambitious and had expressed particular concern over the stockmarket. The 8.10 riot was grist to the conservative mill and Zhu was openly criticised in a State Council meeting for his support of it. Jiang Zemin, still finding his feet as general secretary, must also have been worried since it was he who had authorised the first official trading site in Shanghai back in 1986. The day was saved by Deng, who stood by his reform agenda, ensured that the stock exchanges remained open for business, and backed Zhu and Jiang. In July 1993 Li Guixian, the central bank governor who had spoken out against Zhu in the State Council, was sacked and Zhu took the reins of the PBOC himself. It was now Zhu's job to sort out the economic mess – primarily high rates of inflation – that Deng's *nanxun* (southern tour) had sparked. In August 1993, he launched China's first comprehensive plan for economic reform. At its heart was the recentralisation of monetary and fiscal powers. Credit quotas were reduced and local party and bank officials threatened with the sack if they failed to rein in local bank lending and stock issuance. The stockmarket was also slated for reorganisation. But despite the monetary chaos, Deng had achieved one very important thing: China's movement towards a market was now confirmed.

The creation of non-tradable shares

In the aftermath of the riots China's stockmarket lost some of its radicalism. As well as implementing stricter controls over share issuance, Zhu oversaw the creation of three different share categories and a dedicated share quota. Share categories had been used before, but they were now better defined and more rigidly enforced. Any SOE converting into a shareholding company would now have to divide up its share capital into three parts, each roughly equal. This requirement is still in place.

About one-third of shares can be publicly issued, owned by individuals and legal persons (LPs), and freely traded. These shares are known as individual person (or IP) shares (*geren gu*).

About one-third of a company's equity is made up of state shares (*guojia gu*). The ultimate owner is the State Council, but these shares are managed by bureaus of the MOF (previously by the State Asset Management Administration), as well as by SOEs wholly owned by the state. Only representatives of the state can own them, and they are not freely tradable: authorisation is required from the MOF to transfer them.

Legal person shares (*faren gu*) make up the final third of the average listed firm's equity structure. Only LPs can own them. They are allocated to SOEs that contribute capital to the restructuring company before the IPO, mostly stockholding companies, NBFIS (non-bank financial institutions) and SOEs with at least one non-state owner. Some LP shares are also held by government bureaus (which has created much confusion over the exact difference with state shares). They cannot be traded on the stockmarket, although they can be transferred between legal persons subject to the agreement of the stock exchange where the firm is listed. It was only, however, after August 2000 that such transfers became popular, a subject examined in Chapter 5. The different categories of share are shown in Table 2.1.

There were a couple of attempts to set up sites for the trading of LP shares in the early 1990s. The Securities Trading Automated Quotation System (or STAQS) was established in October 1990 by the Stock Exchange Executive Council (or SEEC), a group formed by the Wall

Table 2.1 **China's share categories**

Type	Description
Individual A-shares	Shares of Mainland companies traded in Shanghai and Shenzhen that are denominated in renminbi and owned by individuals and legal persons (LPS). They make up about one-third of a typical listed company's equity capital. Foreign nationals and companies may not yet own these shares, though the QFII system, due to start in 2003, will allow limited holdings.
Individual B-shares	Shares of Mainland companies traded in Shanghai and Shenzhen that are denominated in US$ in Shanghai and HK$ in Shenzhen. Only a small number of companies have issued B-shares. Their advantage is that a company can raise hard currency; the disadvantage is that the B-share market is highly illiquid. Initially reserved for foreign investors, domestic individuals and companies quickly found ways of buying them. The market is now open to domestic individuals (though not institutions).
Legal person (LP) shares	About a third of every listed firm's equity is sold to domestic institutions (securities companies and SOES with at least one non-state owner) and becomes LP shares. These can not be traded on the stockmarket. During late 2000 an active auction market in LP shares developed and sales of LP shares in one-to-one contracts have become popular.
State shares	About a third of equity is transferred to state organs, usually now to the local bureau of the MOF, though sometimes to other central and local government bureaus as well as SOES wholly owned by the state. The ultimate owner of state shares is the State Council. They are not tradable, though two attempts have now been made to sell and simultaneously convert them into individual shares.
H-shares	Shares of PRC-registered companies listed in Hong Kong. The State Council has chosen some of its most important and impressive SOES to list in Hong Kong and elsewhere. These companies are taking advantage of the greater capital available in more developed capital markets, but are forced to undergo more radical restructuring than they would if they listed domestically and are held to higher standards of corporate governance and disclosure. Mainland Chinese firms listed in New York and London are sometimes called N-shares and L-shares (though the term H-shares is also used).
Red-chips	Shares of Chinese companies registered overseas and listed abroad (principally in Hong Kong), having substantial Mainland interests and controlled by affiliates or bureaus of the government. Red-chips boomed during 1996–97 and have since then bombed. Most now trade below their issuance price.

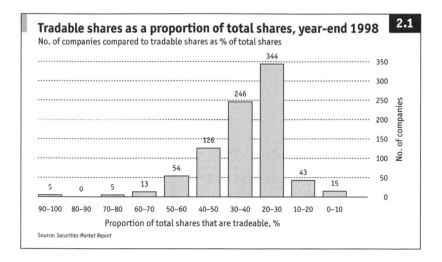

2.1

Tradable shares as a proportion of total shares, year-end 1998
No. of companies compared to tradable shares as % of total shares

Proportion of total shares that are tradeable, %

Source: *Securities Market Report*

Street returnees, initially as a bond trading network. In 1992 it started listing LP shares, Guangxia Yuchai Machinery, Hainan Hengtong Real Estate and Sichuan Shudou Mansion being the first. By 1993 the system had 160 members and electronic links to 38 cities. It enjoyed greater autonomy from the government than the two exchanges. Xin Xueqing, the Stock Exchange Executive Council official in charge, claimed at the time that STAQS "[will not] become the third stockmarket. We are the only national market in China and we believe out future looks promising." It was not: rather than evolving into China's NASDAQ, in 1993 the State Council ordered a ban on further listings of LP shares, and although the STAQS remained in existence till the late 1990s, trading volume quickly died. The PBOC's National Electronic Trading System (or NETS), a similar network, suffered a similar fate.

This shareholding structure meant that the state remained the dominant shareholder of any restructured SOE. Figure 2.1 shows the results of the policy. By 1998 the majority of listed companies had only 20-40% of their shares trading on the market. Only 77 companies, some 9% of those listed, had more than 50% of their shares openly trading. Figure 2.2 shows how unusual this ownership structure is compared with other stockmarkets. Even in other emerging markets the free float makes up, on average, over three-quarters of total share capital.

The other measure that was put in place in late 1992 was the annual share quota (the limit on the number of shares that could be issued each year). Before that, the PBOC had run a quota governing all securities

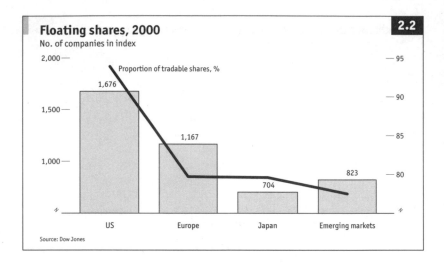

Floating shares, 2000
No. of companies in index

2.2

Proportion of tradable shares, %

US — 1,676
Europe — 1,167
Japan — 704
Emerging markets — 823

Source: Dow Jones

(including bonds), but this was poorly implemented. The new quota (bonds now being dealt with separately) was determined on a national level by the State Planning Commission (SPC). Each province was then allocated a part of it by the CSRC, the south and east of the country being favoured with larger chunks. Some central ministries and associated bureaus were also allocated small quotas. In most years before 1997 the quota allowed rich provinces to choose between three and five companies to issue shares, and poor provinces one or two. Initially the quota set the value of shares to be issued each year. But in 1996 it was revised so that it determined the number of companies that could issue shares. This change was designed to stop local governments spreading their quotas among a large number of small companies. Larger companies were encouraged to list, and smaller SOEs were given an incentive to merge. The quota system was formally abolished in 2000, but the share categories have remained more or less unchanged. This has greatly weakened standards of corporate governance and has had a harmful effect on liquidity in the secondary market. However, these two institutions did have the effect of containing the stockmarket's rapid growth in the early 1990s and of giving the central government a means of shaping the market's development.

Two dull years and a scandal, 1994–95

China's first bout of share fever was short-lived. In the middle of Zhu's retrenchment campaign during late 1994 and 1995 the central government tightened the share issuance quota and trading volumes slumped. During 1994–95 only Rmb1.6bn ($194m) worth of IPOs was allowed, following Rmb4.3bn in 1993.

Despite the market calm, however, this period did not pass off without incident. Established in December 1992 in the wake of the 8.10 riots, the CSRC had enormous problems implementing its regulatory mandate as it battled entrenched interests in Beijing, Shanghai and Shenzhen. Corruption was rampant. The occasional scandal made it into the press. Of particular note was the case of Mrs Xu Lanfang, who attempted to sue Zhejiang ITIC (an international trust and investment company) in early 1994 after one of the firm's branches had allowed her husband to trade on credit, a practice known in Chinese as *rongzi*. Lending money for share trading, although common, was, and is, illegal. The unfortunate husband lost Rmb110,000 of the family's savings and Rmb420,000 extended to him as a loan, and subsequently committed suicide.

The 327 Treasury-bond futures scandal

Stories of deaths connected with share scandals were soon to fade as a huge new scandal was brewing in Shanghai's wild new Treasury bond (T-bond) futures (TBF) market. When it broke in early 1995, it bankrupted one of China's leading securities companies, threatened the meltdown of Shanghai's financial market and reinforced the view of many in central government that the capital market was inherently speculative and had little economic utility.

Before the crisis, regulation of the TBF market was in a mess. The only regulations governing trading were promulgated by the SHGSE in October 1993, ten months after trading had begun in December 1992. The newly formed CSRC was informed of the first issuance rather than asked to approve the move and at the time there was no effective oversight of the market higher than the SHGSE. The MOF was responsible for T-bond trading, but had no clear jurisdiction over TBFs, and the SPC had an unspecified role in regulating commodity futures, but had no formal role in TBF regulation. In April 1994 the State Council finally placed the supervision of all futures markets under the State Council Securities Commission (SCSC), a ministerial-level body overseeing regulation since late 1992, and day-to-day regulatory work under the CSRC. But the CSRC had few means of monitoring what was going on and its regulatory powers were disputed by other government bodies, such as its power to punish securities firms for bad behaviour, which was opposed by the PBOC who also claimed jurisdiction over these firms.

TBF contract no. 327 was a three-year contract expiring in June 1995. Analysts at Wanguo Securities expected that, as inflation fell, the coupon rates on T-bonds would be set at lower rates, and so sold 327 short. On February 23rd 1995 Wanguo had a short position of some 3m contracts, six times the limit set by the SHGSE. Much of the long position on 327 was taken by China Economic Development TIC, known in Chinese as *Zhongjingkai*, a company owned by the MOF, which it is widely accepted had been tipped off by its parent ministry that interest rates would rise – and so they did. On the evening of February 22nd, the MOF announced higher interest rates than Wanguo had been expecting. Prices of 327 rose on February 23rd and, facing catastrophic losses, Wanguo attempted to manipulate the market price by selling 10.6m contracts in the last eight minutes of trading. TBF trading volume for the day totalled Rmb850bn, more than 20 times that of the previous day. With losses in excess of Rmb1bn, around 20 other financial firms faced bankruptcy as the market closed. The government responded by cancelling all trades in those final eight minutes and eventually forced Shenyin Securities, a conservative Shanghai firm, to absorb what remained of the bankrupt Wanguo. The TBF market, astonishingly, remained open after 327, supported by the CSRC. It was only in May, when another group of firms attempted to manipulate the price of another TBF, contract no. 319, that an exasperated Zhu, under pressure from the party's conservatives, ordered the market to be closed. Since then no official futures trading has taken place, although there are occasional rumours of informal contracts being traded between institutions.

Guan Jinsheng, Wanguo's CEO, was arrested and on February 3rd 1997 was found guilty of abusing public funds and taking bribes and sentenced to 17 years' imprisonment (although he has apparently since been released on parole on medical grounds). He was not the only member of the pioneering generation to be hurt by the scandal. Wei Wenyuan, the first head of the SHGSE who had done much to promote the market's development, was removed from his post later in the year. Although respected by his staff at the SHGSE, people within the CSRC viewed him as dangerously fast and loose with regulation, and Wei did little to placate them. In fact, he openly resented the interference of what he called "those arrogant upstart bureaucrats in Beijing" and on a number of occasions declined to meet senior members of the central government when they visited the exchange. In Beijing Liu Hongru, the impressive and stylish head of the CSRC, was made a scapegoat for 327, removed and parked in the Chinese People's Political Consultative Conference (or CPPCC), a powerless consultative body. He had already been criticised for his promotion of overseas listings and his alleged neglect of the domestic market. The men brought in to replace these pioneers were out-and-out bureaucrats. Yang Xianghai, an official who had worked in the Shanghai planning bureaucracy for most of his career, and who was entirely unfamiliar with the world of finance, replaced Wei at the SHGSE. Zhou Daojiong, a former PBOC deputy-governor who had also acted as vice-chairman of the SCSC, took over the CSRC. He was told to crack down. In the months following his appointment a number of senior staff, including Gao Xiqing, the CSRC's first legal counsel and its deputy chairman during 1998–2002, left, complaining about the new bureaucratic atmosphere at the organisation.

A promising but false start, 1996–97

When Zhu made his first visit to the SHGSE in December 1995 it was something of a long overdue homecoming. He had been present at the exchange's opening ceremony in 1990, but had made a point of not returning since. One reason was political: he did not want to draw attention to his connections with such a sensitive experiment. But a second, and probably more important, reason was that, for all his credentials as a radical economic reformer, Zhu was extremely suspicious of the stockmarket. He felt it was too speculative and of little economic use. Stock exchange staff were privately dismayed when he delivered an extremely conservative speech, emphasising the importance of regulation (and not mentioning growth or development). The words *fazhi, jiangguan, zilu, guifan* (rule of law, supervision, self-discipline, standardisation) he used that day were to become the basis of regulatory work for years to come.

But unknown to his audience, Zhu's thinking on the stockmarket was already changing. Prompted by problems in industrial and bank reform, he was beginning to believe that the market could play a more substantial role in reform. For one thing, reform of the SOE sector was going nowhere. Experiments with profit retention and limited-responsibility contracts – attempts to improve managerial incentives and boost efficiency at SOEs without privatisation – had failed. And while corporatisation had been accepted as an alternative in theory at the 1993 party plenum, it had so far not received strong backing, and was not being rolled out on any scale among the larger SOEs. By 1996, things were getting desperate: in the first quarter of the year the SOE sector as a whole recorded its first ever net loss. And so in 1996 efforts to implement shareholding reforms intensified.

In theory, corporatisation entails the transformation of SOEs with no clear property rights into independent LPs with shareholders who have limited liabilities. It means a clear distribution of assets, the separation of owners and managers, and the establishment of boards of directors, supervisory boards, and regular shareholders' meetings. In short, it is a means of turning a SOE into a modern, efficiently run corporation – or at least that is the theory. Reformers hoped, and continue to do so, that corporate restructuring would create the right incentives for firm managers.

But if corporatisation was supposed to solve the governance problem at SOEs, it still left the other serious problem, financing, in the air. From where were SOEs to get their funds? This problem had its roots in the early 1990s, when the SOEs were weaned off the government's budget and told to borrow from the commercial banks. The largest of these were, and remain, the four state-owned commercial banks: the Industrial and Commercial Bank of China (ICBC), the Agricultural Bank of China (ABC), the Construction Bank of China (CBC) and the Bank of China (BOC). The move from being funded through loans instead of from the budget was intended to instil discipline in the SOEs' use of capital and create mechanisms by which banks could file for the bankruptcy of bad borrowers. The problem – and one that still has to be solved – was that politics became involved in what should have been purely commercial lending decisions. Bank managers, appointed by local party and government officials, were instructed to lend to SOEs whatever their financial situation. This was one of the only ways of keeping SOEs going and workers employed. As a result, bank lending ballooned during the 1990s, almost all of the new loans going – against all economic logic – to SOEs. It grew at above 15% in most years, when economic growth was running at 8–10%. Loans were not called in, little interest was paid and the banks' bad-loan portfolios grew until by the late 1990s they had become insolvent.

By 1996 the policy elite was considering other means of raising funds for SOEs. It did not take them long to come up with a new idea: to use the stockmarket on a much larger scale as a supplementary financing mechanism. Zhu was soon won round. More large national SOEs were earmarked for their shares to be listed and the IPO quota was enlarged. In April 1996 CSRC officials gave the first public signals of the new positive attitude to the stockmarket, ending the period of retrenchment that had proceeded the 327 scandal, and sparking a new period of exuberance.

However, before the new agenda could be put into effect properly, local officials hijacked the market for their own ends. Officials in Shenzhen and Shanghai introduced policies that encouraged a rapid increase in trading volume and speculation. They offered preferential tax rates and bank loans to listed companies, spoke of allowing foreign investors into the market, fought aggressively for new listings, improved services for investors and downplayed regulation. Trading volume at the SHZSE exploded from Rmb382.4m ($46m) in 1995 to Rmb4.9bn in 1996, and continued to climb in 1997. Without the right regulatory institutions in place, the central government was left floundering. Share prices soared on the back of massive speculation. Huge sums of bank deposits were illegally lent to securities companies and invested in shares, all with the implicit approval of the authorities in Shanghai and Shenzhen. The central government responded forcefully in December 1996 with an editorial in the People's Daily. The piece, rumoured to have been edited by Zhu himself, spoke of share prices as "abnormal and irrational" and compared the market with Wall Street just before the 1929 crash. The State Council sent investigative teams to both cities.

Once the scandals broke in the summer of 1997, more people were sacked or became scapegoats. The president of Haitong Securities, Li Huizhen, was sacked, as was Kan Zhidong, the president of Shenyin Wanguo Securities. Shenyin Wanguo, Haitong and Guangfa Securities received one-year bans from proprietary trading for manipulating prices. The head of the ICBC in Shanghai, Shen Roulei, was also dismissed, after it was discovered that some Rmb8bn worth of his bank's funds had been invested in the stockmarket. The president of the SHGSE, Yang Xianghai, was removed, as rumours of improprieties at the exchange (including a large fund run by members of senior management) swept the market. In Beijing the CSRC chairman, Zhou Daojiong, resigned in May 1997, and was replaced by Zhou Zhengqing, a close adviser to Zhu. The latter had previously worked with the premier at the SCSC and at the PBOC. However, this time it was not just the people who were reorganised: it was the institutions of regulation too. The CSRC was given the powers it needed and other government organs, including the PBOC and local governments, had their regulatory powers taken away. These developments are explained more fully in Chapter 6.

Growth with the CSRC in charge, 1998–2002

Stockmarket development since 1997 can be roughly divided into two phases. Between 1997 and 2000 the focus was on increasing the supply of funds to the SOEs, and in 2000, the boom year for achieving this, 139 companies raised Rmb210.3bn from share issues (IPOs, rights and secondary offerings) and the market expanded in size by some 50%. There was a 94% increase in trading volume over 1999. Internet awareness and the buzz surrounding China's new economy (even more "virtual" than that in the United States) added to investor fever.

By the end of 2000, however, the strains were beginning to show. Regulators were concerned over stratospheric price-earnings multiples, and a growing number of scandals were revealing the corruption at the heart of listed companies' accounts as well as the manipulative schemes of large investors. Many recognised that the dramatic increase in share prices in 2000 was not sustainable. New policy priorities, including privatisation, creating a modern pensions system and getting rid of government debt, were coming to the fore, forcing policymakers to re-evaluate the role the stockmarket should play in their reform strategy. The impact of these trends is examined in more detail in Chapter 7. As a result, during 2001 policy appeared to shift. Solving some of the structural problems of the market, including the parlous state of regulation, became a greater priority. While welcome, the shift was to cause a lot of short-term pain. The bubble that inflated during 1999–2000 burst in the second half of 2001 as the CSRC began its most serious crackdown yet on illegal activities. And it was not only this that investors had to deal with. In July the government rolled out a plan to reduce the government's shareholdings. The result of these two moves in 2001 was dramatic and immediate: a 45.6% decline over 2000 in trading volume at the SHZSE, and an 11.5% drop at the SHGSE, as Table 2.2 shows. Shenzhen suffered more as its market had been closed to new A-share listings since September 2000 in anticipation of it establishing an entirely new board for high-tech companies. All new companies went to Shanghai. It was generally expected that the Shenzhen market would eventually be absorbed by Shanghai (although this move is being strongly resisted by the Shenzhen authorities). The result was that liquidity began to leave Shenzhen and head north.

There were precious few signs of recovery in 2002. A-share IPOs raised Rmb68.2bn, down 9% on 2001, while rights share issues plunged 87% in the year to Rmb5.7bn. Total stock turnover was Rmb2.8trn, a decrease of 27% on 2001, and revenues from stamp taxes levied on share transactions totalled only Rmb11.2bn, a fall of 62% on 2002.

The Growth Enterprise Market

The new thinking in 2001 also appeared to undermine plans to establish a Growth Enterprise Market (GEM) based in Shenzhen. Once mooted for

Table 2.2 **Stockmarket collapse, 2001–02**

	2000	2001	2002
Total trading volume, Rmb trn	6.1	3.8	2.8
Share capitalisation (including non-tradable shares), Rmb trn	4.8	4.4	3.8

Source: CSRC

2000, this still awaits approval by the senior leadership. If it does eventually go ahead, it would be the most significant institutional innovation in China's capital market since the two stock exchanges were established in 1990. Somewhat modelled on NASDAQ, the GEM would provide trading facilities to the shares of small and medium-sized, non-state firms. The reason Shenzhen was chosen was that if Shenzhen's main board did move to Shanghai, Shenzhen would be left without a stockmarket and without stamp tax revenues (taxes levied on share transactions). The GEM was supposed to be the compensation for the loss of the board, an entirely political rationale.

But wherever it was based, the GEM would be a useful thing if it could be established, since it would provide much needed finance to non-state firms. In contrast to NASDAQ, the GEM would use a competitive auction-based system (rather than market makers). In terms of its regulatory structure, it would be run more according to Western than Chinese norms. For instance, the SHZSE's own listing committee, rather than the CSRC, would authorise share issuance (although there are rumours that CSRC officials would be transferred to the SHZSE to take charge of this work). The competition for listing places would take place on the basis of merit. Listed companies (most of which would be private) would not have LP or state shares. Since all shares would be tradable, this market would therefore be a market in corporate ownership rights. The government has yet to make clear its plans for foreign involvement. According to press reports, at least 300 companies have already applied to list on the GEM.

However, complex political disputes are delaying the project, and might even result in the secondary board never being established. With the meltdown in technology stock prices in 2000–01, problems at secondary boards round the world (including at the one already established in Hong Kong), and the State Council's ambition to promote Shanghai as the Mainland's financial centre, it is unclear what point there would be in a Shenzhen-based GEM. Premier Zhu was reported to be reluctant to establish a new and potentially problematic market before his retirement in March 2003. However, even after Zhu goes, there is no guarantee that the GEM will go ahead. In fact, the longer implementation is postponed, the weaker the rationale for the market becomes. The SHGSE is aggressively listing more private and high-tech firms and the Hong Kong GEM is also speeding up listings, improving liquidity and attracting more Mainland Chinese firms. Many potential GEM firms, faced with immediate financing needs, are now choosing to go to Shanghai or, if they can, escape abroad, mostly to Hong Kong. Soon the only demand for a mainland-based GEM will be coming from Shenzhen government officials scared that they will be left with nothing when their firms give up their listing on the Shenzhen exchange and move to Shanghai in around 2005.

China's stockmarket today

The key role of the stockmarket in China has been – and continues to be – to raise capital for SOEs. The number of companies listing has accelerated since 1996. In 1996 and 1997, over 200 firms were listed annually, and around 100 more were listed each year from 1998 to 2001, as Figure 2.3 shows. The amount of funds raised has also increased steadily since 1996, from Rmb42.5bn ($5.1bn) that year to a peak of Rmb210.3bn in 2000. These figures include international issues and are shown in Figure 2.4. Moreover, firms are each raising more money. The average firm in 2000 raised Rmb626m, compared with Rmb78m in 1995. In 2001, a large company could expect to raise some Rmb1bn–2bn in an IPO.

In spite of its rapid growth, the present size of the market should not be exaggerated, as official statistics on market capitalisation – the size of the market as measured by share prices multiplied by the number of shares – often do. On May 25th 2001 China's stockmarket's official market capitalisation hit Rmb5.27trn, the first time the figure had been higher than that of Hong Kong's, apparently a significant coming of age for the Mainland market. Or at least that was how the official media presented the numbers. However, the Mainland figure was bogus for one important reason: it included non-tradable LP and state shares. These were valued at their supposed market price while in reality they cannot generally be traded. The ones that have been traded at auction and those that have changed hands in one-to-one transactions, have been priced at heavy discounts of 10–20% of the price of tradable shares. This means that the official capitalisation overstates the size of the market. A truer picture of market capitalisation comes when only trad-

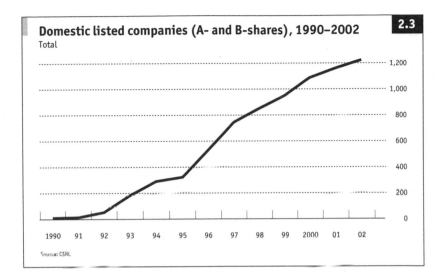

Domestic listed companies (A- and B-shares), 1990–2002 `2.3`
Total

Source: CSRC

able shares are counted. At the end of 2002 (see Table 2.3), they had a value of Rmb1.2bn, making the market about one-third of the size of Hong Kong and only 12% of GDP. In comparison, the stockmarket in the United States is worth over 120% of GDP.

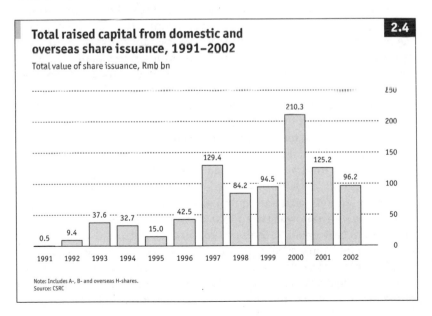

Total raised capital from domestic and overseas share issuance, 1991–2002 `2.4`

Total value of share issuance, Rmb bn

Note: Includes A-, B- and overseas H-shares.
Source: CSRC

Table 2.3 **Stockmarket capitalisation, 1992–2002**

	Market capitalisation (Rmb bn)	Market capitalisation as % GDP	Tradable market capitalisation (Rmb bn)	Tradable capitalisation as % of GDP
1992	104.8	3.9	86.16	3.2
1993	353.3	10.2	96.89	2.8
1994	369.1	7.9	96.5	2.1
1995	347.4	5.9	93.8	1.6
1996	984.2	14.5	286.7	4.2
1997	1,752.9	23.4	520.4	7.0
1998	1,950.6	24.5	574.5	7.2
1999	2,647.1	31.8	821.4	9.9
2000	4,809.1	53.8	1,608.8	18.0
2001	4,352.2	45.4	1,446.3	15.1
2002	3,832.9	37.0	1,248.5	12.0

Source: CSRC

It is also important not to assume that the stockmarket has become the dominant source of funding for industry. It is still the poor cousin of the banking sector in this regard. Figure 2.5 compares the level of financing provided by the market with that provided by banks. In 2001 enterprises raised about Rmb118bn from share issues, while banks lent more than Rmb1.3trn. In 2002, the share of capital provided by the stock market slumped. Share issues raised Rmb74bn, while banks loaned an estimated Rmb1.9trn, meaning that the share market raised only 4% of the money extended by the banks.

One other important use of the market has been to raise revenues for the government budget. Between 1991 and 1997, a stamp tax of 0.3% of the value of shares traded was levied on both the buyer and seller of A-shares, and with the level of share transactions being among the highest in the world, both local and central government benefited enormously. In May 1997 the rate was raised to 0.5%, in June 1998 it dropped to 0.4% and then in November 2001 the CSRC cut the tax from 0.4% to 0.2% for A-shares, and from 0.3% to 0.2% for B-shares. Many of these moves were motivated by a desire to effect a change in investor sentiment. The rise in 1997, for instance, was designed to curb extremely bullish trading; the reduction in 2001 was meant to revive sagging interest in shares.

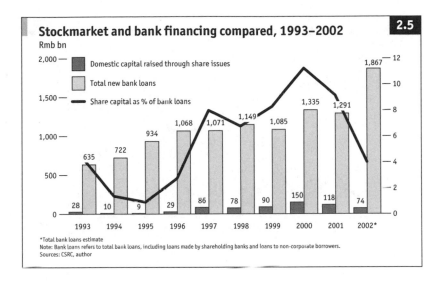

Stockmarket and bank financing compared, 1993–2002   2.5

Rmb bn

■ Domestic capital raised through share issues
▢ Total new bank loans
━ Share capital as % of bank loans

*Total bank loans estimate
Note: Bank loans refers to total bank loans, including loans made by shareholding banks and loans to non-corporate borrowers.
Sources: CSRC, author

Figure 2.6 shows the revenues that the stamp tax on share transactions has brought in. Initially, local governments took all of it but the central government has gradually seized an increasing proportion, and now takes around 97% of the total. The total stamp tax revenue for 2000, a bumper year, was Rmb48.6bn, nearly double the amount raised in 1999, accounting for 3.6% of the government's total financial revenues that year. The bear market that began in August 2001 hit the government's coffers hard. In addition to the lost revenue from taxes on the profits of securities companies, TICs and investment firms, the stamp tax dropped as trading volume plummeted. The government planned to raise some Rmb38bn in stamp tax in 2001, but only reached Rmb29.1bn. In 2002, stamp tax revenues fell to Rmb11.2bn, down by two-thirds on 2001.

Demand for equities and listed-company valuations

Since the purpose of the stockmarket in China has been to channel money to companies favoured by the government, rather than companies which deserve the funds, why have shares had high price-earnings ratios (P/ES), apparently indicating that the equities on offer are valuable assets? A P/E is simply a company's share price divided by earnings in the previous year. As such, in theory, it indicates what premium the market is placing on the company's ability to create value and pay dividends in the future. In Western markets, a high P/E generally indicates that investors are expecting future growth in earnings (but it may also

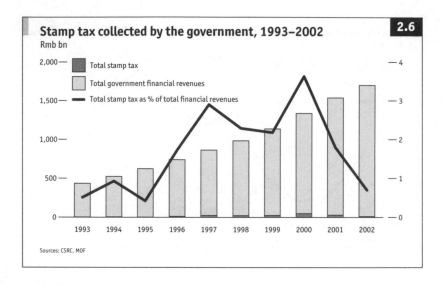

Stamp tax collected by the government, 1993–2002   **2.6**
Rmb bn

■ Total stamp tax
□ Total government financial revenues
━ Total stamp tax as % of total financial revenues

Sources: CSRC, MOF

simply indicate low earnings). In addition to the difficulties of interpretation, there are other drawbacks to P/ES, not least that they are often based on history – past earnings – and investors are more concerned about the future when they value companies. As a rule, P/ES in Western markets float between 10 and 20, as Table 2.4 shows.

In marked comparison, for much of the 1990s P/ES in Mainland China were above 40 and even by the end of 2002, after a sustained fall in prices, at the SHGSE prices averaged 35 times earnings and at the SHZSE 38. Some senior figures in the CSRC, as well as most investors, have long believed that such high P/ES are unjustifiable. This was one reason that many CSRC officials were not over-concerned with the massive price falls of 2001–02.

But why are P/ES so high in China when, at least during the 1990s, 95% of listed companies were state-controlled, and as Chapter 5 shows, had woeful standards of corporate governance and were mostly busy destroy-

Table 2.4 **Selected P/E ratios, October 2001**

	China	Taiwan	South Korea	Hong Kong	UK	US	Japan
P/E ratio	40	20	12	13	19	31	61

Source: author

Table 2.5 **Variations in the one-year household deposit savings rate, May 1996–March 2002**

	May 1996	August 1996	October 1997	March 1998	July 1998	December 1998	June 1999	March 2002
One-year deposit rate	9.18	7.47	5.67	5.22	4.77	3.78	2.25	1.98

Source: PBOC

ing value rather than creating it? The reasons are rooted in the wider problems of China's transitional financial sector. Three factors are particularly important: a lack of alternative investment options, limited company share floats and the soft budget constraints of many institutional investors.

First, government policies designed to provide cheap finance to SOEs have ensured continued demand for SOE equity. Bank deposit interest rates are set low (at 1.98%, after a series of interest rate cuts since May 1996, as seen in Table 2.5) by the PBOC to allow banks to lend cheaply to SOEs. Because of capital account controls, investors cannot easily remit financial assets out of the country (although, of course, many large investors and SOEs do so illegally) to invest in equities overseas. Neither has the corporate bond market been developed much (see below). Thus, the incentive for investing in equities is relatively high.

Second, only a third of the shares of a typical SOE are tradable in the market. This, with the quota system, limits the supply of shares considerably. During the late 1990s, the proportion of shares being issued by listed companies actually fell, often to only 20–25% of a company's total equity capital. There are similarities here with Japan's stockmarket, where the majority of listed stock is held by large conglomerates in an informal system of interlocking shareholdings. In practice, a large amount of equity is not traded, giving rise to artificially high valuations (see Table 2.4). This practice was particularly common in the 1980s in Japan before the stockmarket crash of 1989. In fact, with P/Es commonly at above 150, at one point Japan's stockmarket capitalisation exceeded the total capitalisation of the rest of the world's markets put together. China's market suffers from a similar lack of liquidity, and this pushes up valuations of the shares that do float. As the experiment in selling off state shares in 2001 suggested, share prices fall dramatically when the number of shares sold off in a flotation is increased, emphasising the serious flaw in using market prices to value non-tradable shares.

Third, many SOEs and local governments use public funds to speculate in shares. Soft controls over their budgets mean that any profits they make can be skimmed off into informal accounts and retained, while losses can be put through their books and replaced by budgetary transfers or loans from the state banks. During the 1990s it was standard practice for a newly listed company to take a large slice of the revenues from its IPO and use it to trade both its own shares and the shares of other companies. Many SOEs have bought shares on a much larger scale than would otherwise have been the case. This drives up prices to levels that would be unsustainable in a market where investors have to operate under Western-style financial constraints.

China's stockmarket and the world

The rise of China's stockmarket fascinates not only because of its strangeness in a supposedly communist country, but also because of the size the market has apparently assumed in such a short period of time. Figure 2.7 shows the world's largest equity markets at year-end 2001 in terms of market capitalisation: China ranks eighth, an extraordinary achievement for a market only 15 years young. However, this figure uses the official market capitalisation figure, the one that includes non-tradable shares valued at market prices, and therefore gives a false impression. If a more realistic market capitalisation figure of $170bn is used, China then comes in 20th place, trailing after Brazil, Finland, Argentina and Taiwan. Another statistic that puts the size of China's stockmarket into perspective is that at end-2001 it was 1.2% the size of that of the United States.

Compared with other emerging markets, China's stockmarket at the end of 2001 was ranked fourth in terms of the number of companies listed, after India, Romania and South Korea (see Figure 2.8). However, in India and Romania many listed firms were small. In terms of market size, if a readjusted figure for its market capitalisation is used, compared with other emerging markets, China comes in fifth, after Taiwan, South Korea, Argentina and Brazil (Figure 2.9). Looked at regionally, China's stockmarket comes fifth in size after Japan, Hong Kong, Taiwan and South Korea (Figure 2.10).

Comparison with other post-socialist states is not flattering either. During their transition to the market, 20 out of the 26 states from Eastern Europe and the former Soviet Union have opened, or reopened, stock exchanges. To effect rapid privatisation, many of these countries organised voucher schemes in which millions of tokens were issued to the public. These tokens could then be exchanged for shares in newly pri-

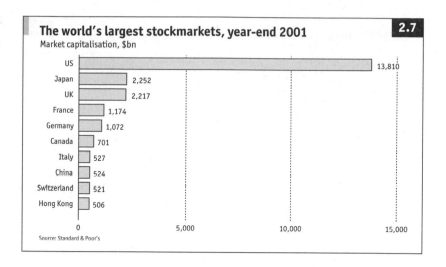

The world's largest stockmarkets, year-end 2001 2.7
Market capitalisation, $bn

US	13,810
Japan	2,252
UK	2,217
France	1,174
Germany	1,072
Canada	701
Italy	527
China	524
Switzerland	521
Hong Kong	506

0   5,000   10,000   15,000

Source: Standard & Poor's

valised SOEs. In some countries, including the Czech Republic, there was "big bang" stockmarket creation: thousands of SOEs were all privatised at once and instantly listed. Many of these companies, however, were of poor quality and were simply not large enough for a public listing, so numerous delistings quickly followed. The Czech Republic's market listed over 1,600 companies in 1995, but over 90% have since been delisted. Other countries took a different approach to privatisation and stockmarket creation. In Russia, Ukraine and Azerbaijan there was

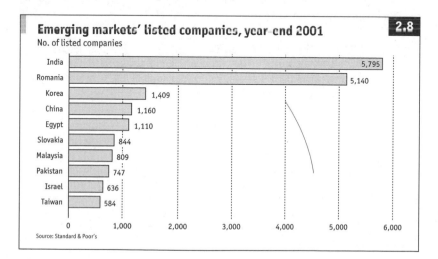

Emerging markets' listed companies, year-end 2001 2.8
No. of listed companies

India	5,795
Romania	5,140
Korea	1,409
China	1,160
Egypt	1,110
Slovakia	844
Malaysia	809
Pakistan	747
Israel	636
Taiwan	584

0   1,000   2,000   3,000   4,000   5,000   6,000

Source: Standard & Poor's

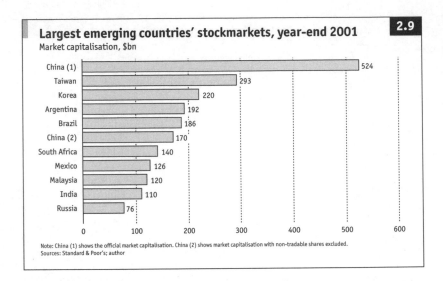

Largest emerging countries' stockmarkets, year-end 2001   2.9
Market capitalisation, $bn

China (1) — 524
Taiwan — 293
Korea — 220
Argentina — 192
Brazil — 186
China (2) — 170
South Africa — 140
Mexico — 126
Malaysia — 120
India — 110
Russia — 76

0   100   200   300   400   500   600

Note: China (1) shows the official market capitalisation. China (2) shows market capitalisation with non-tradable shares excluded.
Sources: Standard & Poor's; author

a similar mass privatisation voucher scheme, but companies were then only gradually listed. In others, notably Croatia, Hungary and Poland, the entire privatisation process took place over a longer period, and companies were listed through traditional IPOs. (Several countries, including Albania, Georgia and Tajikistan, did not set up stock exchanges at all.) In terms of its gross size, China's stockmarket domi-

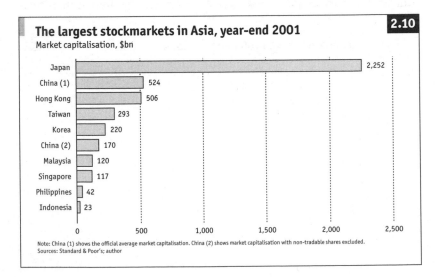

The largest stockmarkets in Asia, year-end 2001   2.10
Market capitalisation, $bn

Japan — 2,252
China (1) — 524
Hong Kong — 506
Taiwan — 293
Korea — 220
China (2) — 170
Malaysia — 120
Singapore — 117
Philippines — 42
Indonesia — 23

0   500   1,000   1,500   2,000   2,500

Note: China (1) shows the official average market capitalisation. China (2) shows market capitalisation with non-tradable shares excluded.
Sources: Standard & Poor's; author

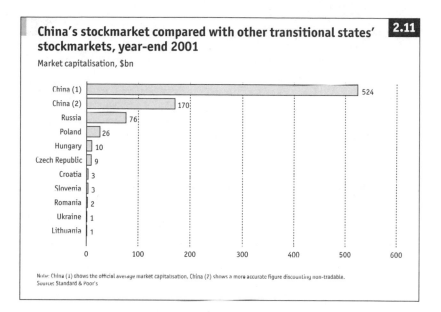

China's stockmarket compared with other transitional states' stockmarkets, year-end 2001   `2.11`

Market capitalisation, $bn

China (1)	524
China (2)	170
Russia	76
Poland	26
Hungary	10
Czech Republic	9
Croatia	3
Slovenia	3
Romania	2
Ukraine	1
Lithuania	1

Note: China (1) shows the official average market capitalisation. China (2) shows a more accurate figure discounting non-tradable.
Source: Standard & Poor's

nates those of transitional Europe (Figure 2.11). However, when looked at as a proportion of the size of the domestic economy, China's market was worth only 15% of GDP, compared with, for example, 34% in Hungary and 25% in the Czech Republic. Russia's stockmarket had a capitalisation of $76bn at end-2001, some 25% of its GDP. As in so much else in China, the sheer size impresses and the comparative size disappoints.

As befits its status as a developing country, companies listed in China are small compared with those listed in more developed markets. In terms of the size of companies listed in these markets, the average Chinese firm was around a quarter the size of a Hong Kong firm, one-sixth the size of a Japanese listed firm and one-fifteenth of the size of a firm listed in the United States. However, Chinese firms were large compared with emerging market firms, having an average tradable market capitalisation of some $147m compared with an average of $103m (Figure 2.12).

In summary, China's stockmarket is not yet as large or as economically important as many commentators say it is. But this is not to diminish its achievement, potential and significance for economic reform. Eastern Europe's stockmarkets benefited from new politics and a general acceptance of privatisation, and Asia's markets grew up alongside the region's economic growth miracle, but China's stockmarket was created in the midst of – and in spite of – a large number of obstacles. Stijn

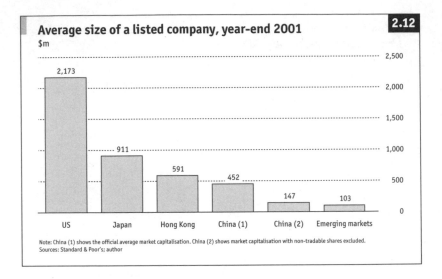

Average size of a listed company, year-end 2001 `2.12`

$m

Note: China (1) shows the official average market capitalisation. China (2) shows market capitalisation with non-tradable shares excluded.
Sources: Standard & Poor's; author

Claessens, an economist formerly with the World Bank, has shown that stockmarket development in transitional countries is strongly correlated with low inflation, a legal framework that protects minority shareholders' rights and the existence of sizeable institutional investors. In contrast, China's market coped with a Communist government, two very serious bouts of inflation in 1988–89 and 1992–93, few institutional investors and poor regulation coupled with weak enforcement. Moreover, the potential of the market is extraordinary, if China's economy continues to grow at 8–10% a year. According to Goldman Sachs, an investment bank, China's GDP will be some $5trn by 2020 (compared with $20trn projected for the United States). If China's stockmarket grows to 50% of GDP by that time it will be worth some $2.5trn, some ten times its present value.

China's bond market

A bond market is fundamental to a well-functioning market economy. Bonds allow governments to finance budget deficits and private companies to raise investment capital. They help investors construct better portfolios: equities are risky, bank deposits are dull, whereas bonds can be said to provide for a healthy mix of risks and returns. In addition, the Treasury bond (T-bond) market lies at the heart of government's monetary policy: monitoring T-bond prices is one of the ways a central bank can effectively set interest rates. It is for these reasons that the Ministry of Finance (MOF) and CSRC are now seeking to develop the bond market after years of neglect.

Treasury bonds

Official bond issuance began in the early 1980s in China as a form of taxation. A yearly quota of T-bonds was set by the MOF and each province had to buy its share, adding in effect to its fiscal contribution to the central government's budget. However, most budgetary finance was still sourced through borrowing from the central bank. This changed in 1994 when the central government banned itself from borrowing money from the PBOC and turned to issuing T-bonds to the public and institutional investors to raise funds to cover the deficit. This was a positive move since it created, if at least notionally, the sense that government was borrowing money which had a cost associated with it, and should have thus created some discipline in its finances. The government moved rapidly to expand T-bond issuance from an annual amount of around Rmb20bn ($8.7bn) in the late 1980s to Rmb40bn during 1991–93 to Rmb300bn by 1998 (see Figure 2.13). Since then the government has also issued special bonds for particular projects, including infrastructure and recapitalising the banks. The price of all these bonds is set administratively, not by means of an auction as in the United States and elsewhere.

Budgetary revenues are not sufficient to cover the government's spending. China's budget deficit for 2002 was some Rmb310bn ($37.5bn), up from Rmb260bn in the previous year. To fund this deficit, the government issues long-term bonds. Although this makes appropriate fiscal policy, it does not help monetary policy. The problem is that all the debt is long-term. This means that a yield curve, a curve that shows what returns will be produced by bonds with different maturities, cannot be plotted. In the United States, in contrast, the Federal Reserve organises regular auctions of T-bonds of three and six months' maturity. Since the prices paid for these bonds reveal the market's demand for bonds (and thus its sentiment on inflation and growth), a yield curve can be plotted, and the Fed is then able to set the interest rate on a market basis. Like many other developing countries, however, China's MOF does not yet have a cash management system that allows it to predict its short-term cash needs. Instead of issuing short-term paper, therefore, it relies on its account with the PBOC for borrowing money in the short term, simply borrowing and repaying funds as needed. It is also restricted by the annual bond quota set by the State Development and Planning Commission (SDPC). This would need to be eliminated if short-term issues

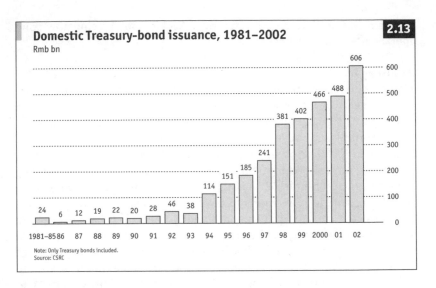

Domestic Treasury-bond issuance, 1981–2002   2.13
Rmb bn

Note: Only Treasury bonds included.
Source: CSRC

were to become more common. Once such a cash management system is set up – and the MOF is working on it – short-term bond issuance can begin. This is important because only when the MOF can plot a yield curve can interest rates be liberalised, and this is one of the most important steps towards building a market economy.

China's three bond markets

At the start of 2002 China had three bond markets, none of them particularly liquid or efficient. The oldest one was based at the SHGSE (where by the end of 2002 bond trading volume was larger than share trading volume), but the largest was the over-the-counter (OTC) market of which banks, insurers and rural credit cooperatives were members. The term OTC simply indicates the type of trading system used: unlike the SHGSE's competitive bidding, the large interbank market players are market makers; they offer to buy and sell bonds in a quote-based system. Since September 1999 some securities and fund companies have also been allowed to participate in this market. The third market, the certificate bond market, which was not much of a market at all since these bonds could only be bought and not sold, was for individuals. However, in February 2002 new rules allowed the trading of new certificate bonds.

The interbank bond market was established in August 1997, after commercial banks were banned from the stock exchanges for lending money through repurchase contracts (or repos) to securities companies, which was illegal. The new market grew quickly: by the end of 1999, it was larger than the one based at the SHGSE. In 2000 the MOF issued Rmb390.4bn of T-bonds here, nearly two-thirds of the year's total issuance. However, despite its size, this market suffers from a number of problems. One is that the vast majority of trading is in repos, in which funds are borrowed in the short term using bonds as collateral. Total trading volume on the OTC market was some Rmb4trn in 2001, two and half times the figure for 2000, but this was made up of Rmb3.96trn in repos, and only Rmb83bn in normal spot trading. In other words, the OTC market is treated mainly as a money market, a market in which companies raise funds for less than one year, in contrast to a capital market in which assets are held for the medium to long term. So while the OTC market helps banks solve their short-term liquidity problems, it plays a limited role in helping them restructure their financial assets, as a good bond market should. Part of the reason is the short supply of T-bonds. There were some Rmb2trn worth of bonds in the OTC market by the end of 2001, an amount that did little to meet the huge demand of China's financial institutions for bonds. There is therefore a general reluctance to sell, and this results in an illiquid spot market. In late 2002 the authorities attempted to improve liquidity with a number of new measures, including a one-day T-bond repo and the promise of repo trading in corporate bonds. Commission rates were also lowered.

Looking forward, however, the PBOC sees the interbank bond market as a potential source of problems for the banks. Several times in the course of the second half of 2002 it tightened credit in the money market to try to stop them from buying bonds. In September, for instance, the central bank withdrew some Rmb25bn of the finance available to banks, meaning that the banks found it difficult to buy the Rmb22bn worth of bonds the MOF was then selling.

The problem, as the PBOC saw it, was that banks, with lots of idle cash, were keen buyers of bonds, but with demand for bonds high, their interest rates had been forced low. The central bank worries that any return of inflation would wipe out the value of the bonds that banks have bought so many of during 2001–02. By the end of 2002 there were signs that the PBOC was winning as the banks began extending more loans and buying fewer bonds.

In contrast to the OTC, the SHGSE allows non-financial companies the opportunity to trade bonds. As a result, spot trading at the SHGSE is more active than at the OTC. By the end of 2002 the SHGSE listed some Rmb257bn of T-bonds. Securities and fund management companies prefer to trade here because it is easier for them to shift between equities and bonds. Less than 30% of fund companies' bonds were held on the OTC market in 2001 (where they trade repos mostly in order to raise short-term funds to subscribe to new shares). However, since 1998 trading volume at the SHGSE has been in steady decline. Spot trading fell from Rmb605bn in 1998 to Rmb366bn in 2000 and has remained at around that level since. Again, a lack of liquidity is to blame.

China's third bond market was never really a market at all. Up till February 2002 the only way for ordinary people to buy T-bonds was through certificates. Issued by the MOF and sold by the banks, certificate T-bonds could not be traded but were still popular because the rates they offered were higher than bank deposit rates. By the late 1990s, 60% of all government debt was held by individuals, in contrast to more developed markets where institutions are the dominant holders of official debt. But these certificates were not ideal because individuals were obliged to hold bonds until maturity, which meant that the government had to offer certificate T-bonds at higher rates than those offered on the OTC market. This was to change in February 2002 when the PBOC allowed institutions and individuals to trade bonds on the interbank market (although bonds issued before February were still not allowed to be traded). However, take-up was low, a result largely blamed on the low interest rate offered. Despite this initial lack of enthusiasm the move should increase aggregate demand for bonds over the medium term since individuals will have an exit option before the bond matures. It should also lower the cost to the MOF to issue debt in the first place. Banks, who provide the intermediary services, can earn income from commissions. However, there are risks for the banks since they are now obliged to buy all the T-bonds that investors want to sell, and to sell all of their holdings if the market so demands.

The World Bank argues that the three markets – the interbank bond market, the stock exchange bond market and the certificate bond market – need to be unified in order to increase liquidity, spread risk and create more rational pricing structures. But where? In more developed markets, including the United States, an OTC market is usually preferred. Bond trading, in which banks make massive ad hoc trades and where individuals often buy and then hold for a long time, requires market makers since there are not enough frequent small trades to facilitate an auction system. (The share market, in contrast, usually operates through a competitive auction system where trades are smaller in size and more frequent. Both the SHGSE and SHZSE operate such a system.) That means China's interbank market would be an ideal place to host all of the country's bond trading. However, the SHGSE, armed with a state-of-the-art trading system and the backing of the CSRC, is also fighting for the privilege. Ever diplomatic, the World Bank argues that if both sites are allowed to develop, they must be connected, allowing all instruments to be traded on both.

Corporate bonds

China's bond market, like the share market, is state-dominated. For the most part, only the government, via the MOF and the two major policy banks, has issued bonds, and companies, even state-owned ones, have been largely excluded. But change is afoot here too.

After mass corporate bond (CB) issuance by local governments during 1992–93, the central government clamped down. It set up a system by which the SDPC sets an annual quota for CB issuance, the PBOC controls their interest rates and the CSRC supervises the trading of the few bonds that make it to market. Figure 2.14 shows the official CSRC statistics on CB issuance. However, these include things not normally classified as CBs, such as house construction bonds and state investment bonds. Table 2.6 provides a more accurate picture, as well as indicating the size of the annual CB quota between 1990 and 1997.

Bond issuance has been low relative to equity issuance. During 1995–97, China issued Rmb46.4bn ($5.6bn) worth of CBs compared with

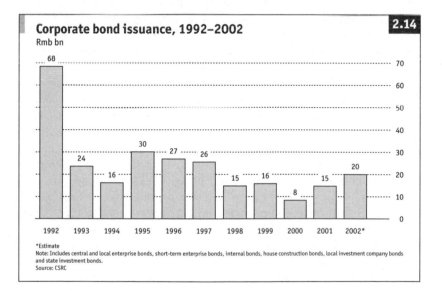

Corporate bond issuance, 1992–2002   **2.14**

Rmb bn

*Estimate
Note: Includes central and local enterprise bonds, short-term enterprise bonds, internal bonds, house construction bonds, local investment company bonds and state investment bonds.
Source: CSRC

Table 2.6 **Enterprise bond issuance, 1990–97 (Rmb bn)**

Year	Quota	Actual issuance volume	Total outstanding debt
1990	17.5	7.6	15.1
1991	25.0	14.6	24.2
1992	35.0	44.9	61.6
1993	49.0	2.0	55.7
1994	4.5	3.8	50.4
1995	13.0	13.0	47.1
1996	25.0	14.8	45.2
1997	30.0	18.6	45.2

Note: Includes the debt of central enterprises, local enterprises, as well as internal debt issuance and local investment company debt. It does not include short-term financing liabilities.
Source: *Capital Market Magazine*

Rmb123.6bn in equities. During 1998–2000, using the (exaggerated) CSRC figures, the proportion was Rmb38.9bn to Rmb317.4bn in equities. It has also been low compared with the quota. While the annual CB quota for 1994–97 was Rmb72.5bn, actual issuance was only Rmb57.4bn.

Such small CB volumes have been convenient for the government since, unlike in Western capital markets, shares are a cheaper financing mechanism than bonds. In the West, the original owners dilute their share of the company's profits, and their control rights, by creating other shareholders. While shareholders then demand dividends and a say in how the company is run, debt holders receive only a fixed interest payment, which is generally cheaper to finance since the debt holder is taking on less risk. In China's capital markets, however, because corporate governance has been so poor, dividend payments low and equity so far has entailed no real ownership rights, shares are relatively cheap for SOEs to issue. So favoured has equity been that during 1998–99, all CB issuance was simply suspended (the CSRC figures for these years are made up entirely of nonstandard bond issues). Daily CB trading volume at the stock exchanges averaged only Rmb50m during 2000–01. By the end of December 2002 only Rmb20.9bn worth of CBs were listed on the two stock exchanges (compared to a tradable capitalisation of A-Shares of Rmb125bn). Table 2.7 shows the situation. This hostile policy supports SOEs but damages China's capital market. Companies find it extremely useful to diversify their sources of finance, and banks, insurance firms and investment firms also suffer a lack of opportunities to diversify their portfolios.

Table 2.7 **China's corporate bond market, end-2002 (Rmb bn)**

Number listed	20
Total capital raised at issuance	27.9
Market capitalisation	20.9

Source: www.p5w.net

But there are signs of change. In September 2001 nine SOEs were allowed to issue Rmb19.5bn of CBs and the number has since climbed. According to the China Development Bank, at least Rmb23bn of CBs were to be issued in 2002. Other sources stated that in September 2002 the SDPC authorised Rmb27bn of CBs to be issued by ten companies. Shortly after, Guangdong Mobile, a subsidiary of China Mobile, made the largest CB issue yet, an offering worth Rmb8bn. In addition to the greater scale, the bond market is becoming increasingly sophisticated. In July 2000, for example, the Three Gorges Development Company issued the first floating rate bond, and since then companies have also offered a fixed premium on a floating bank deposit rate. The Rmb5bn China Telecom issue in June 2001 was the first CB issue to use market pricing, rather than having its issue price set administratively. Maturities are becoming more varied, extending to 15 years on a Three Gorges issue. Another innovation is that since 1999 most CBs have paid their interest yearly. Previously, all interest had been paid at maturity.

A consensus appears to have formed in the government to develop this market. There are at least three reasons for this policy shift. First, since the bear market in equities began in July 2001, SOE managers have become frustrated by their inability to raise capital. With investors unwilling to buy into their share offerings, many have lobbied the CSRC and PBOC to be allowed to issue CBs instead. The bet is that investors will be keener to buy something with a guaranteed return. Second, interest rates are low. China's consumer price index fell 0.8% year-on-year during the first half of 2002, and by the summer analysts were talking about the possibility of a ninth drop in nominal rates before the end of the year. This means that the current costs of CB issuance are very low. Third, there is demand for CBs among institutional investors. Currently, investment funds and securities companies are restricted to buying high-risk, high-return equity and low-risk, low-return bank deposits. CBs offer a mixture of risk and return that helps support the construction of efficient portfolios. Banks, currently restricted to holding Treasury bonds, would also benefit from access to a deeper bond market. Many small investors are looking for a new place to park their funds after a new CSRC ruling in 2002 raised the costs of buying shares at their IPO. One firm, China Fund Management, established the first bond fund in late 2002. Others are working on setting up a bond index.

To ensure the development of an effective CB market, there are a number of areas that need to be worked on. The SDPC needs to relax the CB approval system to allow more state and non-state companies to issue and list debt. Current rules restrict issuance to only large SOEs. More flexibility here would be useful. The PBOC should allow also more flexibility in the rates CBs can offer, although not enough to undermine the bank deposit interest rate structure. Currently CBs are restricted to within some 40% of the relevant bank deposit rate. The problem with this is that bond pricing cannot properly account for the additional risks involved in holding the bond. There are also a whole number of wider issues. Credit rating agencies (or CRAs), the companies which assess the risks associated with a company's debt, should be made more independent and more reliable: institutional investors will buy bonds only if they are assured of their quality. There are also complex legal issues to be addressed, including the rules governing bankruptcy: bondholders need to be assured of protection in the event of bankruptcy, something that they currently are not. Like the share market, bond market development very much depends on the necessary institutions being put in place.

Convertible bonds

The CSRC is also actively supporting the development of the convertible bond (CV) market. A CV is simply a CB that includes an option for the holder to convert the bond into equity at a fixed date, at a fixed price. Since CVs allow holders to buy the company's equity at a discount to the market price, it allows bondholders to take advantage of any share price appreciation while at the same time ensuring minimal risk (since the CV still pays a guaranteed interest rate and need not be converted). CVs are thus often issued at lower rates than CBs, and thus can be more cost-effective for the issuer, although the company may have to promise to buy back the CV if the conversion price is not reached.

In recent years there has been some experiment with CVs. Nanning Chemical Industry issued the first in August 1998, raising Rmb150m ($18.1m). However, by the end of 2001 only two CVs were trading pub-

Table 2.8 **China's convertible bond market, end-2002 (Rmb bn)**

Number listed	9
Total capital raised at issuance	7.2
Market capitalisation	7.4

Source: www.p5w.net

licly: Shanghai Hongqiao Airport and Maolian, a steel firm. At year-end 2002, seven more had made it to the boards, as Table 2.8 shows. There is thus much room for growth. In April 2001 the CSRC issued new rules that signalled its intention to nurture this market, but on the basis of tough criteria. It limited the issuance of CVs to listed companies (whereas previously non-listed SOEs had also been allowed). Companies must have recently distributed cash dividends, have an outstanding performance (as judged by the CSRC), had no recent asset reorganisations or disclosure problems, and in the previous three years had sufficient profits to pay interest on a CB. Their return on equity (ROE) must be 10% (or 7% if the enterprise is involved in energy, infrastructure or natural resources) and their debt-equity ratio must be less than 70%, a measure which only 85 of the 1,160 listed companies satisfied at year-end 2001. Despite these restrictions, some 61 companies had stated their intention to apply to issue CVs by July 2002, raising at least Rmb4obn in total. Haier, a white goods manufacturer, hoped to raise Rmb2.6bn, Minsheng Bank Rmb2.3bn. It was reported in June 2002 that over 50 had received permission to proceed. The first to go ahead since the 2001 rules was Shenzhen Wanke. It issued Rmb1.5bn in CVs with a 1.5% coupon rate in June 2002.

Some analysts complain that these conditions are too restrictive. Only some 20% of CVs in the United States are considered by a credit rating agency to be of investment grade (although in Europe the proportion is 90%), and the majority are issued by small- and medium-sized companies. However, given the immature nature of China's capital market, the weak rule of law and the large expense which goes into evaluating companies that issue CVs in the United States, the CSRC's tough stance should signal to investors that CVs are worthy of their attention.

3 Foreign investors and Chinese equity: the B- and H-share markets

For any country, one important reason for having a stockmarket is to attract foreign investment. This rationale has been especially important since the 1980s when a worldwide boom in privatisation began, combined with widespread liberalisation in investment regulations and a huge increase in portfolio capital flows between countries. The first surge in capital flows to emerging markets in recent times took place in the 1970s, mostly in the form of syndicated bank loans to Latin America. Most of the loans were extended to governments, many of which went on to waste the money. Following a global rise in interest rates in the early 1980s, many of these loans became unserviceable and the developing world's debt crisis began. When capital flows restarted in the late 1980s they were dominated by portfolio capital (capital that does not buy control of assets but buys financial assets like shares and bonds) and foreign direct investment (FDI – foreign investment is classified as FDI when it takes an ownership stake in a company). This way foreign investors had more control over the use of their funds: in the case of a crisis, fixed assets purchased with FDI could be sold and portfolio capital could be quickly pulled out. With their fast growth rates emerging markets again became hot destinations for rich-world investors. Portfolio capital accounted for about 40% of all the financial flows to emerging markets in the 1990s. Investors were seduced by the double-digit growth rates in much of Asia, and by the start of 1997 rich world mutual funds held some $77bn worth of Asian equities. The Asian financial crisis of 1997–98 triggered a dramatic collapse in portfolio flows to the region however. Net portfolio investment in the region peaked at $27bn in 1996, and fell to $8.9bn in 1997, turning negative in 1998. By 2001 a mild recovery was under way with $3.2bn flowing into the region during the year.

In addition to encouraging inflows of foreign capital, many firms in developing economies have gone abroad in search of finance. By the end of 1999, 72 companies from Eastern Europe and the former Soviet Union had American Depositary Receipts (ADRs) listed on the NYSE and NASDAQ, and 61 listed in London. A depository receipt is a way of allowing shares issued domestically to be listed in a foreign market. The incentive to do this was particularly strong for large firms that needed larger sums of capital which small local stockmarkets could not provide. By the end of the 1990s seven of Russia's ten largest domestically-listed companies had issued ADRs. However, it is worth noting that depository receipts hurt a country's domestic market since they reduce liquidity and lower the incentives for foreign portfolio managers to become involved.

China's path to financial globalisation

China has done things a little differently. Although the government has been deliberately coy about opening up the stockmarket to foreign capital, it has pursued three other strategies for attracting foreign investment. It has tried hard to maximise FDI inflows, it has set up a share market dedicated to foreign investors and it has been a keen issuer of equity abroad.

FDI gives a foreign entity "control" of domestic assets. When exactly control is achieved is a matter of some interpretation. In the United States a foreign entity gaining a 10% stake in a firm qualifies as FDI. In China the investment counts as FDI only when it takes a 25% stake. FDI can take two forms: greenfield investments, in which new capacity is built, or the acquisition of assets of local firms. If economic success were all about importing huge sums of FDI, then China would be home and dry. In 2001 it attracted some $50bn, a record, and in 2002 it looked on course to attract even more. The country's total stock of FDI totalled some $369.3bn at the end of 2001, some 20% of all FDI in the developing world. But there are at least two provisos to this story. First, relative to the size of the economy, this is still a small figure, some $300 of FDI per head of population, compared with $670 for Thailand and $2,400 for Malaysia. Even Indonesia ($280) gives China a run for its money. China's FDI is concentrated in the east and south of the country. Second, a large chunk, some 10-20% of total FDI, is thought to be domestic capital round-tripping through Hong Kong to take advantage of preferential tax rates for foreign investors. However, with WTO entry secured, investment from the major Western economies is increasing and as tax rates harmonise, the incentive for round-tripping will decrease. More FDI from Western multinationals should mean more technology transfer, which should in turn lead to higher rates of productivity, benefiting the wider economy.

The second, far less successful, means of attracting of attracting foreign capital has been via a special foreigner-only B-share market set up

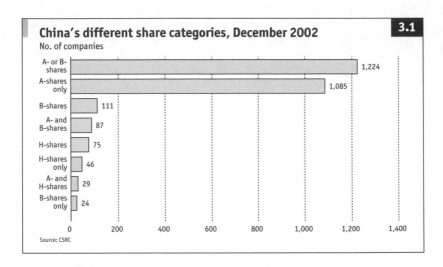

China's different share categories, December 2002   `3.1`

No. of companies

A- or B-shares	1,224
A-shares only	1,085
B-shares	111
A- and B-shares	87
H-shares	75
H-shares only	46
A- and H-shares	29
B-shares only	24

Source: CSRC

in 1991. By December 2002, 112 companies had issued B-shares. However, as this chapter shows, the B-share market has been a failure for a number of technical and political reasons. Third, unlike smaller countries, China has been able to leverage enough worldwide excitement about its reforms and its future prospects to raise money abroad. By the end of 2002, China had listed 75 companies abroad, mostly in Hong Kong. Figure 3.1 shows Mainland companies issuing shares to foreign investors, both outside China (H-shares) and inside China (B-shares).

Table 3.1 compares the three sources of financing. FDI is clearly the most important, growing steadily over the past decade. Overseas share issuance has waxed and waned, becoming more important in recent years. In 2000 it accounted for 17% of FDI. The B-share market has simply flopped. In 1997, its peak year, B-shares only attracted 2.2% of the amount that FDI did, and has since declined.

This three-pronged strategy has had at least one important benefit. Large volumes of foreign capital have been attracted, but with the capital account closed, China has been able to avoid the crisis that engulfed almost all of its Asian neighbours during 1997–98. No volatile portfolio flows out of the country undermined its stockmarket or destabilised its currency. Open capital accounts (that is, with a freely convertible currency) helped destabilise East Asia in 1997 (although domestic problems were at the core of the crisis) and also Argentina in 2001.

However, China's present policy bears a number of costs. First, attention appears to have been focused on maximising FDI to the detriment of

Table 3.1 **Capital raised from equity issuance abroad and FDI, 1991–2002**

	Overseas share issues (Rmb bn)	B-share issuance (Rmb bn)	Foreign direct investment (Rmb bn)
1991	–	–	–
1992	–	4.4	–
1993	6.1	3.8	–
1994	18.9	3.8	280.5
1995	3.2	3.3	297.1
1996	8.4	4.7	332.8
1997	36.0	8.1	366.9
1998	3.8	2.6	363.5
1999	4.7	0.4	322.0
2000	56.2	1.4	318.7
2001	7.0	0.0	365.2
2002	18.2	0.0	431.6*

* Estimate
Note: Share issues exclude rights and secondary issues.
Sources: CSRC; IMF; Economist Intelligence Unit

sorting out the domestic financial system. A look at the country's huge household savings – some Rmb8.3bn ($1bn) in July 2002 – suggests that the problem the economy faces is not lack of capital, but an institutional problem in getting this capital to work. Yasheng Huang at the Harvard Business School takes this observation one step further and argues that China's huge FDI inflows are a sign of weakness. They indicate a banking system and capital market unable to allocate this capital sitting in savings accounts efficiently to where it is needed most, forcing entrepreneurs to seek capital from overseas by selling equity in their firms.

Second, the government has allowed only a few chosen firms – mostly SOEs – access to foreign capital markets, thus channelling foreign funds to its favourite firms, a highly inefficient means of allocating foreign capital. Allowing firms, whatever their ownership structure, to compete openly for foreign capital would be much healthier. It would help instil a greater desire to improve performance and transparency among China's large firms.

The third benefit lost is that this system has limited the import of international standards of accounting, corporate governance and regulation. Foreign analysts are more likely to be objective, even given their standard conflicts of interests (so well displayed in recent scandals involving Western investment banks whose research departments made recommendations to help the corporate side of their bank's business), than analysts employed by domestic state-owned companies.

The B-share market

The B-share market, the market in shares denominated in foreign currency which was, at least initially, created exclusively for foreign investors has been a failure. It remains small and only 112 firms had issued B-shares by December 2002, all but 24 of which had also issued A-shares. By this time A-share IPOs had raised Rmb460.9bn and A-share rights issues had raised Rmb209.7bn, while B-share IPOs had raised only Rmb38.2bn and B-share rights Rmb2.7bn, some 8% and 1.3% respectively, of the A-share volumes, as Figure 3.2 shows. Figure 3.3 shows a decline of B-share issues in the late 1990s, and none in 2001 and 2002. Domestic investors – individuals legally and institutions illegally – now dominate the trading that still exists and ownership. Hampered by low liquidity and poor-quality listed companies, the market never really got off the ground following its creation in 1991 and is now well and truly dead. The main issue now facing the CSRC is how to bury it.

The B-share market has its roots in the exuberance that existed in the late 1980s about the prospects for China's share market. Back then anything seemed possible. A number of financiers working at Shenyin Securities in Shanghai began pushing for foreign capital to be allowed into the nascent stockmarket. There are reports that Taiwanese capital, using locally registered companies, was already investing in Mainland Chinese shares by 1988. Shenyin's proposal was heard by the Shanghai party secretary, Jiang Zemin, who was positive but remained unconvinced about the existence of demand from foreign investors. Research began at the PBOC in Shanghai, and Shenyin started preparing a couple of companies to make experimental issues of "foreign" shares issued in-country. The Tiananmen protests in June 1989 put the proposal on hold, but things got under way again in late 1991 with the first B-share offering, Shanghai Vacuum, a television tube manufacturer. Investors jammed phone lines to get hold of a piece of the company and even at 17-times 1991 earnings, the share price doubled in a short while.

The choice of a category of share exclusively reserved for foreign investors was odd. In order to introduce foreign capital in an orderly and gradual fashion, most other emerging markets have established variations of the Qualified Foreign Institutional Investor (QFII) frame-

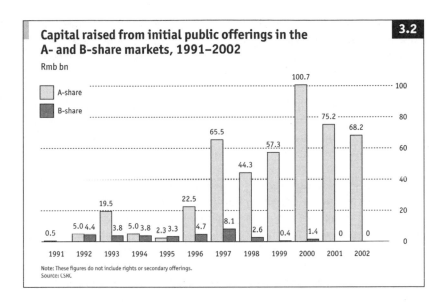

Capital raised from initial public offerings in the A- and B-share markets, 1991–2002   **3.2**

Rmb bn

- A-share
- B-share

Note: These figures do not include rights or secondary offerings.
Source: CSRC

work (see also Chapter 8). In QFII, a small amount of foreign capital is remitted into the country (through a "hole" managed by the central bank in the otherwise closed capital account), which is allowed to be invested in listed companies, with certain restrictions. Thus, although domestic and international capital use different accounts, they trade the same shares: there is one price and all shareholders are treated equally.

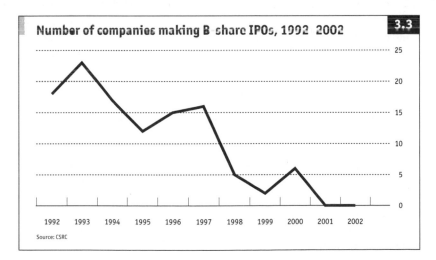

Number of companies making B-share IPOs, 1992–2002   **3.3**

Source: CSRC

When considering such schemes, however, China's policymakers had to cope with the ideological legacy of communism. While FDI, which bought fixed assets and employed people, could just about be accepted, portfolio investment was still seen as intrinsically speculative and unproductive. It was only by keeping foreign portfolio separate and by setting up a separate authorisation system for companies who wanted access to it, that ideological opposition could be neutralised. The B-share system also calmed the fears of those worried about the stability of the renminbi since no currency conversion would be required. The result was, despite official claims to the contrary, a market with shares with different prices and different rights from domestic shares.

After the excitement of Shanghai Vacuum, investors' sentiment for B-shares soon soured. In July 1992 Shanghai Chlor-Alkali Chemical's issue of B-shares priced at 20-times earnings was met with indifference: the share price fell by half within a week. Investors lost confidence in Shanghai Vacuum after reports came out about how it had wasted its funds, and its share price dropped some 50% in the early months of 1992. Shanghai Compressor issued B-shares in December 1992, which at 8.7-times 1992 earnings was the most realistically priced B-share so far, but that did not stop the price falling soon after issue. The following April, Shenzhen Wanke's B-share IPO flopped, with only half of the shares purchased. Hong Kong-based China funds, many of which had championed B-shares in early 1992, now avoided the market. By late November 1992 only 20% of their assets was invested in B-shares, and that proportion was to fall further as the decade progressed. The problem was that most of these companies, chosen by the Shanghai and Shenzhen governments up until 1996, were former SOEs and were of terrible quality. The other crippling factor was that the former government's plans for the market were never clear.

Not to be: B-share policy, 1993–97
Since 1993 the government's policy on B-shares has been disorganised, to put it politely. While numerous schemes for developing it have been floated, only a few have been implemented, and then usually badly. In the absence of foreigners, it has been domestic investors, speculating on rumour and hoping to take advantage of the arbitrage opportunities with A-shares, which have kept the market alive, if barely. Domestic investors quickly got involved, particularly in Shenzhen, where they used the passports of friends and relatives resident in Hong Kong to open B-share accounts.

Table 3.2 **B-share mid-year results, 2000–01 (Rmb)**

	——— SHGSE ———		——— SHZSE ———	
	2001	*2000*	*2001*	*2000*
EPS	0.074	0.072	0.099	0.111
ROE	2.028	2.605	2.68	2.96
NAV per share	2.54	2.356	3.73	–

Sources: Stock exchanges; press reports

Why were they keen when foreign investors were not? B-shares have always traded at a significant discount to A-shares, in contrast to most other emerging markets where shares which foreign investors are allowed to buy commonly trade at a premium. This is because of excess domestic demand for equity in China, a problem examined in Chapter 2, and a lack of demand for B-shares among foreigners. Since they can invest mostly anywhere in the world, in any number of financial instruments, foreign investors' appetite for China's poor-quality, illiquid B-shares has been low compared with trapped domestic investors. The discount to A-shares has encouraged domestic investors to buy B-shares in the hope that the CSRC would combine the two markets and their B-share prices would rise to the same level as A-shares. The central government has made periodic attempts to crack down on domestic investors active in B-shares, but has usually failed, announcing finally in 2001 that individual Chinese could invest legally in the market.

But it was hardly an appetising prospect. The average profit per share of B-share companies, at Rmb0.5 in 1999, was 48% lower than in 1998, and the 2001 results were even worse. Net profits fell 92% year-on-year to an average of Rmb5.3m per company. Table 3.2 compares mid-year results for 2001 with the previous year. Return on equity (ROE) declined at both exchanges, though earnings per share (EPS) appears to have stabilised at Rmb0.07 at the SHGSE and Rmb0.1 in Shenzhen.

Even some of the market's best performers have disappointed. China Bicycle and Shenzhen Lionda, a lighting-equipment manufacturer, reported huge losses in 2001. Konka, a consumer electronics firm based in Shenzhen, made a net loss of Rmb699.8m, down from a net profit of Rmb214.4m in 2000. It had overestimated domestic demand for televisions and was hit badly by competitive price cutting. The only B-share companies to produce respectable earnings in 2001 were in the power sector. Heilongjiang Electric Power's net profits grew 23%, Guangdong Electric Power was up 9% and Nanshan Power rose 40%.

How to bury the B-share market?

Rather than accept that the B-share market needs to be closed down as soon as possible, some commentators, and some within the CSRC, argue that it should be revived. Their proposals include boosting the market through listings of larger, better-quality companies, making adjustment to the fees levied on B-share trading and setting preferential tax policies for companies listed there. However, these proposals have not been acted upon, and given that 2001–02 saw no new listings at all, the weight of opinion appears to be in favour of closure rather than revival, probably via a merger with the A-share market. But no one is rushing to set this in train, and it will be tricky to organise.

This is because of the foreign-currency denomination of B-shares and foreign ownership restrictions on A-shares. B-shares are denominated in Hong Kong dollars in Shenzhen and in United States dollars in Shanghai, and A-shares are all traded in renminbi. The two currencies cannot be exchanged freely at present. And even if they could be, the two categories of shares could not simply be merged since that would mean foreign investors gaining immediate and unrestricted access to A-shares.

Of course, when the QFII framework is up and running the problem should be easier to solve: the B-shares held by foreigners would simply become A-shares and would be transferred into the investors' QFII accounts. In 1999 Jardine Fleming, then a British brokerage house, came up with a proposal to do just that. It suggested reviving the B-share market by allowing Chinese citizens with foreign exchange to invest in B-shares via dedicated mutual funds. If, the logic went, Chinese investors were encouraged to believe that this was the first step towards a merger of the two markets, B-share prices would quickly rise to the level of A-shares. The QFII system could then be introduced. Foreign institutions holding B-shares would receive QFII licences and remit dollars into China, and B-shares would be redenominated into renminbi at the official exchange rate. At this point the A- and B-share markets would be effectively merged. Of course, although Jardine's scheme was workable, it did mean that all holders of B-shares, including Jardine, would have to be automatically granted QFII licences. At the time of writing, with the QFII system just about to start, it was unclear if the CSRC was thinking of taking up the plan.

There are other proposals on the table for sorting out the B-share market. One involves listed companies buying back their B-shares. Although this sounds simple, the pricing of such re-purchases, and whether or not they would be compulsory, would be difficult issues to resolve. Most B-share listed companies would struggle to find the requisite funds. One variation on this idea would be for companies to buy back only those B-shares held by foreign investors, now a small proportion of the total. Estimates in 2000 put the level of foreign ownership of B-shares at 40% of the market's tradable capitalisation, but after profit-taking in 2001, this proportion is now probably nearer 20%. After foreign investors were bought out, outstanding B-shares could then easily be reclassified as A-shares. Of course, there is no need for a "one-solution-fits-all" approach and the CSRC might choose this method for those companies with low levels of foreign ownership and other methods for others.

In 2001 the CSRC took steps to revive interest in B-shares, apparently with another aim in mind. On February 20th 2001 it formally allowed Chinese individuals with forex accounts to buy B-shares (many having done so illegally much earlier). In the space of two days, February 26th and 27th, a total of 340,000 new accounts were opened, and heavy buying led to the A-/B-share discount narrowing significantly. Officially this move was meant to soak up some of China's domestically-held foreign exchange. Since 1998 households' forex deposits have grown at an annual rate of 20–30% to total around $144bn at the end of July 2002, while renminbi deposits had only grown at 8% a year. (A further $50bn was thought to be held in the banks by corporate entities.) It was hoped that by allowing access to B-shares these deposits could be coaxed out of the banks, invested in domestic industry and prevented from escaping abroad.

But the CSRC's policy soon backfired. Although the sudden spurt in B-share prices suggested large sums of money had been attracted, the rally faltered on June 1st 2001, when individuals without foreign-exchange accounts opened before the February deadline were also allowed to purchase B-shares. Prices spent the rest of the year in decline. B-share P/ES fell from an average of 45 in March 2001 at the SHGSE to 31 a year later. No significant forex funds were coaxed out of the banks in the long term. In fact, many foreign investors used the rally to exit the market completely, many with profits. Going the other way were thousands of domestic investors hoping for a quick merger and instant profits as B-shares rose in price to the level of A-shares. They are now trapped and disillusioned.

Table 3.3 **Distribution of China's foreign-listed shares, December 2002**

	Only in United States	Only in London	Only in Singapore	Only in Hong Kong	HK and US	HK and London	HK and Singapore
No. of companies	1	0	1	59	12	3	0

Source: CSRC

Overseas share issuance

The government has been keen for companies to issue equity in capital markets overseas, mostly in Hong Kong and the United States. Such issues are important: not only do they provide access to deeper markets and therefore more funds, but the companies that do this are important ambassadors abroad for China's industrial reforms. For these reasons, international issues have been mostly reserved for large, strategically important and relatively successful SOEs. By December 2002, 75 PRC-registered companies had listed H-shares in Hong Kong, New York and London, raising a total of $20.4bn. 46 of these companies had issued shares only overseas, while 29 had also issued shares at home too, as Table 3.1 (see page 49) shows.

In addition to these H-shares, by early 2002 there were also some 60 "red-chips" listed in Hong Kong, companies with their headquarters in Hong Kong but which were controlled by the PRC government, or entities connected to it, and which had their dominant operations located in the Mainland. The advantage of overseas issuance, aside from the funds it provides, has been that it has forced these companies to undergo thorough restructuring, to have been audited to international standards and to be disciplined and monitored by, for most of the time at least, a demanding investment community. However, the romance between China and the international financial markets has had its ups and downs. The first fling began with Deng Xiaoping's reformist *nanxun* comments in early 1992.

The 1992 equity boom

As Chapter 2 explained, in early 1992 a frail Deng, concerned that conservatives were again wrecking the economy, decided to go on holiday to the coast. But this was no ordinary vacation. After a quick round of golf, Deng began visiting factories and speaking to government officials, singing the merits of economic growth. He set off an unstoppable stampede towards reform. When this hit the radar screens of international investors, there was a gold rush for Chinese equity. During the year, 37 Hong Kong-based China funds were established, raising some $1.8bn. Barton Biggs, who visited China for Morgan Stanley, wrote:

> [I was] stunned by the enormous size of China. Sometimes you have to spend time in a country to get really focused on the investment case. After eight days in China, I'm tuned in, overfed and bullish.

But frustratingly, China remained closed to foreign portfolio capital. Biggs solved the problem by recommending increased investment in Hong Kong stocks. Others wanted China to come to them. Investment banks foraged China for restructured SOEs wanting to go overseas to raise capital. Qingdao Brewery was visited by 25 investment bankers in the space of two months during 1992, leading to official notices banning foreign bankers, lawyers and accountants from approaching these companies about international listings. The world's major stock exchanges joined in: the New York, NASDAQ, Hong Kong, Singapore and Vancouver exchanges all sent delegations to the Mainland during 1992–94 to attract listings. The competition between them was intense. Vancouver officials were said to be ready to create a separate board to accommodate the "unique" accounting standards of Mainland companies. And the NYSE probably went one step too far with the listing of Shandong Huaneng Power Development in October 1994, allowing the company to provide only one year of audited accounts and two years of unaudited accounts. Normally, it required three years of audited accounts. Although the United States Securities and Exchange Commission (SEC) claimed that it was unreasonable to expect such accounts from a freshly restructured SOE, Hong Kong bankers had cause for complaint: all nine of the H-shares listed in the territory by that time had provided three years of audited accounts.

The one in front: Brilliance Automotive

The first real Mainland play to hit the international capital markets was Brilliance China Automotive Holdings. It issued 5m shares on October 9th 1992 in New York, raising some $72m after the accountants, lawyers and underwriters had been paid. The issue was 12 times oversubscribed and Brilliance was the second most active stock on Wall Street on its first day, rising from $16 a share to just over $20. Such huge demand was for a company which had only one asset: a 51% holding (which, as it turned out, was not really a controlling interest) in a small mini-bus manufacturer in northern China, Shenyang Jinbei Passenger Automotive Manufacturing Company. Jinbei was the exclusive manufacturer of deluxe mini-buses (from kits provided by Toyota) in China. In 1991 Jinbei's turnover was only $114.4m and its net income was only $8.4m. Envious investment bankers, together with some at the Hong Kong Stock Exchange (HKEX), argued that Brilliance was not actually a first. As the company was incorporated in Bermuda, and had its headquarters in Hong Kong, according to NYSE rules it was actually a Hong Kong, not a PRC, company. Qingdao Beer, listing in Hong Kong in July 1993, would officially become the first Mainland company to list overseas. But at the time, with its 51,375 employees and manufacturing operations in Shenyang, Liaoning province, China Brilliance was as close as a foreign investor could get to Mainland China from the comfort of his Wall Street trading desk.

Preparing Brilliance to list was a gargantuan struggle. The main challenge, which fell to one man, Yang Rong, the founder of the Brilliance Group, was entirely political: how to win approval from the government? During 1992 government officials were engaged in an intense struggle over stockmarket regulation. Riots in Shenzhen in August 1992 (see Chapter 2) had discredited the PBOC and moves were already under way to create a new regulatory body. However, while negotiations were going on, the PBOC retained its power to approve all issuance applications, which was convenient since the PBOC had an indirect ownership stake in Brilliance through the Chinese Financial Education Development Foundation (CFEDF), an "educational" subsidiary set up by the PBOC. While Yang Rong was winning over the powerful in Beijing, accountants and underwriters sweated the details. Converting three years of financial statements from Chinese to American GAAP standards required 11,000 man-hours from Arthur Andersen. Inventory was written off and allowances for depreciation increased, deflating the company's assets considerably. Another problem required considerable guile: re-organising the ownership structure. Before the listing the CFEDF had owned 78.4% of the group. Jinbei Automobile, a company owned by the Shenyang municipality, held the remaining 21.6%. Brilliance initially only had a 25% stake in Shenyang Automotive. This was a problem since without a majority stake Brilliance could not attract investors – it had no other assets. A 15% stake was acquired from Hainan Huajin TIC for $12m, but Jinbei, the majority owner, refused to reduce its 60% stake. To solve the problem, a cross-ownership structure was established. 11% of Jinbei's stake in Shenyang Automotive was exchanged with Brilliance in return for a 21.6% stake in Brilliance itself. The result was that on paper Brilliance owned a 51% stake in Shenyang Automotive, while in practice Jinbei retained a 49% stake, and de facto control over Brilliance itself. When the public was offered a 28.75% stake in Brilliance, and CFEDF's stake was reduced to 55.8%, and Jinbei's stake was reduced to 15.37%.

Where Brilliance blazed a trail, other companies were desperate to follow. China Tyre Holdings, a subsidiary of China Strategic Investment, a conglomerate run by Oei Hong Leong with interests in more than 100 companies in the PRC, listed on the NYSE in July 1993, raising close to $100m. Bermuda-incorporated Ek-Chor China Motorcycle followed, raising $16.5m before expenses, most of which was passed down to its subsidiary, Shanghai Motorcycle. But within a year the enthusiasm for foreign listings had waned. For one thing, the leadership in Beijing was having second thoughts and the CSRC chairman, Liu Hongru, was ordered to limit the number of foreign listings because of fears that the development of the domestic market was suffering. By mid-1993 the Mainland economy was having to retrench, and foreign investors ran for cover. By June 1994 the share prices of Brilliance, Ek-Chor and China Tyre were all at least 30% lower than their heady peaks.

After its successful IPO, Brilliance hit trouble during 1993–94 as its buyers tightened their budgets in response to monetary retrenchment. A revival in its business in the late 1990s led to a listing in Hong Kong. But by 2000 Brilliance was again suffering, this time from suspicions over a multitude of deals involving Yang Rong, further confusion over its ownership structure and reports of corruption. The HKEX and NYSE suspended trading in the company's shares on June 21st 2002 after Yang Rong was removed from management. Yang reportedly fled to the United States, claiming persecution from officialdom, and his stake in Brilliance was frozen by a Ningbo City court.

The 1996–97 "red-chip" bonanza
The second flush of enthusiasm for foreign listings came in 1996, and the object of desire this time was the "red-chips". With the imminent return of Hong Kong to Mainland control in July 1997 and the resurgence of economic growth in China, a new wave of positive sentiment from investors hit Mainland stocks in Hong Kong. The word was out too from Beijing that a bull run in the British territory would be ideal for the run-up to the return of the territory to China (anything less would constitute

a loss of face for the new rulers). Companies such as GITIC Enterprises, a marble and real-estate business based in Guangdong province, led the way. In March 1997 investors put up $13bn in subscriptions for its IPO. In the week the company held the funds before it issued the shares it earned $8m in bank interest, more than its entire profits for 1996. By early 1997 there were some 45 red-chips listed in Hong Kong. Their popularity derived principally from their political connections, their *guanxi*. Hu Zhaoguang, Beijing's deputy mayor, was the vice-chairman of Beijing Enterprises Holdings, which listed in Hong Kong in 1997. Larry Yung, the son of Rong Yiren, formerly China's vice-president, bought an inactive HKSE-listed company, injected two large blocks of shares in Hong Kong Telecom and Cathy Pacific, and renamed the company CITIC Pacific. He then went on a buying binge funded by the loans from the Bank of China to form the most powerful of all the red-chips. CITIC Pacific's market capitalisation of $150m in 1990 had risen some 6,600% to over $10bn by early 1997, before Hong Kong was handed back to China.

Such crazy valuations were short-lived. After the establishment of the Hong Kong Special Administrative Region (of China, the HKSAR), share values plummeted. Media stories of red-chip corruption became rife and by March 2002 only ten of the 100-plus red-chips and H-shares listed in Hong Kong were trading above their issue price.

Share issuance in the United States

Outside Hong Kong, the United States has been the favoured location for PRC companies escaping abroad. Including four Hong Kong-listed red-chips, by June 2002 China's total of 17 companies listed in New York was more than any other developing country outside the Americas (see Table 3.4). CSFB, the investment bank, estimates that by June 2002 the market capitalisation of Chinese companies listed abroad was some $170bn.

The American Depositary Receipt (ADR) has been a favourite vehicle. An ADR is simply a negotiable instrument, listed in the United States and settled in US dollars, that represents an ownership interest in the shares of a non-American company. They enable investors in the United States to gain exposure to foreign companies without the costs of cross-border transactions. In addition, institutional investors, who face regulatory restrictions on their holdings of equities overseas, are free to buy them. JP Morgan created the first ADR in 1927 for Selfridges, a British retailer. Since then numerous firms such as BP, Nokia, Unilever, GlaxoSmithKline and Taiwan Semiconductor, have issued ADRs to tap into the world's largest equity market. At the end of 2001, JP Morgan estimated

Table 3.4 **Non-US companies listed on the NYSE, June 2002**

Country	No. of companies
Brazil	33
China	13
Hong Kong	11*
India	8
Indonesia	3
Japan	17
South Korea	5
Mexico	25
Russia	5
Singapore	1
Taiwan	4

* Of which four are red-chips.
Note: Companies that have listed multiple share types are counted only once.
Source: NYSE

that the total capitalisation of the 2,200 odd ADRs was $500bn, accounting for about one-third of all American investment in foreign equities.

There are four different types of ADR, each involving its own regulatory standards and conferring different benefits (see Glossary): Level I, Level II, Level III and Rule 144A.

Up until June 2002, 31 Mainland companies and at least nine Hong Kong-registered red chips had issued ADRs in the United States. Of these, 14 of them had raised capital via Level-III ADRs and had their shares listed on the NYSE, as Tables 3.5 and 3.6 show. JP Morgan predicts that by 2007 ADRs originating in the PRC will account for more than half of all ADRs coming out of Asia.

During the 1990s, heavy industry, energy and infrastructure stocks came to be listed in New York. But in 2000 foreign investors fell head over heels for stocks that combined the two things that promised untrammelled wealth: China and the Internet. Dozens of Internet Content Providers (ICPs) and e-commerce firms in China looked longingly at NASDAQ as the answer to their financing and publicity problems, and NASDAQ investors gazed back, mesmerised by the speed of IT development in China and the potential size of the e-commerce market. China's government was much more shy, and it was not hard to see why. For one thing, in a media sector previously monopolised by state-owned organs, websites like Sina.com

Table 3.5 **Mainland China ADRs, June 2002**

Company	Market	Date of listing
Aluminium Corp of China	NYSE	12/01
Beijing Datang Power	OTC	
China Eastern Airlines	NYSE	02/97
China Petroleum & Chemical (Sinopec)	NYSE	10/00
China Shipping Development	PORTAL*	
China Southern Airlines	NYSE	07/97
Greater China Technology	OTC	
Guangshen Railway	NYSE	05/96
Guangzhou Shipyard International	OTC	
Harbin Power Equipment	PORTAL	
Huaneng Power International	NYSE	10/94
Jiangling Motors	None	
Jilin Chemical Industrial	NYSE	05/95
Maanshan Iron and Steel	PORTAL	
Qingling Motors	PORTAL	
Shanghai Chlor-Alkali Chemical	OTC	
Shanghai Erfangji	OTC	
Shanghai Haixing Shipping	OTC	
Shanghai Jinqiao Export Processing	OTC	
Shanghai Lujiazui Finance Trade Zone	OTC	
Shanghai Outer Gaoqiao Freetrade Zone	OTC	
Shanghai Tyre and Rubber	OTC	
Shenzhen Special Economic Zone	OTC	
Sinopec Beijing Yanhua Petrochemical	NYSE	07/97
Sinopec Shanghai Petrochemical	NYSE	07/93
Sinopec Yizheng Chemical	PORTAL	
Tianjin Automotive Xiali	–	
Tsingtao Brewery	OTC	
Yanzhou Coal Mining	NYSE	03/98
Zhejiang Southeast Electric Power	PORTAL	

* PORTAL: Private Offering Resale and Trading through Automated Linkage, where private placement shares trade on the NASDAQ.
Sources: www.adr.com; NYSE

Table 3.6 **Red-chip ADRs, June 2002**

Company	Market	Date of listing
Beijing Enterprises	OTC	
China Resources Enterprises	OTC	
China Unicom	NYSE	06/00
CNOOC	NYSE	02/01
Guangdong Investment	OTC	
Legend Holdings	OTC	
PetroChina	NYSE	06/00
Shanghai Industrial Holdings	OTC	
Zhejiang Expressway	OTC	

Sources: www.adr.com; NYSE

were proving immensely popular. This was a threat to the profits of other operators like Xinhua, a government propaganda organ which has recently sought to ramp up its commercial operations. For another, these sites reported news and views without CCP-appointed editors looking over the copy and this was a political threat. Allowing such companies access to foreign finance was dangerous, it was thought, not only because it provided them with additional resources to outspend their government rivals, but also because it opened the media sector up to foreign influence.

Sina, the most popular Chinese ICP, had an enormous struggle to gain approval from China's authorities to list in the United States, despite its attempts to deflect attention away from its news content ("we have chat rooms, games and email facilities too"). The compromise eventually reached involved Sina restructuring to separate its content from the listing vehicle. It established a company in the Cayman Islands into which it inserted its Taiwan, Hong Kong and United States websites, and it was this company which listed on NASDAQ in April 2000. The Mainland site remained 100% Mainland-owned. Sina enjoyed a 21% jump in its share price on the first day of trading. Alongside Chinadotcom, which had listed in 1999, it was soon joined by Netease, the second most popular Chinese portal at the time of its listing in June 2000.

But the bursting of the tech bubble in early 2001 wrecked China's hopes for its e-businesses and also exposed some of their flaws. Netease was discovered to have learnt some tricks from its American peers: it exaggerated its 2000 profits by $4.2m and had its shares suspended in

September 2001. In October 2001 several shareholders launched a class-action suit against its management and underwriters for false disclosure. But by April 2002, even with the law suit continuing, things were looking up for Netease. Its shares had been relisted and revenues for the first quarter were Rmb24m ($2.9m), a 376% increase on the same period in 2000. However, the collapse of confidence in the Internet sector had dashed the listing hopes of a large number of other Mainland start-ups. Meetchina.com, Dangdang.com and IT-retailer 8848.com were all forced to postpone planned listings. By the end of 2001, there were only six Chinese companies listed on NASDAQ: Netease, Soho, Sina, Chinadotcom, Asiainfo and UTstarcom.

P-chip fever

No matter, a new hot investment concept for Chinese equity was just round the corner: China's private sector. Accounting for more than half of all economic activity, non-state businesses are growing fast and the capacity of domestic banks and investors to provide funds for them lags behind. So it is no surprise that many of China's private companies (p-chips) want to raise funds abroad. When they do, foreign investors get excited for a number of reasons. First, these companies are often run by entrepreneurs rather than the bureaucrats who generally ran the red-chips. Second, many of these firms operate in high-tech sectors and have good growth prospects because of, for example, their patents on medicines or expertise in software.

At the start of 2000 at least ten Mainland firms were waiting to list on the Hong Kong's new Growth Enterprise Market (GEM), a market initially established for high-tech start-ups but which quickly extended its reach to small and medium-sized enterprises (SMEs), whatever their line of business. However, they were being prevented from listing. China's Securities Law, article 29, states that when a domestic enterprise lists abroad, it needs regulatory approval. Yuxing, a computer and DVD player manufacturer based in Beijing, reorganised itself in order to avoid the need for the CSRC's approval. Its parent firm, Beijing Golden Yuxing Electronics, set up a holding company in Bermuda, Yuxing Technologies, and the controlling shareholders gained residency rights overseas as well. It applied to the HKEX GEM and gained permission to list. The CSRC then intervened, announcing that all firms with Mainland operations, no matter where they were based or registered, had to receive its approval before seeking an overseas listing. Having made its point, the CSRC allowed Yuxing to go ahead. It listed on January 31st 2000.

Table 3.7 **UBS Warburg's p-chip index in 2002**

P-chip	Performance first half 2002	Performance second half 2002
AsiaInfo	–38%	–46%
Chaoda Modern	+29%	–50%
China Rare Earth	+4%	–55%
Euro-Asia Agriculture	+74%	Suspended
Global Bio-Chem	+29%	–29%
Greencool Technology	–20%	–71%
People's Food	+16%	–42%
Phoenix TV	–56%	0%
United Food	+4%	–57%
UTStarcom	–33%	–10%
Wah Sang Gas	+68%	–33%
Xinao Gas	+50%	–39%
Average	+11%	–40%
Hang Seng Index	–1.3%	–16%

Note: HKGEM-listed, except AsiaInfo and UTStarcom (NASDAQ-listed) and People's Food and United Food (Singapore-listed). The average price change is not weighted.
Sources: Nasdaq; author's calculations

Since then several dozen medium-sized private firms in the PRC have gone abroad for financing, mainly to the HKEX and its new market, the GEM. The former requires a company to have at least three years of operations and profits of HK$30m ($3.8m) in the two years before listing. In contrast, the GEM offers companies a much easier time: it does not require them to have a track record of profits, and it only demands two years of operations, although this rule is frequently not applied. A dozen or so other p-chips have gone to the Singapore Exchange. The authorities there are aiming for ten PRC firms to list in 2003, and 20 a year after that.

Joe Zhang, head of China research at UBS Warburg, established a p-chip index in July 2001 consisting of 12 private Mainland firms (since expanded to 20), weighted in terms of their market capitalisation. NASDAQ-listed UTStarcom, a successful maker of equipment for wireless phone networks, had a market capitalisation of some $2.6bn and thus accounted for one-third of the index. The other firms had market values of $72m–672m. The performance of the index was initially impressive, rising 58% over the course of 2001, compared with the broader Hang Seng index, which fell 22%. Things continued well in the first half of

2002, when the average p-chip rose in price by 11%, while the Hang Seng index fell by 1.3%, as Table 3.7 shows.

However, despite the hype surrounding them in 2001 and early 2002, p-chips were also a risky investment, for a number of reasons. First, these are young companies, and young companies are more likely to fail than succeed, something that is true in any area of the world. Second, because they often operate in new industries, they are vulnerable to disruptive regulatory moves by the government. Third, because intellectual property rights are still weakly protected, the firms that rely on bio-tech or IT-related patents are vulnerable to piracy. Fourth, due to the weak rule of law in China generally, protection of minority ownership is still patchy, transparency is very poor and incentives for corruption legion. One popular p-chip, Euro-Asia Agriculture, a practitioner of accounting tricks that have become common in the Mainland stockmarket, was found out and its shares were suspended. There is also political risk. Despite being privately owned, many of the p-chips rely on good political connections for at least some of their success. But as the red-chips proved so well, *guanxi* can destroy companies just as easily as it can make them. In the second half of 2002, as investors realised that p-chips were subject to all these problems, their prices fell fast. The average p-chip price fell 40% during these six months, compared with the Hang Seng index, which only fell 16%.

Greencool Technology, which listed on the GEM in July 2000, is a prime example of some of the risks involved. It puts energy-efficient and CFC-free refrigerants into commercial refrigeration and air-conditioning systems. In March 2002 35% of the company's shares were tradable, and 62.6% was owned by Gu Chujun, the company's chairman. Greencool's results for 2001 were good: net profits were up 17%, Rmb314m ($37.8m) on a turnover of Rmb516m. It was in fact a star p-chip performer. However, some of the sheen came off the company in December 2001 when an article appeared in *Caijing* magazine questioning the efficiency of its refrigerants and the accuracy of its accounts. Greencool launched a robust defence, organising press conferences at which its customers, flanked by Gu, expressed their satisfaction with Greencool products. At the end of April Gu stepped down as CEO (but not as chairman). There was more trouble in May when the HKEX began investigating a payment of Rmb230m made by Greencool to another company owned by Gu, Tianjin Greencool. The suspicion was that the transaction may have broken HKEX rules about transactions with affiliated entities. All this hit Greencool's share price.

The share price of Euro-Asia, another p-chip, suffered when rumours of the company diverting funds into a Dutch theme park run by its chairman, Yang Bin, leaked out in early 2002. Since then, tax authorities in Shenyang have accused a number of other companies owned by Yang, one of China's richest men, of tax evasion to the tune of Rmb10m, and Yang has sold 82m shares in Euro-Asia to fund his pet theme park project (bringing down his stake in Euro-Asia to 49.1%). The CSRC reportedly informed the HKEX that Euro-Asia had inflated its sales figures some 21-times during 1998–2000. Between July and early October 2002, the share price fell by 84%, and was then suspended.

The future of overseas issuance
A few large SOEs will continue to come to market in the West in the next decade. However, there will be no deluge, for a number of reasons. First, many of the firms hoping to list in New York will face huge challenges meeting the listing requirements and raising sufficient investor interest. The state-owned banks want to go public and many would jump at the chance of an international listing. However, the Bank of China's July 2002 listing in Hong Kong was not a precedent: the listing vehicle only included the BOC's Hong Kong operations. Resolving the huge portfolios of NPLs of the Mainland operations of the BOC and other banks will take at least five years, probably longer. The Three Gorges dam project has expressed an interest in an overseas listing after a domestic issue in Shanghai in late 2003. However, it would undoubtedly attract protests from environmental groups. Furthermore, foreign investors continue to worry about the probity of accounting and weak legal protection in China. Although firms like PetroChina, a firm with fairly reliable access to energy resources, will continue to excite, other firms with less surefire ways of generating profits will find it harder to go overseas. The only way to generate sufficient interest in the future will be if these equity sales are parts of a genuine privatisation programme.

Second, in terms of the cost of capital, overseas markets are expensive. Often, after the exuberance around the IPO, a more sober look at the firm and its operating environment makes investors more cautious. The price usually then drops. As a result of this and the huge (if artificial) domestic demand for equity, overseas shares trade at big discounts to A-shares. During 1996–2000, the average H-share traded at a P/E ratio of between 7 and 15, and A-shares traded at between 31 and 59. Table 3.8 shows the relative valuations of four companies with both H- and A-share listings. Based on these, considering its financing options in 2001, a firm could reasonably expect to raise double the

Table 3.8 **P/Es of selected firms listed at home and abroad, year-end 2001**

	A-share P/E	H-share P/E
PetroChina	16.7	5.6
Shanghai Petrochemical	79.5	22.3
Huaneng Power	12.5	8.5
Qingdao Beer	7.1	16.2

Source: *Capital Markets Magazine*

amount of capital domestically than it would overseas for the same number of shares.

Because of this discrepancy, for companies listed at home and abroad the choice of where to make a rights or secondary issue is often obvious. For those with only an overseas listing, the next step is also fairly obvious: go home. In the last two years a number of overseas-listed Mainland companies have done so through getting a dual listing in Shanghai. Now that the PRC domestic market has grown in size, a few sizeable issues are possible each year there. New York- and Hong Kong-listed Sinopec went public in Shanghai in April 2001, raising Rmb11.8bn. New York- and Hong Kong-listed Huaneng Power issued 350m A-shares in Shanghai in November 2001 and Shenzhen Expressway followed. In March 2002 the Hong Kong-listed Tianjin Capital Environmental Protection, a sewage treatment company, announced that it would raise Rmb1.2bn through a convertible bond issue in the Mainland rather than in Hong Kong. In late 2002 China Unicom Group listed in Shanghai: it was heavily oversubscribed and raised about Rmb20bn. At the same time, there were rumours that its competitor, China Telecom, which raised £1.4bn in Hong Kong and New York in late 2002, was also considering a domestic A-share offering.

In addition, in early 2002, there were reports that a number of H-share companies, including China Mobile, Legend, Beijing Enterprises and Shanghai Industrial Holdings were planning to issue China Depository Receipts (CDRs) in Shanghai (although this proposal later ran into opposition). A major oil company, CNOOC, made its first public issue in Shanghai rather than overseas like Sinopec and PetroChina, proving that the domestic market could provide sufficient funds for large companies, even if the market is only deep enough for a handful of such issues each year. In 2001 a major firm could hope to raise about

Rmb2.5bn abroad, but a listing at home would only provide it with some Rmb500m. Another factor in favour of a domestic listing is cost. A listing on the HKEX GEM, for instance, can entail costs for underwriters, lawyers and accountants of about 20% of the total funds raised. A NASDAQ listing costs around $500,000–750,000. A domestic issue is cheaper, because it is helped by a low underwriting fee set by the CSRC, something of particular interest to small firms.

But one barrier for red-chips (in contrast to H-shares) wanting to return home is that China's company law currently prevents foreign-registered companies listing in the Mainland. Until it is revised, there are two options for red-chips: setting up and listing a subsidiary or holding company in the Mainland, or issuing CDRs. China Unicom restructured during 2002 to enable a listing by the former method. An SHGSE-listed special-purpose vehicle was created, but was largely empty of assets, while the company listed in Hong Kong retains control of operations and the major assets. CDRs are examined in more detail in Chapter 8.

The obvious danger of these two trends – p-chips going abroad and SOEs staying at home – is that China's stockmarket will not help the country's transition to a market economy: it will remain a support for the old economy. The suspicion with which foreign investors view government-linked enterprises will continue to mean that they are valued cheaply overseas. Faced with this, together with the higher disclosure standards that are demanded overseas, the government may have decided that it would be most efficient to use the domestic stockmarket to continue funding SOEs and to allow private companies to escape abroad. During 2001 more than 200 Chinese companies applied to the CSRC to make overseas issues, and by May 2002 the CSRC was reported to have authorised 120 of them, most of them private. Given a global stockmarket recovery, and continued interest in China, it is possible that by 2005 over 300 private firms will have their shares listed abroad, the majority in Hong Kong and some in the United States. At the same time, though some 60 non-state companies had listed in Shanghai and Shenzhen by the end of 2002, all the indications are that former SOEs will continue to account for the large majority of listings in 2003–05, an issue which Chapter 5 looks at in more detail. This would seriously hinder the development of China's stockmarket since it would deprive it of what it needs most: non-state companies with growth prospects. Allowing p-chips – encouraging them even – to list abroad is a perverse policy if a vibrant modern stockmarket is the long-term objective of the Chinese leadership.

4 The investors

"Seven lose, two even, one wins." A favourite saying among China's share investors: out of every ten of them, seven lose money, two break even and one makes some money – and he is sure to have institutional backing and some inside information. Of course, the common image of crowds gazing at the screens in securities brokerages suggests that small investors, most of them pensioners, dominate this market and that institutional investors are only marginally important. It is then easy to explain the high trading volumes and the great volatility of prices. It is only a short step from there to explaining the fundamental problems of the market by the types of investors it attracts. It is common to hear small investors blamed and institutional investors welcomed as the market's saviours. However, closer analysis reveals that individuals are fewer, and institutional investors more numerous and more significant, than most accounts suggest. From very early on the market was controlled by institutional investors, whether they were formally registered or not. Small investors are those who are regularly sacrificed in their manipulative schemes. In fact, *xishengpin* (sacrificial objects) is a phrase commonly used to describe them. Given the dominance of institutional investors, it is clear that it is not the investors who are to blame for the problems of this market, but the regulatory institutions and the goods – the listed companies – that are on sale.

Formal institutional investors include securities companies, investment funds, TICs and insurance funds. As in other emerging stockmarkets, there are few of them in China. For instance, at the end of 1999, accounts officially opened by individuals at the SHGSE held Rmb367.3bn ($44.4bn), worth of stocks, some 89% of market capitalisation, but the institutions' share accounts held only Rmb43.9bn of stocks, 11% of market value. However, institutions are not a minor presence in this market for a number of reasons. First, the statistics lie. Informal institutional investors, the type that do not show up in these statistics because they use individual accounts, now account for about 50% of market capitalisation. Formal institutions also make extensive use of fraudulently-opened individual accounts. Second, both types of institutions dominate trading and the profits that are made, through their access to huge sums of capital and inside information.

This chapter takes a close look at all the different types of investors:

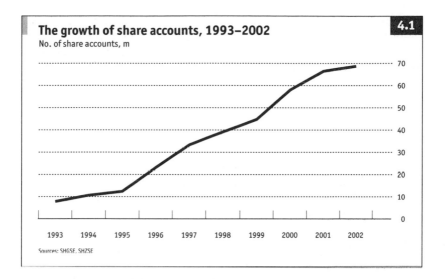

The growth of share accounts, 1993–2002
No. of share accounts, m

Sources: SHGSE, SHZSE

individuals, securities companies, investment funds, insurance companies and the informal privately-raised funds (*simu jijin*). The securities companies are given special attention, with their business models, competitiveness and future prospects dealt with in depth. The chapter ends by considering the development of China's financial conglomerates and their likely impact on the stockmarket.

Individual share investors

Domestic and foreign press reports are fond of claiming that China has over 60m share investors, basing the number on the fact that over 68.7m share accounts had been opened at the two exchanges by the end of 2002, as Figure 4.1 shows.

However, this figure represents the number of share accounts and not the number of investors. The two differ enormously for a number of reasons.

First, millions of investors have opened accounts at both stock exchanges. A survey carried out by the SHZSE's Research Institute of some 2,500 investors in 2001 found that 91% of them had opened two accounts.

Second, a large proportion of accounts were opened for the express purpose of entering the "IPO lottery". Till mid-2002 anyone with a registered securities account could enter this competition to buy IPO shares. The CSRC held a competition among these accounts, and the winners won the right to buy IPO shares. Since the IPO was commonly priced at a huge discount to secondary market prices, anyone lucky enough to win the lottery was guaranteed instant profits on the first day of trading. Millions of accounts were used simply to play this lottery, and when an investor won, they would rarely hold on to the shares for long. Accounts opened for this purpose should therefore be omitted from calculations of the number of investors active in the market. It was not only individuals who took part; many SOEs and financial institutions did so too. Shenzhen Venture Capital, one of the country's leading venture-capital firms, for instance, made profits of Rmb12.1m ($1.4m) in 1999 and Rmb91.6m in 2000. According to its management, all the 1999 profit and two-thirds of that made in 2000 were derived from this lottery. The CSRC has made efforts to limit this risk-free play. In April 2000 it issued a regulation that required a minimum holding of Rmb10,000 worth of A-shares in the secondary market before an investor could enter the lottery. However, owing to technical problems in calculating the amount of an investor's shareholdings and transmitting these data to the underwriters, the scheme was suspended until May 2002. Since then, however, the scheme appears to have worked rather well. The CSRC has only allowed a small number of important issues, like the A-share offer by CITIC Securities, the first brokerage to issue shares, to be exempt from this rule. For all other issues though, it is now necessary to own shares to take part in the lottery.

Third, wealthy individuals and institutional investors have fraudulently opened several million share accounts to allow them to engage in complex schemes, including matching orders, to manipulate share prices. It is a matter of much speculation exactly how many accounts are fake, opened using the ID cards of rural people, or opened before regulations required ID cards to be presented, but industry estimates put the figure at 20m–40m at the end of 2001. As a result, at that date there may have been only 10m–20m individual investors active in the market, a tiny proportion – some 0.8–1.6% – of China's total population of 1.3bn, or some 5% of households. Perhaps during the bull market of 2000 the figure approached 30m. It is also a matter of debate what proportion of market capitalisation they would be holding, although it is highly unlikely to be more than 30%. Compare this with the United States where, according to the Investment Company Institute, by the end of 2001 52.7m households, some 50% of the total, owned shares of one sort or another or mutual funds, inside or outside an employer-sponsored retirement plan. Of these, some 36m households owned shares (or mutual funds) directly, outside these employer schemes, and 21m held individual shares (not mutuals) directly (outside any pension plan). In other words, some 20% households were involved in investing in the share market. So while China has a reputation as a share market dominated by individuals, individual participation is nowhere near the level of the United States.

An investor profile

Quite a bit is known about individual investors, thanks to a number of recent surveys.

How old are they? Another fallacy is that among individual investors, pensioners dominate. In fact, the 2001 SHZSE survey found that 78% of its sample of investors were aged 25–55, and that only 17% were over 55 years of age. (In the United States, some 27% of investors were over 55 years old at the end of 2001, although this figure did include a large number of passive mutual fund investors as well as active share-pickers). It is the younger professionals, operating from home or working from their rented offices in the securities companies, who dominate the individual trading crowd. They are often extremely sophisticated in their use of computers and trading strategies. They are certainly not fools in need of institutions. For their part, pensioners play the market rather like bingo. Most are not playing with their retirement savings, but are simply spending their days with their friends out of the house. Many of their grown-up children will give them share pocket-money to keep them occupied.

For how long do they hold shares? One widely held belief about individual investors is true: they do not hold on to their shares for long. Individual investors commonly keep shares they have bought for less than one month. This fact is often used to suggest that individuals are responsible for the huge churn. The trading turnover ratio was 422% at the SHGSE and 372% at the SHZSE in 1999, while trading ratios in New York, London and Tokyo were between 50 and 70% during the 1990s. However, as explained below, it is not individuals alone who are responsible for these figures.

Where are they trading? It is no surprise that investors are concentrated in the well-developed areas of Shanghai and Guangdong province, as Table 4.1 shows. Curiously, however, Sichuan, an inland province, and Liaoning, part of China's northern rust-belt where unemployment runs high, also appear high in the rankings.

How much money do they have to trade? Individual investors vary in

Table 4.1 **Regional distribution of investors at the Shanghai Stock Exchange, year-end 2001**

Province/city	No. of investor accounts (m)	% of total
Shanghai	4.8	14
Guangdong	3.2	10
Jiangsu	3.2	9
Sichuan	2.3	7
Shandong	2.1	6
Liaoning	2.1	6
Zhejiang	1.7	5
Beijing	1.5	4
Hubei	1.1	3
Fujian	1.1	3
Henan	1.0	3
Heilongjiang	1.0	3
Hunan	0.9	3
Shaanxi	0.8	2
Anhui	0.8	2
Tianjin	0.8	2
Hebei	0.8	2
Jilin	0.6	2
Jiangxi	0.6	2
Shanxi	0.5	2
Xinjiang	0.4	1
Guangxi	0.4	1
Hainan	0.4	1
Gansu	0.3	1
Yunan	0.3	1
Inner Mongolia	0.2	1
Qinghai	0.2	1
Guizhou	0.2	–
Chongqing	0.1	–
Ningxia	0.1	–
Tibet	0.02	–
Total	33.3	

Source: SHGSE

size, of course. As a rough guide, small investors in 1999 had less than Rmb200,000 ($24,000) available to trade, medium-sized had Rmb200,000–500,000 and large individual investors were those with over Rmb500,000 in investment capital available. The SHZSE survey found that over half of investors had an annual income of less than Rmb20,000, and that the proportion of this used to trade was high compared with other countries.

Where do they get the money from? Most of their funds are savings, pocket-money or money lent by friends or relatives. In addition, although securities companies have long been banned from lending to their customers, and the CSRC has made some progress in cracking down on this practice in recent years, it is still common, especially with regular investors. In 2002, as a partial response to the meltdown in prices, CSRC and PBOC officials introduced a scheme in which individuals can borrow money from commercial banks using their shares and bonds as securities, and then use this money to invest in shares.

What is their investment strategy? It is simple: to profit from changes in share prices. The SHZSE survey found that only 12% of individuals made investments in order to make money from dividend payments. One of the most common techniques is to try and spot a share on the rise (often one that is being manipulated) and ride it up. Many small investors, however, jump on and off too late, and lose money as a result.

Do they make money? Not much. At the end of 1999, one official survey reported that only 34% of individual investors profited from share-dealing in the previous year: 16% broke even and 50% lost money. This was despite a bull market and index rises of 14% and 19% on the SHZSE and SHGSE respectively. Investors, probably correctly, blame external factors for these losses: changes in government policy, fake company disclosures and price manipulation.

Online: The future of trading for individual investors?

Few countries beat China in the theatre of trading. Walk a few blocks around Shanghai on a weekday and you are sure to stumble across a brokerage filled with people entranced by a screen of prices. However, in fact, most trading does not take place here, but in back offices at the securities firms, at home on the phone and, increasingly, over the Internet. Online trading has developed rapidly in China since 2000. IDC, a consultancy, estimates that by 2005 more than one-fifth of all share accounts will be online. By that time China will have 21m online accounts, the highest number in Asia.

Established in late 1996 by the Stock Exchange Executive Council, Hexun was the first securities-dedicated website and remains the most authoritative source for financial news and analysis. It was quickly followed by other high-quality sites, such as Stockstar, Kangxi, Go Trade and Genius. Because a CSRC licence is required for any brokerage activity, these sites remained providers of information and real-time quotes only, despite their ambitions to broker shares online. However, the people behind them quickly realised that they could sell their frustrated technical expertise to securities companies who needed to set up trading platforms. Stock2000, for instance, has been highly successful in providing support services for more than 60 securities firms. It was only in March 2002 that the CSRC moved to dismantle the monopoly that securities companies had on the sector by beginning to accept applications for online brokerage businesses from IT companies. Sohu became the first portal to sign up for a joint venture with Guolian Securities, a medium-sized firm owned by the Wuxi City government, to provide online trading services. Homeway also had ambitions for a platform of its own.

In April 2000 the CSRC issued its first regulations on online trading, and in February 2001 it certified 23 securities companies to offer online trading facilities, with a handful more authorisations following later in the year. By the end of March 2001, ever keen to prove their independence, more than 70 firms had launched trading platforms. The move was initially very popular and 2.3m accounts, about 8% of the total number, had been opened by May. Nearly 20% of all accounts opened in the first quarter of the year were online ones. By the end of 2001 there were 3.3m online accounts, a figure some analysts believed represented 10–20% of the active trading population. Online trading totalled Rmb357.8bn ($43bn) for the year, still only some 4.4% of the total trading volume, but double the figure for 2000 in spite of a 50% drop in trading volume. And the growth continued. By July 2002 there were 4.7m online accounts, accounting for some 11% of trading.

China lags behind other countries in its take-up of online trading, but not by much. In South Korea, the most wired country in the world, big mobile phone penetration, broadband access and low commissions meant that by the end of 2001 about 60% of share trades were conducted via the Internet. In comparison, in Hong Kong the figure was 10% for the same period; in the United States by the end of the 1990s about 40% of households had online access, with about one-third of active investors – some 10m people – trading online. As China's personal com-

Table 4.2 **The location of China's securities companies, year-end 1999**

Province/city	No. of SHGSE members
Guangdong	40
Beijing	28
Liaoning	27
Jiangsu	24
Zhejiang	17
Henan	14
Shandong	13
Fujian	13
Sichuan	12
Shanghai	11
Heilongjiang	9
Hainan	9
Shaanxi	8
Jilin	8
Hubei	8
Guangxi	7
Hunan	6
Hebei	6
Tianjin	5
Shanxi	5
Jiangxi	5
Gansu	5
Anhui	5
Yunnan	4
Xinjiang	4
Ningxia	4
Inner Mongolia	3
Guizhou	3
Chongqing	3
Qinghai	2
Tibet	1

Source: SHGSE

Table 4.3 **Securities companies brokerages in the ten largest provinces, year-end 1999**

Province/city	No. of brokerage outlets
Shanghai	480
Guangdong	390
Liaoning	162
Sichuan	143
Jiangsu	137
Zhejiang	122
Hubei	120
Shandong	99
Beijing	99
Tianjin	94

Source: SHGSE

puters and online populations of some 12.5m and 34m respectively expand, the take-up of online trading will also increase. As the market matures, fund management services will also migrate online.

Securities companies

By the end of 2002 there were some 120 securities companies operating in China, with some Rmb120bn in total capital. Their business is concentrated in the south and east of the country, as Table 4.2 shows. Securities companies in Guangdong, Beijing, Liaoning and Jiangsu had the largest number of trading seats at the SHGSE in December 1999. In the central and western regions only Henan and Sichuan had significant numbers of seats.

Each securities company operates a number of brokerage branches (*yingyebu*) where investors go to trade shares, watch share prices on large electronic boards and exchange information. Table 4.3 shows the top ten provinces in terms of the numbers of these branches at the end of 1999. Not surprisingly, economically developed Shanghai and Guangdong were the sites of most of them. Liaoning and Sichuan, two provinces that are not nearly as prosperous or fast-growing but where shareholding reforms started early, are in third and fourth place respectively, reflecting the high number of individual investors there. Coastal Jiangsu and Zhejiang follow.

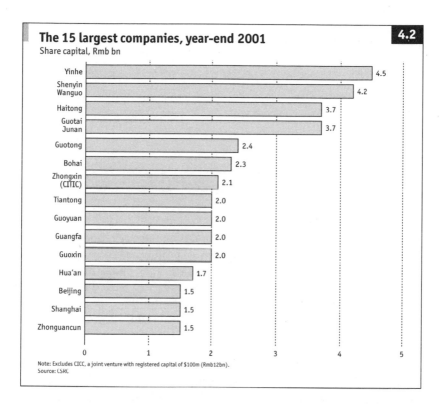

The 15 largest companies, year-end 2001   **4.2**
Share capital, Rmb bn

Yinhe	4.5
Shenyin Wanguo	4.2
Haitong	3.7
Guotai Junan	3.7
Guotong	2.4
Bohai	2.3
Zhongxin (CITIC)	2.1
Tiantong	2.0
Guoyuan	2.0
Guangfa	2.0
Guoxin	2.0
Hua'an	1.7
Beijing	1.5
Shanghai	1.5
Zhonguancun	1.5

Note: Excludes CICC, a joint venture with registered capital of $100m (Rmb12bn).
Source: CSRC

Since 1998 securities companies have dramatically increased in number and size. Figure 4.2 shows the 15 largest securities companies at the end of 2001 in terms of their registered share capital. Yinhe (Galaxy) Securities, the result of the merger of five TICs formerly owned by the four national commercial banks and an insurance firm, was the largest.

In the good times, securities companies are money-making machines. Table 4.4 shows the consolidated profits for 89 firms in the sector during 1999–2001. The average company made a net profit in 2000 – a huge bull year – of Rmb146m and paid Rmb69.7m in taxes. In the bad times though, these firms are vulnerable: it is widely believed that most firms made losses in 2001 because of their exposure to falling share prices. Nanfang (Southern) Securities lost over Rmb1bn from its proprietary and asset management businesses, forcing the Shenzhen authorities who own it to replace management and provide loans (which will probably not be repaid). Securities companies only underwrote Rmb77.8bn worth of shares in 2002, a drop of 30% on 2001 and daily trading

Table 4.4 **Profits of 89 securities companies*, 1999–2001**

Year	Total net profits (Rmb bn)	Average profit per company (Rmb m)	Total tax contribution (Rmb bn)	Average tax contribution (Rmb m)
1999	5.0	56.2	2.7	30.3
2000	13.1	147.2	6.2	69.7
2001	6.5	56.5	2.0	17.4

*Figures for 89 securities companies on which the SHZSE provided data.
Note: 2001 figures are for all securities companies.
Sources: SHZSE, press reports

turnover fell 27%. Their underwriting and brokerage revenues were thus hit hard. CITIC Securities, the second most profitable brokerage in 2001, warned in its 2002 listing prospectus that earnings had dropped 83% in the first 11 months of 2002 compared with the same period in the previous year. As 2003 dawned, and the market hit a three-and-a-half year low, the end of the suffering did not appear in sight.

The ownership of securities companies

After the founding of the first dedicated company, Shenzhen Special Economic Zone Securities, in September 1989, the securities industry grew quickly. Companies were founded by different parts of government or state-owned entities. Some, including Nanfang (Southern) and Haitong, were established by banks, insurance firms or non-bank financial institutions (NBFIS). Others, such as Shenyin in Shanghai and Beijing Securities, were set up by local bureaus of the MOF. A third group, which includes Shanghai Finance Securities, were formed by hiving off the securities operations of local government bureaus. And others, like CITIC Securities and Everbright, owe their existence to TICs establishing securities arms. All the provincial governments and many cities established companies in the early 1990s and local protectionism continues to prevent the consolidation of an industry that suffers from a huge overcapacity. Such is the dominance of local government that only one dedicated securities firm, Galaxy Securities, which belongs to the MOF, is owned by a central government organ.

Most securities companies began life as SOEs (*guoyou rongzi gongsi*), rather than shareholding companies. After the passage of the Company Law in 1994, however, most restructured into limited responsibility

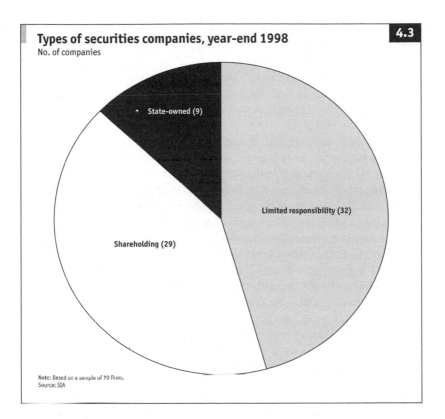

Types of securities companies, year-end 1998 · **4.3**
No. of companies

State-owned (9)

Limited responsibility (32)

Shareholding (29)

Note: Based on a sample of 70 firms.
Source: SIA

(*youxian zeren gongsi*) or limited liability shareholding (*gufen youxian gongsi*) companies. As Figure 4.3 shows, by the end of 1998 most had restructured, and more followed after the Securities Law was promulgated in July 1999.

Attempted privatisation: the strange case of Junan Securities
Up until a couple of years ago privatisation was not permitted, as the case of Shenzhen-based Junan Securities in 1997 made clear. Junan Securities was based in Shenzhen and was run by Zhang Guoqing, a respected pioneer in the finance industry who had previously worked at the Shenzhen branch of the PBOC. After the fall of Wanguo Securities with the 327 T-bond futures scandal in early 1995, Junan became China's leading securities company. During 1996–98 it led the underwriting of 117 IPOs, more than any other company. Given this success, the senior management became greedy for more control and secretly attempted to

privatise the firm. Zhang and his colleagues transferred Junan shares to companies controlled by themselves. But in July 1998 the CSRC was tipped off about Junan's privatisation by a discontented employee. The State Audit Bureau, Hong Kong's Independent Commission against Corruption, the CSRC's own investigators and officers from the party's Central Discipline and Inspection Commission descended on Shenzhen to investigate the case.

According to one report, the investigators were placed under house arrest by Junan "security guards" (there were rumours of PLA involvement in the scam). Vice-Premier Zhu Rongji is reported to have written on the report of the incident: "It is said that military-backed Junan is like a tiger whose butt cannot be touched, but I have to touch it. But I have no backing." Although the connection is hazy, it seems that one of Junan's founding shareholders was a former high-ranking member of the army. The report then went to President Jiang Zemin, who allegedly wrote, "I support Zhu Rongji. Investigate with severity." Security personnel finally caught up with Zhang in Macao. However, when police attempted to arrest him, he reportedly threatened that if they did so he would have his American lawyers release a disk that contained details of corruption in Beijing and Shenzhen on the part of senior officials. His bluff was called, and he was detained. No more was ever heard of the disk. Zhang was later sentenced to a prison term.

The CSRC renationalised Junan. Shares held by the companies linked to Zhang were transferred to the Shenzhen government. A CSRC staffer, Yao Gang, was appointed to represent Junan in merger talks and the shareholders of Guotai Securities were steamrollered into agreeing to a merger with Junan. This took place on August 18th 1999 and Yao became deputy president of the merged entity, Guotai Junan Securities, in March 1999. The new company has two major shareholders, the Shanghai Finance Bureau (16.4%) and the Shenzhen City Investment Management Company (15.7%); the rest of the shares were distributed among over 100 government-owned or affiliated organs. Dispersing control so far and wide was designed to prevent any repeat of the privatisation debacle. In 2002, Liu Huimin, formerly deputy president of the SHGSE and a CSRC staffer, took over as CEO of Guotai Junan.

Since then a small number of companies have had the majority of their shares bought up by private companies. According to research by *Xin Caifu* (New Fortune) magazine, some 13% of the total ownership of all securities companies was held privately at year-end 2002. Qinghui, Datong, Aijian and Minsheng Securities are all privately controlled.

Ownership concentration and political influence

Although most securities companies remain state-owned there has been much change in the ownership structure. The present trend is a dispersal of ownership stakes, and with it, perhaps, administrative influence over these firms will be reduced. Since 1993 state-owned banks and insurance companies have been forced to sell or transfer their ownership stakes in securities companies, many of which they set up from scratch themselves. And since 1998 the TICs have also been encouraged to disengage from the sector. Many of these ownership stakes were divided up and sold to other government organs and enterprises.

The concentration of shareholdings does vary considerably now. Many firms, like Huaxia, Guotai Junan and Lianhe (United) have a very dispersed shareholding structure, with the largest ten shareholders owning less than 70% of the shares. Some firms, such as Haitong, Xiangcai and Guotong, have their shares concentrated in a small number of hands, with the largest shareholder owning more than 20% of the stock, and the largest ten holding over 80%. A small number of firms, like Shanghai Finance Securities and CITIC Securities, are fully owned by a single shareholder.

As part of their search for additional capital, securities companies have been keen to attract investment from cash-rich listed companies. In the first half of 2002 alone, at least 14 listed companies spent Rmb961m acquiring stakes in securities companies. For instance, in August 2002 Beijing University Founder Group moved to buy a controlling stake in the near-bankrupt Zhejiang Securities from Zhejiang ITIC. This dispersal trend is important since it makes it more difficult for government officials to interfere in the operations of these companies. Moreover, as these owners are themselves privatised, it will be difficult to prevent more securities companies themselves also being privatised.

However, it is not only through state ownership that the government exerts its control over these companies. The appointments of senior managers in the large companies are authorised by party organs within the CSRC and the Central Committee's Financial Work Committee (FWC), a special organ established in 1998 to oversee political work in the financial sector. All large firms operate party committees of which the CEO is usually secretary. However, the influence of the local party and central government is not uniform across the sector. Some firms are more impervious to the influence of CSRC than others, and there is evidence of growing independence. It often depends on the shareholding structure. According to insiders, the CSRC cannot now appoint the CEOS

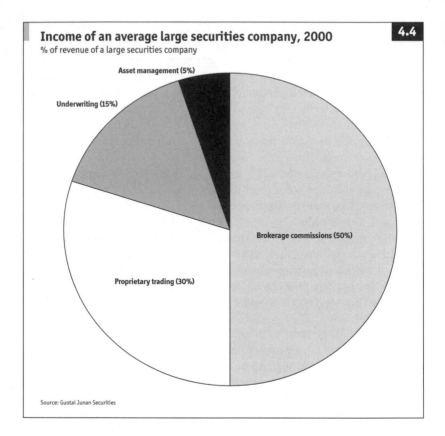

Income of an average large securities company, 2000 `4.4`
% of revenue of a large securities company

Asset management (5%)

Underwriting (15%)

Brokerage commissions (50%)

Proprietary trading (30%)

Source: Guotai Junan Securities

of financial firms (but can only confirm the decision of shareholders), and nor can it remove them without cause. But even despite this constraint on its powers the regulator does have enormous influence, and few professionals working in the sector want to get on its wrong side.

The business scope of securities companies

After the speculative investments in real estate (also light manufacturing, hotels, pleasure parks, etc) of securities companies and TICs in the late 1980s and early 1990s, the State Council decided to force them to focus on their core business. As a result, from 1992 securities firms were formally banned from taking deposits, managing payments transactions, making direct investments or engaging in the insurance business. These limitations were laid out in the Commercial Bank Law of 1995. The three main businesses of securities companies are now underwrit-

Table 4.5 **Top three securities companies in each sector, 2001**

Company	Gross revenue (Rmb bn)	Brokerage revenue (Rmb bn)	Underwriting revenue (Rmb m)
Guotai Junan	2.55	2.17	380
China Galaxy	2.19	2.17	-
Haitong	2.00	1.92	-
Southern	-	-	243
Guoxin	-	-	167

Source: China Online

ing, brokering shares for clients and proprietary trading. Most have also quietly moved into asset management, although by December 2002 this business still had neither legal recognition nor a regulatory framework. Figure 4.4 shows the average breakdown of revenue for each of the businesses in 2000. Table 4.5 shows a breakdown of revenues for the top three domestic firms in 2001. As is obvious from both charts, brokerage dominates. On average it accounts for some 50% of revenues. However, Guotai Junan, China Galaxy and Haitong all had gross revenues of Rmb2bn or more, and in these companies brokerage revenues made up some 85–95% of gross revenue.

Brokering

Some individual investors spend their days standing around in the brokerage branches, but most stay at home and trade over the Internet or phone. A less public but equally distinctive part of China's brokerage business is found inside the offices of securities companies. All the main firms provide dedicated private trading facilities for their richer clients. Some sit in large rooms filled with row upon row of computers and telephones; other rooms, for the well-off who value their privacy, hold only two or three traders. Such rooms are dotted all over China. For such customers, going to trade shares on a daily basis is a little like going to the office. Typically there is no fee for using these facilities: the trader only guarantees to trade a certain volume of stocks, which in turns creates enough commissions to satisfy the host company.

By June 2000 China had 2,623 brokerage outlets. Table 4.6 shows the firms with the largest brokerage networks at the end of 2000. Unsurprisingly, Guotai Junan and Shenyin Wanguo, the results of mergers of

Table 4.6 **Securities companies with the largest brokerage outlet network, year-end 2000**

Company	No. of brokerage outlets	% of total outlets
Yinhe (Galaxy)	174	6.6
Guotai Junan	126	4.8
Shenyin Wanguo	108	4.1
Huaxia	93	3.6
Haitong	90	3.4
Nanfang (Southern)	68	2.6
Xinda TIC	52	2.0
Guangfa	49	1.9
Dongfang TIC	42	1.6
Lianhe (United)	41	1.6
Dongfang (Orient)	38	1.5

Source: SIA

already sizeable securities firms, and Galaxy had the most, together controlling about 15% of all outlets.

Having a large network is important because, although the value-added component on such services approximates to zero, companies make between about one-half and two-thirds of their revenue from brokerage commissions. For small companies unable to underwrite, the proportion is often more than 80%. Table 4.7 shows the most successful brokers in 2001. Shenyin Wanguo appears to be not converting its network into income. Haitong, in contrast, did much better than its number of branches would have suggested.

This business line was hit hard by the 2001–02 bear market. Tens of thousands of small investors stopped trading from July onwards and the trading volume fell to Rmb3.8trn for the year, compared with Rmb6.1trn in 2000, a decrease of 37%. Total commissions to brokerages would have totalled some Rmb13.3bn in 2001. Shared among 2,623 branches, the annual income per branch in 2001 works out to be around Rmb5m, with the estimated yearly cost of running a branch Rmb4m. In 2002, trading volume fell to Rmb2.8trn, and total commissions would have reached some Rmb9.8bn. That would have provided only Rmb3.7m per branch. In future, many branches will be closed as the use of the phone and the Internet becomes more common, investment

Table 4.7 **Top ten securities companies in the brokerage business, 2001**

Rank	Company	Volume of 2001 brokerage transactions, (Rmb bn)	Volume of brokerage transactions, 2000 (Rmb bn)	Rank, 2000
1	Haitong	958.7	1,281.7	1
2	Yinhe	704.8	911.4	2
3	Guotai Junan	673.6	870.2	3
4	Nanfang	553.3	792.6	4
5	Huaxia	547.8	756.4	5
6	Shenyin Wanguo	542.2	754.8	6
7	CITIC	424.3	343.8	8
8	Guangfa	316.9	441.7	7
9	Guotong	219.2	252.5	10
10	Tiantong	207.2	260.4	9

Note: Includes income from the brokerage of shares, funds and bonds.
Source: *China Securities News*

funds turn active speculators into passive investors, and securities companies merge. In addition, securities companies are increasingly linking up with banks to allow bank customers to use their deposit account to trade shares. This further undermines the rationale of operating dedicated brokerage branches.

Commission rates

Up until early 2002 brokerage commissions were fixed by the CSRC at 0.35%. However, many companies have in practice disregarded these rules. It has been common for securities companies to reduce the standard fee on traditional transactions by one-fifth and by one-half for trading carried out online, in order to attract and retain customers. At various intervals during the 1990s, price wars flared up. In February 2002 a new round of price-cutting erupted when the newly established Tiantong Securities began offering a 70% across-the-board commission discount on trades carried out on its online trading platform. Tiantong, based in Guangzhou and owned by Shandong Securities, had invested some Rmb100m in its systems and had linked up with local bank branches at which customers could open accounts. It thus avoided the need to establish a brokerage network of its own and after only a couple of years of operations, the firm made it into the brokerage top ten, as Table 4.7 shows. Tiantong's competitors complained to the CSRC about

Table 4.8 **Brokerage commissions across Asia, 2000**

Country	Brokerage commission
Hong Kong	0.25–0.5%
Indonesia	1%
Japan	Completely liberalised since September 1999
Malaysia	1%
South Korea	Upper limit of 0.6%
Taiwan	Completely liberalised since July 1996
Thailand	Lower limit of 0.5%

Source: SIA

its behaviour, hoping that enforcement of the commission rate rules would protect them.

Instead, in May 2002 the CSRC moved to cut brokerage fees, not only in response to the Tiantong affair, but also with the aim of adding some life to a depressed share market. For normal trades, the rate was cut to a maximum of 0.3% for A-shares and B-shares, lower for bulk and online transactions. The CSRC appears flexible in how these rules are applied. According to the *People's Daily*, after the new rules were announced Jiangnan Securities, a small firm, offered free trades to customers who paid an annual fee. For example, a customer owning shares worth less than Rmb100,000 would pay Rmb360 for a year's brokerage services. A small brokerage firm in Sichuan Province was also reported to have cut its commissions to 0.02%. Other countries in Asia, including Taiwan, have already liberalised their commission rates, as Table 4.8 shows.

The CSRC's move was clearly designed to trigger further consolidation in the brokerage sector. Brokerage income now looks likely to fall by some 30% as a result of the change. Large securities companies, able to subsidise their brokerage business with revenues from underwriting and asset management, will be freer to undercut smaller companies, encouraging small companies to sell out to their larger competitors.

Proprietary trading

A large firm typically makes around 30% of its income from trading shares on its own account. Practices common in Western markets such as fundamental analysis and portfolio investment are only slowly being taken up. Rather, during the 1990s traders at securities companies were engaged in extensive manipulation and insider trading. Often together with a small number of their richer customers, they frequently organised manipulation scams, choosing companies to manipulate, visiting them (often bringing management on board) and then gradually buying up the stock. They would then spread rumours about its great growth prospects and wait for the stock to soar before selling out. While the *dahu*, rich investors, dominated the market in the early 1990s, as the securities companies grew in size they took over the mantle of market leaders. One reason securities companies are reluctant to enter into joint ventures with Western firms is that they already understand how China's stockmarket really works.

Another problem has been that during the 1990s it was common practice for cash-strapped securities firms to "borrow" funds from their brokerage customers' accounts. These funds would be used for in-house proprietary trading or would be lent to other customers. CSRC officials estimated that by the end of 2000 the use of such funds to trade shares had fallen from 23% of funds on account at the end of 1997 to only 2.3%, some Rmb8.6bn. But blatant abuses continue despite the CSRC crackdown. After the 2002 Yinguangxia scandal, several investors claimed that funds in their accounts had been used to buy shares in the firm as the share price fell, causing them losses of Rmb1.3m. Presumably this allowed the price to be supported while others sold their holdings. A regulation which came into force in January 2002 said that securities companies must keep their customers' share-trading deposits in a completely separate account from their own capital. It is too early to assess what effect this ruling will have. Another problem is that very porous "Chinese" firewalls between brokerage and proprietary trading has meant that front-running – when the broker trades on his own account before the customer's trade is executed, thus taking advantage of any price changes – has also been common.

Most securities companies lost money during 2001–02 on their proprietary trading as prices slumped and the CSRC's crackdown on illegal trading practices caused additional losses. For example, in December 2001 the CSRC revealed that Zhejiang Securities had used Rmb630m from its customers' accounts to trade shares, and that between January and October it had illegally lent customers Rmb461m with which to trade. The regulator also found Zhejiang guilty of using 56 individual share accounts to trade the shares of Zhenjiang Qianjiang Biochemical. It was a classic "matched orders" scam. By buying and selling a company's shares between its own accounts, Zhejiang created the illusion of demand for the shares, caused their price to rise and thus encouraged other investors to buy in. It then sold its holdings, making some Rmb42m in profit. (Such matched orders trading sometimes involves hundreds of accounts, as in the case of Zhongke Chuangye in 2000, examined in Chapter 7.) As punishment, the CSRC withdrew Zhejiang's licence to trade shares and fined it Rmb500m, with senior personnel receiving fines of Rmb30,000–100,000 each. Such fines were among the heaviest so far in the industry and threatened to bankrupt Zhejiang Securities.

Underwriting

Historically, 15–30% of the revenues of a typical securities company have been derived from underwriting initial, rights and secondary share issues. However, because of the low margins involved, IPOs have largely become loss leaders, more often undertaken for their prestige than profit margins. There are three reasons. First, underwriting fees are set at a mandatory 2.5% of the capital raised. In Hong Kong the fee, set by market players, is also around 2.5%. But in the United States, it is typically much higher, usually around 7%. Second, as Chapter 2 explained, IPO prices themselves have been set low. CSRC policy during 1993–97 was that IPO shares should sell for P/E ratios of 14–18, whatever the quality of the company, the market's valuation of the industry sector or the firm's growth potential. In other words, no market-based valuation of the company or its discounted future revenue was made. This limited the funds that could be raised, and thereby also the size of the fee. During 2000, however, the CSRC relaxed rules on IPO pricing. By the end of the year, P/Es were being set by the underwriter and issuing company, and rose to an average of 20–30, with some high-tech firms even issuing at ratios of 60–80. As a result, underwriting has become more profitable, but at the same time much riskier. Third, the extensive work involved in converting the average SOE into a shareholding company, reorganising its accounts and fulfilling the CSRC's now extensive disclosure requirements, places a heavy burden on the underwriter.

Before the enactment of the Securities Law, which came into effect in July 1999, there were no legislative constraints on which companies could underwrite securities, although the CSRC had promulgated regulations in June 1996 that established a qualification system for companies wishing to do so. Although there was little risk of them ending up buying the shares they underwrote (since IPO prices were set so low), this weak regulation did lead to irregularities. Many listing companies,

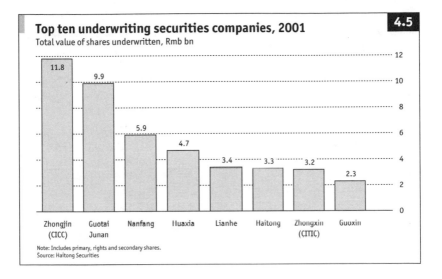

Top ten underwriting securities companies, 2001 4.5

Total value of shares underwritten, Rmb bn

Note: Includes primary, rights and secondary shares.
Source: Haitong Securities

in cooperation with their underwriters, accountants and lawyers, issued shares on the back of falsified accounts, a problem discussed in Chapter 5. In order to modernise the industry, protect investors and encourage consolidation, the Securities Law divided securities companies into two types. Firms with a registered capital of Rmb500m are now termed comprehensive (zonghe) firms, and can engage in brokering, proprietary trading and underwriting securities. At the end of 2001 there were 109 securities companies, 69 of which had the requisite capital to engage in underwriting and proprietary trading. Firms with capital below this requirement can only broker shares.

Figure 4.5 shows the top performers in the underwriting business in 2001, a bad year. With the loss of demand for equities, only 74 new companies made IPOs during the year, raising Rmb119.2bn in capital, one-fifth less than 2000. Several securities firms were left paying for rights shares and investment fund units that they had underwritten because they failed to find sufficient buyers. Things got worse in 2002. More companies issued shares, but together raised only Rmb73.9bn in IPOs.

Asset management

Asset management is an increasingly important business for many securities companies. All the major securities companies now manage *simu jijin* (privately-raised funds) on behalf of non-financial firms, including many SOEs, and their individual customers. Companies have secured

Table 4.9 **Top ten securities companies with funds under management from listed companies, year-end 2001**

Company	No. of listed companies	Funds under management (Rmb m)
Guotai Junan	20	2,273
Nanfang	11	950
Guotong	4	850
Haitong	10	663
Xingye	5	630
Guoxin	5	575
Xinan	5	506
Yinhe	5	500
Shenyin Wanguo	-	494
Changjiang	3	39

Source: press reports

these funds mostly since 1997, often promising annual returns of 6% or more. During 1998–2000 they scooped up considerable profits, but since July 2001 they have been floundering to meet promised levels of returns.

Estimating the size of the funds under management is extremely difficult because of the quasi-legal status of the business. By September 2002, the CSRC had yet to issue rules, and officials at securities firms were uncomfortable talking about the business openly. In early 2001, Xia Bin, an official at the PBOC, carried out a survey of the sector, including funds managed by financial consultancies (examined below). He estimated that securities companies had about Rmb150bn–300bn under management in total, some 12% of tradable market capitalisation. That was, on average, some Rmb2bn–3bn each. Another study by Shenzhen Securities Information (SSI), a consultancy, found that 164 securities companies had conducted asset management business during 2001, with 57 conducting business worth more than Rmb100m, 14 managing more than Rmb500m and four more than Rmb1bn. In mid-2001 Nanfang Securities was widely reported to have at least Rmb10bn under management. Table 4.9 shows the results of a survey carried out by Shanghai Securities News at around the same time. Guotai Junan was far and away the most successful company in terms of raising *simu* funds, with Rmb2.3bn; Nanfang and Guotong came second and third. Of course, these numbers should be treated with some care since securities companies had incentives for not reporting the true scale of their involvement. Moreover, since 2001 the bear market has significantly reduced the profits that can be made and many customers have withdrawn their funds as a result. One report estimated that by the end of 2002 securities companies were only managing some Rmb60bn worth of outside assets. No data are available on what rates of return were made on these investments.

The CSRC has moved gently to extend its influence over the asset management business. In March 1999 it allowed securities companies, in theory, to manage financial assets. And in January 2002 it released rules that, subject to authorisation, allowed them to establish asset management subsidiaries in which they had at least a 51% stake. In anticipation of these new rules, Galaxy Securities, China's largest securities company, set up Galaxy Fund Management with four large non-financial SOEs. The directive also allowed securities companies to take majority stakes in venture-capital firms. However, at least by December 2002, no detailed rules had been issued and the business remained a grey area. It seems likely that the Investment Fund Law, under discussion in the NPC since 1998 and due out in 2003 if all goes well, will not cover *simu* funds in any detail, and that the CSRC will have to issue its own detailed regulations on the business in the future.

Asset management is a useful business for securities companies. However, the CSRC is extremely concerned about where these funds are coming from. While managing individuals' savings and the liquid assets of corporations earned through ongoing operations is positive, the CSRC is (rightly) suspicious of listed companies entrusting revenues from IPOs, rights and secondary issues to securities companies and others to invest in shares. This is extremely common, and is worrying because it signals that these companies are raising too many funds. By December 2001, SSI reported that 205 listed companies had entrusted some Rmb24.6bn to securities companies for investment. Seventy listed firms had entrusted more than Rmb100m, 30 companies Rmb200m and three firms, Shanghai Changhong Electric, Liaohe Oilfield and Baoshan Iron and Steel, had reportedly each entrusted more than Rmb1bn. This would not be so much of a problem in an open and competitive market for IPOs, but since this market is controlled, it suggests that the firms who are winning IPO places are not using the funds for the projects described in their prospectuses.

In response, in October 2001 the CSRC instructed listing companies to reduce the amount of funds they raised at IPO. Soon after, the regulator banned listed companies from entrusting the proceeds from share offerings to securities companies or other management companies entirely, and instructed them to recover all the funds that they had previously entrusted to outside managers. This ruling was more than a little tricky to implement: the bear market at the time meant that shares had to be liquidated at very low prices. By the end of 2001 only 95 listed companies had managed to recover the funds; 43 securities companies had returned the funds; and 54 had returned about half of the funds. The returns of listed companies that recovered funds in the first half of 2001 averaged 9%. That ratio would have fallen to below zero in the second half of the year and in 2002. Since securities companies had guaranteed levels of return of say some 6% or 10%, some lent listed firms money out of their own accounts to meet the shortfall.

Are China's securities companies competitive?

Everyone in the securities industry knows that China's securities companies are no match for the international investment banks. Their deficiencies range too widely, from their limited size to their restricted scope of business, from their inexperience in a wide range of transactions to their China-centric focus and bureaucratic management styles. Even after another ten years of protection and preferential government policies, it is unlikely that they would cause Goldman Sachs or Morgan Stanley anything to worry about.

By the end of 2000, only three of China's 101-odd wannabe investment banks had registered capital of Rmb3bn or above. They were tiny in comparison with their international peers: the capital of the largest of them was less than one-thirtieth of that of Merrill Lynch, Goldman Sachs or Morgan Stanley. This is shown clearly in Table 4.10.

But size is not everything: the strength of a financial firm is also rooted in the extent to which its sources of revenue are diversified. A well-diversified firm, like a well-diversified share portfolio, is protected from hard times in one of its businesses. International firms, as Table 4.11 shows, are relatively well diversified. The obvious difference with their Chinese counterparts is the very limited amount brokerage revenues contribute to the revenues of international banks. Even Merrill Lynch, the world's leading broker, derived only 29% of its income in 1999 from this side of its business. On the whole, although their profiles are different, the international banks are much better diversified: income is spread across their business lines. Of course, in a prolonged downturn where profits from several financial activities (underwriting,

Table 4.10 **Assets of China securities companies and international investment banks, year-end 1999 ($ bn)**

Company	Total assets ($ bn)	Company	Total assets ($ bn)
Yinhe (Galaxy)	-	Merrill Lynch	328.1
Guotai Junan	4.0	Morgan Stanley	367.0
Liantong (United)	2.0	Lehman Bros.	192.2
Nanfang (Southern)	2.5	CSFB	278.6
Guotong	0.7	Goldman Sachs	250.5

Sources: SIA, *Institutional Investor*

brokerage and proprietary trading) all decline, such firms also suffer. However, even in such an environment the returns on direct investments, as well as fees charged on corporate advisory and asset management services, can serve to supplement income. Moreover, since these firms are global, although they rely heavily on the North American market, they are well protected from regional difficulties. In contrast, even leading firms such as Guotai Junan are almost entirely exposed to one activity, brokerage – and, of course, to one country, China. As Table 4.12 shows, Haitong and Nanfang, two of the largest firms, are also exposed to their brokerage and proprietary operations. And in the investment-banking sector in China, underwriting dominates: as yet corporate advisory is an unprofitable business.

Many of the weaknesses of China's securities firms are typical of

Table 4.11 **Breakdown of the income of three international investment banks, 1999 (% of total income)**

Income	Merrill Lynch	Goldman Sachs	Morgan Stanley
Brokerage commissions	29	11	9
Investment banking: underwriting	11	16	8
Investment banking: advisory	6	17	6
Asset management	22	7	10
Proprietary trading	23	43	20
Other	9	6	47

Source: SIA

Table 4.12 **Breakdown of the income of three large Mainland securities firms, 1999**

Income	Guotai Junan	%	Haitong	%	Nanfang	%
Brokerage commissions	1,282	68	896	43	1,058	47
Investment banking (underwriting)	247	13	234	11	185	8
Proprietary trading	351	19	951	46	1,030	45
Total	1,880	-	2,081	-	2,273	-

Note: Commission income is calculated using a fee rate of 0.35%, underwriting at a rate of 2.5% of total issuance. Any income from asset management is not included.
Source: SIA

firms in developing markets. However, other weaknesses reflect the limits set by the State Council. For instance, up to 2001, the government was not keen on securities firms establishing non-traditional businesses like venture capital. The PBOC has for a long time prevented securities firms from gaining access to funds from the banking system. Help is now at hand. The CSRC is intent upon nurturing these firms in a variety of ways, and it has State Council backing to do so. It is supporting the consolidation of the sector as well as encouraging individual companies to expand their capital. It is also intent on facilitating the development of other businesses like asset management and venture capital.

Consolidation
The CSRC is keen to encourage consolidation. Since 1998 it has overseen and, in many cases, organised mergers of dozens of firms, large and small. In June 2001 Bohai Securities became China's fifth-largest securities company after the merger of a Tianjin-based securities company and several TICs. Everbright Securities and Shenyin Wanguo will likely merge, and Huaxia Securities and Beijing Securities, as well as Guangfa Securities and Guangdong Securities, are said to have held talks. The CSRC reportedly aims to create a core of 8–10 national firms each with capital in the Rmb6bn–8bn range by 2006. The next five years should therefore see plenty more acquisitions. However, this does depend on whether the CSRC can persuade provincial governments, which have traditionally protected local firms from takeovers from firms in other areas, to cooperate.

Expanding capital
Most securities companies in China lack funds. In the early 1990s they were banned from borrowing money from commercial banks, and the

1995 Commercial Bank Law created a separation (like the American Glass-Steagall law) between the two parts of the banking industry. This was motivated by senior policymakers' concerns over minimising the destabilising effects of huge movements of bank deposit funds into the share market. However, despite attempts to crack down, bank lending continued to be a popular source of securities companies' funds throughout the 1990s. The problem is now less common, but anecdotal evidence suggests that it still goes on. During the drafting of the Securities Law, securities companies lobbied hard against a blanket ban on their borrowing funds from banks, and won a loophole in the legislation that allows the State Council flexibility to rule on the issue itself.

One important route for raising funds has been through the increase of registered capital. Some companies expand their capital by merging; others invite new companies to become shareholders; yet others encourage old shareholders to stump up more capital. Up till the end of 2000 only 22 securities companies had expanded their capital, but in 2001 alone some 35 companies did so. One result was the creation of eight companies with capital in excess of Rmb2bn: Shenyin Wanguo, Haitong, Bohai, Xinan, Tiantong, Guoyuan, Xingye and Guotong. In early 2002 the CSRC, keen to keep the expansions going (and wanting to help the many companies that were in need), relaxed its demand that securities companies needed three years with an ROE of 10% and a blameless record before they could apply to expand. No longer: the CSRC announced it would approve all applications. Total capital for the industry totalled Rmb80bn at the end of 2001, up from Rmb50bn a year before. In July 2002 there were reports that Haitong, China's most profitable brokerage, would raise Rmb3bn through issuing new shares to its existing shareholders, including Shanghai Industrial Investment Group (the investment arm of the Shanghai government), to fund an expansion of business and several new subsidiaries, including one in Hong Kong. By the end of 2002, China's securities firms had total capital of Rmb120bn.

The CSRC has also sought other means of augmenting securities companies' funds. Since August 1999, for instance, it has allowed several large, well-run firms to enter the interbank market for funds. Here they can sell T-bonds to banks on a repo basis, thus enabling them to raise short-term funds. In February 2000 the CSRC and PBOC allowed some comprehensive securities firms to borrow funds from banks using shares as collateral. A company can borrow funds worth 60% of the value of the shares, though they cannot use certain stocks as collateral, including those of loss-making companies and those whose prices have fluctuated by more than 200% in the previous six months. By the end of 2000 Guangfa, Huatai, Xiangcai and CITIC Securities had each borrowed Rmb14m–80m each, mostly from the ICBC. Up to the end of 2001 securities companies in total had borrowed some Rmb18bn.

Some banks have also been authorised to make ad hoc loans to needy companies. In December 1999, for example, the ICBC lent Rmb800m to Huaxia Securities for an underwriting project. In June 2000 a commercial bank in Beijing agreed to create a Rmb100m finance facility for CITIC Securities. Another route for raising funds is, of course, the stockmarket itself. Only two firms, both small, Hongyuan Securities and Anshan Trust and Investment Company (TIC) (purchased by Haier, the white-goods firm that has conglomerate ambitions, in August 2001) were publicly traded by 2001. When Hongyuan issued it was a TIC, but was then restructured. In December 2002 CITIC Securities became the Mainland's first dedicated securities firm to go public, raising Rmb1.8bn with a 400m share offer. It is likely that during 2003–04 a number of larger firms will follow them. Galaxy, Haitong, Guangfa, Guotong and Eagle have all been recognised as possible candidates. Even CICC, the China Construction Bank/Morgan Stanley joint venture, has been rumoured to be seeking a listing.

Trust and investment companies

At the end of 2002 there were some 200 trust and investment companies (TICs) involved in the securities industry. Established in the 1980s and early 1990s, TICs offered a quick and easy way for the government to raise and channel capital to fast growing parts of the economy. Part bank, part government investment arm, part get-rich-quick schemes, they were so popular that their numbers ballooned to nearly 1,000 by 1992. They financed everything from airports to share trading. It was only in the mid-1990s that the central government came to regret their development. Huge mismanagement, corruption and overinvestment in real estate had led the whole sector to pile up a mountain of debt. By 1998 TICs had become, in the words of a senior member of the CSRC, "the most serious threat facing China's financial sector". The PBOC is in the midst of its fifth attempt to resolve the problem.

One reason for their many troubles was that their securities activities were never kept firewalled off from their other businesses. This led to numerous cases of share-related problems spreading to other areas of their business, and vice versa. For instance, when funds were needed at TIC headquarters to cover, say, a failed property investment, customers' accounts from the brokerage arm were often raided. This left the brokerage bit of the business insolvent. A serious systemic risk was thus created. If the customers of one large TIC brokerage had discovered that the firm had "lost" their funds, and then rushed to TIC to withdraw funds, runs at other TICs and other financial institutions could easily be triggered.

Resolution of the TIC issue has been complicated by rivalries between the CSRC and the PBOC. Although regulatory authority over securities firms was clarified in 1998 when all powers were concentrated in the CSRC, authority over the TICs has remained divided. The central bank retains responsibilities for the bank and investment functions of the TICs, and the CSRC has responsibility for their securities operations. This has caused problems. In one case in 2000, the CSRC attempted to force a TIC headquarters to return customers' funds to its brokerage arm. The PBOC refused to cooperate and the TIC was let off. In another case, the CSRC traced customers' "borrowed" funds to an account hundreds of miles away from the TIC's brokerage arm. But the provincial government had frozen the funds and refused to let the CSRC transfer them back to the securities operation. The TIC in question was in arrears on a debt to an SOE under that provincial government's control.

Since 2000 the PBOC's strategy for dealing with the TICs has involved the following actions.

- All TICs lost their commercial banking and securities businesses. TIC securities operations were merged, a process managed by the CSRC, and new companies, like the recently established Yinhe (Galaxy) Securities, were created. Banking assets and debts were transferred to commercial banks or their asset management companies (AMCs).
- Some TICs were restructured and merged to form new trust or finance companies, both with reduced scope of business and a minimum capital requirement of Rmb300m.
- After resolution of their debt, a minority of TICs were closed. Guangdong ITIC was ordered to be closed in October 1998. Hainan ITIC and the Everbright TIC followed.
- The hoped-for result is to reduce the 239 TIC operations in the late 1990s to only 40–50, one per province, together with three TICs run from Beijing. Provincial governments will retain control of the first group, and the three others will fall under the supervision of the PBOC and the CCP's Central Committee's Financial Work Committee (FWC).

Investment funds

Institutional investors – mutual funds, pension funds and insurance companies – are increasingly important participants in the world's capital markets. In many developed countries the value of pension fund assets is equal to over 50% of GDP, insurance assets 20–30% of GDP and mutual funds 10–20% of GDP. The global mutual fund industry grew enormously, from a net asset value of $705bn in 1989 to over $3.6trn by 1999. During the 1990s the composition of their portfolios changed, as they increasingly shifted into equities and out of debt instruments, so that by the end of 1998, on average 68% of the world's mutual fund assets were invested in shares. The United States, with mutual funds worth over 50% of GDP, accounts for around two-thirds of all the world's funds.

One priority for many developing countries is to nurture institutional investors at home, because they can have a number of good effects. For one thing, they enable private financial assets to be managed more intelligently than bank deposits, and thus provide one of the few means by which pensions and insurance assets can be grown to cover future needs. Second, there is the competitive effect: these companies intensify competition for financial assets, forcing commercial banks and other financial service providers to improve services for their customers. Third, they can have a healthy influence on listed firms' corporate governance and performance, since funds often buy large enough stakes to make a difference at shareholders' meetings.

Closed and open-ended fund development

Since 1997 the CSRC has prioritised the development of the investment fund sector. By December 2002 it had overseen the establishment of some 54 closed-ended investment funds and 17 open-ended funds issued by 19 investment fund management companies. By the end of December 2002 formal investment funds had net assets of over Rmb130bn, some 10% of tradable market capitalisation, compared with 50% in the United States.

As well as the positive impacts outlined above, this policy has three aims. The first is to draw more investors out of the banks and into the share market so that their capital can be more efficiently allocated. By the end of 2002 savings deposits totalled Rmb8.5trn, an increase of Rmb1.2trn over the year, but these funds are not mediated efficiently. They do not get to the most dynamic sector of the economy: the non-state-owned firms. By the end of 2000 private business had borrowed only Rmb65.5bn from formal financial institutions, some 0.7% of all loans. Political bias is not the only problem. Entrepreneurs frequently have little to offer in collateral, and their accounts are often unreliable. In addition, bank managers can add only 30% on to the PBOC's lending rate for SMEs, not enough usually to cover the additional risks involved.

The 1996 idea of boosting the funding of industry through share issuance has become all the more attractive since that date. It is only by drawing in private depositors that the market can grow over the long term. Investment funds have been proved to be the best means of achieving this elsewhere in the world.

Second, officials want to alter the style of the market from one dominated by short-term speculation to one of long-term, professionally managed investment. This will, they hope, reduce price volatility and mature the market. Only in such a context can the government's plans for pension fund development work. As Chapter 7 argues, though, this policy can work only if the quality of listed companies improves in tandem with the development of funds. A third, more cynical, reason for the government's support of investment funds is that they provide a means by which senior leaders can potentially shape stockmarket sentiment. The CSRC maintains significant mechanisms of influence over the funds, since it approves the appointments of fund management firms' CEOs and the fund managers themselves, and thereby can retain some influence over their trading strategies and the market's indices. Obviously, however, as the market grows in size, this becomes more difficult.

There have been two phases of investment fund development in reform China. During the first phase between 1990 and 1997, local governments at the provincial, city and county levels set up some 75 small closed funds with the aim of raising capital for diverse local projects. The funds were badly managed (investing in everything from real estate to light industry), had chaotic governance (many lacked distinct trustees and/or custodians) and were poorly regulated (they fell under PBOC jurisdiction but the capacity of local PBOC branches to supervise them effectively was extremely limited). The central government attempted to provide some order in 1994 by banning the establishment of new funds, but it did not put the sector as a whole to rights until 1997.

This is when the second phase began. On November 14th 1997 the central government issued new regulations which laid down the legal basis for reinventing the sector, this time under tight CSRC control. These measures stated that all funds had to receive CSRC approval before they could be established, a measure which sidelined local governments. Fund management firms now require only Rmb10m ($1.2m)

Table 4.13 **China's fund management companies and their shareholders, year-end 2001**

Company	Major shareholders
Boshi	China Great Wall TIC, China Everbright Securities, Jinhua TIC, Guotong Securities
Changsheng	CITIC Securities, Hubei Securities, Anhui TIC, Tianjin Northern ITIC
Dacheng	Everbright Securities, Guangdong Securities, China Eagle Securities, China Economic Development TIC
Fuguo	Haitong Securities, Shenyin Wanguo Securities, Jiangsu Securities, Fujian ITIC
Guotai	Guotai Junan Securities, Shanghai Aijian TIC, Zhejiang ITIC, Xinjiang Hongyuan TIC, China Electric Power Finance
Hua'an	Zhejiang Securities, Shanghai Finance Securities
Huaxia	China Securities, Beijing Securities, China Science & Technology ITIC
Jinshi	Guangfa Securities, Beijing Securities, Jilin TIC, Zhongmei TIC
Nanfang	Southern Securities, Guangxi TIC, Xiamen International
Penghua	Guosen Securities, Zhejiang Securities, Anshan TIC, Anhui ITIC

Source: Panorama

in registered capital, although most have Rmb120m–200m. The funds themselves must have paid-up capital of Rmb300m and have a minimum term of five years: 80% of fund assets must be held in securities, 20% in domestic T-bonds, and no direct investments (such as in real estate) are permitted. Another requirement designed to protect investors is that 90% of the funds' returns have to be distributed to investors in the form of dividends. On this footing, the CSRC has overseen the establishment of dozens of new funds and the restructuring of the old ones.

The CSRC enlisted the support of large securities companies in its new project, allowing favoured ones to set up fund management companies (see Table 4.13). In 2002 the CSRC determined that each financial institution should not have a controlling stake in more than one investment fund company, a ruling that will force sales of stakes in some funds as new fund companies are set up – with the purchasers of the stakes including entities not allowed to buy them under the rules. Already, at the beginning of 2003, there were reports of an unofficial market for shares in the fund companies developing. In March 1998 the first second-phase funds Jintai and Kaiyuan, managed by the Guotai and Nanfang fund management companies

Table 4.14 **Investment management companies, year-end 2001**

Company	Registered capital (Rmb m)	No. of funds managed
Baosheng	-	2
Boshi	100	5
Changcheng	-	0
Changsheng	80	4
Dacheng	100	5
Fuguo	100	4
Guotai	110	4
Hefeng	-	0
Hua'an	150	5
Huaxia	138	6
Jinshi	60	1
Nanfang	100	5
Penghua	80	4
Rongtong	-	2
Yifangda	-	1
Yinhe	-	0
Yinhua	-	1
Zhongrong	-	0

Sources: CSRC, author's research

respectively, were launched. These were 15-year closed-ended funds and had capital of Rmb2bn each. Since then, over 25 new closed-ended funds have been established with capital of Rmb2bn–3bn. Another 30 of the funds created since 1997 are smaller, with Rmb200m–300m in registered units, and are the results of restructuring the old funds. Many of these were taken over, reorganised and recapitalised by the fund management companies under CSRC direction. During 2001 the combined total of closed-ended and open-ended fund issuance was Rmb25bn. In 2002, the total was only Rmb18bn. Table 4.14 shows the registered capital and number of funds under management at end-2001. Figure 4.6 shows the two phases of fund development clearly: the number of funds grew rapidly after 1998, as did trading volume. The decline in the number of funds in 2000 was due to many old funds being delisted, merged and restructured.

The bear market that began in the second half of 2001 took its toll, even if the funds performed well in relative terms. According to research

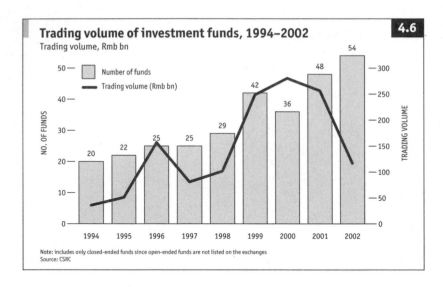

Trading volume of investment funds, 1994–2002   `4.6`

Trading volume, Rmb bn

Note: includes only closed-ended funds since open-ended funds are not listed on the exchanges
Source: CSRC

by Huatai Securities, in the third quarter of the year small funds (Rmb500m or less) sustained an average loss of 10% of their net asset value (NAV), and larger ones (more than Rmb1.5bn) experienced an average NAV fall of 13.6%. In relative terms, this was impressive: it compared to an index decline of some 30% over the period. The best performer, Huaxia's Xinghua fund, lost only 9% of its value, between April 2001 and May 2002, and the worst performer, Dacheng's Jinhong fund, lost 27%.

The total net assets of the 33 funds in existence at the beginning of 2001 fell from Rmb68bn at the start of the year to Rmb57bn at the end, a loss of over Rmb10bn. By the end of 2001, two-thirds of the funds' NAVs were trading under face value, and less than half of the 50-odd funds managed to make dividend payments in 2001. 28 funds made no final dividend payment in 2002. In the bear market, demand for new funds also fell. In May 2002 Hua'an Fund Management's Anjiu Fund announced the results of its rights issue. The product of the restructuring of one of the small funds set up in the early 1990s, Anjiu originally issued Rmb200m worth of units. It now wanted to issue another 297m units, but only 1.7m units were subscribed to, leaving Haitong Securities, the underwriter, obliged to buy the rest. Haitong became the unhappy owner of 56.7% of all Anjiu's shares. This was not an isolated incident: Yifangda's Kerui fund's IPO issue and Dacheng's Jingye fund rights issue were also undersubscribed. This was, of course, not great news for the underwriters, whose capital was tied up and who would lose money if the fund price continued to trade below the issue price. It also broke the CSRC rule that no single investor can own more than 4% of a fund. The regulator looked the other way.

Development of the fund sector has run into four problems. First, there is public distrust. There is little experience of the trust relationship in China, entrusting your assets to strangers who claim to have expertise in asset management. Many investors believe that fund managers (who, after all, work for state-owned companies) are simply another way for the government to profit from or steal their savings. Even the less cynical often do not believe that the professionals can manage their money better than they can – and recent evidence of corruption in the sector suggest that they may be right.

Second, there is still no proper legal framework. An Investment Fund Law is being drafted but has become the subject of much dispute and is unlikely to be passed by the NPC for some time. Industry insiders say the law, having undergone at least ten redrafts, will cover funds on a general basis, leaving it to the State Council and its bureaus to issue detailed administrative regulations on securities, industrial and venture funds. At present, the securities fund sector is run on the basis of CSRC-issued rules.

Bad practice and ineffective regulation is the third issue. In March 2001 the CSRC released the findings of its investigation into illegal trading practices at ten fund management companies. Managers at Boshi, Dacheng, Changsheng and several other companies were found to have ramped up stock prices by selling shares between accounts under their control. A number of staff were removed, demoted or otherwise disciplined. Bad practice, of course, continued. In January 2002 an exasperated Zhang Jinghua, director of the CSRC's fund management department, wrote an open letter to the fund management companies. He complained that they had broken regulations with regard to Shenzhen Expressway's A-share IPO, to which 47 funds had subscribed to shares worth Rmb105.6bn. CSRC rules state that funds can only subscribe to IPOs up to an amount equivalent to 10% of their own net assets. However, in this case the funds attempted to buy IPO shares worth 13-times their limit. Zhang singled out Huaxia, Nanfang and Changsheng (again) for particular criticism. Another alleged scam involved a fund management firm's SOE shareholder using the fund for its own ends. According to industry sources, a major SOE forced a certain fund to use about a third of its available cash to buy shares in Yinguangxia, just at the time when the SOE wanted to exit the stock. This occurred a few months before Yinguangxia's shares crashed, and left the fund's shareholders hugely vulnerable. There have been several other accusations of funds helping large investors exit their positions. Such abuses have done much to destroy public confidence in the market.

Fourth, the industry offers only limited investment options. Fund managers have had scant access to corporate bonds and other financial instruments. It has thus been hard to offer different styles of funds, and it is even harder to offer the choice of low-risk or high-risk funds, since most Chinese equities are volatile. Moreover, fund managers can only trade "long" (buying and selling now), and have not been able to sell shares short (selling shares you do not own in anticipation of buying them at a later date for a lower price), a common practice in more developed markets. Short selling is extremely useful since it permits hedging against falling prices, but it can also introduce additional downward pressure on prices. Regulators suspect that short trading could cause havoc in the market (though there are reports that informal short contracts already exist). Another important hedging mechanism which is currently lacking is the index future contract, an instrument that allows hedging a portfolio of stocks against a general decline in prices. In late 2001, however, progress was made when an All-China index was set up on a trial basis. This combined the major shares at the Shanghai and Shenzhen exchanges into one index, the two cities having previously run their own separate indices. Once this is in place, the way appears open not only for index-linked funds (funds that track the index and are thus only passively managed) and for index futures. However, after the debacle involving Treasury bond futures in 1995, considerable suspicion over the use of futures still has to be overcome.

Open-ended funds

One area where foreign expertise has been particularly useful is in setting up open-ended funds (OEFs). The difference between these and closed-ended funds is that the latter have a fixed number of units and are traded on the stock exchange. Their price can rise or fall to be at a discount, or premium, to the net value of the assets held by the fund. In contrast, with OEFs (known as mutual funds in the United States), the fund's size varies according to how many units are bought or sold by investors, while the unit price is always the same as the NAV. OEFs are the dominant type of funds bought by individual investors in more developed markets. This is partly because they offer the security of knowing that the price of the fund is directly linked to the value of the assets held by the fund. However, in young stockmarkets their use often trails behind that of closed-ended funds for two reasons. First, OEFs are more complicated to manage since the firm's back office must organise the continual buying and selling of the units of the funds and the stocks that comprise the fund's units. Second, there are often fears about the extra volatility that OEFs introduce into the market. This is because OEFs buy back units whenever holders wish to redeem them, so in a market downturn, fund holders sell their units and the fund is forced to liquidate its positions, pushing prices further down. In contrast, in a downturn, closed-ended funds can hold or buy stocks, thus absorbing some of the downward pressure, instead of contributing to it (and can thus be more susceptible to administrative influence).

Chinese fund companies, all of whom have benefited from the backing of foreign firms, had launched 17 OEFs by December 2002. On September 18th 2001 Hua'an launched the first, the Rmb3bn ($360m) Hua'an Innovation Fund. During 2001, all China's funds raised around Rmb25bn, of which only Rmb7bn was by OEFs. In 2002, however, OEFs began to dominate, with 14 new funds raising some Rmb16.5bn, according to Taiyang Securities.

Privately-raised funds (simu jijin)

Since 1995 several thousand financial management and financial trust companies have been established in China. They have secured funds from rich individuals, non-state firms and SOEs, and now engage in asset management on a huge scale. They are known as *simu jijin* (privately-raised funds). According to research by Xia Bin, then a senior official at the PBOC (and a former president of the SHZSE), there were at least 7,000 of these companies operating in Shanghai, Shenzhen and Beijing and probably dozens, if not hundreds, more dotted around the country at the end of 2000. According to Xia Bin's research, the most detailed yet, in total (including those funds raised by securities companies), *simu jijin* were worth about Rmb700bn, over 40% of total tradable market capitalisation, as Table 4.15 shows. It is likely that since the onset of the bear market, the funds available for investment have declined considerably. Considering the fund sector as a whole, one interviewee estimated in mid-2002 that about a third of the total volume of China's funds were managed by the formally recognised fund companies; a third by securities companies managing individual and corporate assets; and a third by these dedicated trust, financial management and consultancy companies.

Table 4.15 **Market capitalisation of formal funds and simu jijin, year-end 2000**

	Formal funds	Simu jijin
Market capitalisation	80	700
Proportion of tradable market capitalisation, %	5	43

Sources: Xia Bin, CSRC

On average, each of this last group of companies manages about Rmb150m of funds which are entrusted to it by around 5–50 clients. Some funds are made up of cash entrusted by one or two corporate clients (Rmb200m–1bn). In this scenario the firm often promises a minimum level of return and then scoops up the extra profit made. Most offered returns of 6–10% during 2000 and early 2001, some up to 50%, well above the one-year bank deposit rate of 2.25%. Others are formed by 50 or more smaller investors, and in this format the company often takes its income in the form of a fee, making it less vulnerable to a market downturn. The largest *simu* funds manage assets in amounts comparable with the largest formal fund companies. Delong Investment, for instance, has an estimated Rmb3bn–5bn under management. It is estimated that there are around five firms, mainly in Shanghai, that are of a similar size. This compares with a large formal fund company like Hua'an that had issued funds worth just over Rmb5bn by the end of 2001.

As a whole, these *simu jijin* companies are a worthwhile development. For one thing, they increase the number of long-term participants in the share market and so are a force for stability. Moreover, many of these companies are professionally run and highly competitive. Most of the fund managers involved have passed CSRC exams. This is no guarantee of quality, of course, but it is worth considering that the larger *simu jijin* companies have built their businesses based solely on the quality of their service, rather than on the basis of a government-issued licence, like the formal funds. Indeed, one interviewee involved in the sector ranked them above the official fund companies. "These guys actually go and visit listed companies," he observed. In addition, he claimed that the informal fund companies often had better results, and with fewer overheads than the formal firms, could pass more of their profits on to their customers. The CSRC has yet to issue detailed regulations on this sector: most of these companies are currently covered only by the Company Law and do not even fall under the CSRC's formal purview. However, it appears likely that the regulator's strategy will be to support the *simu jijin* and bring them into the formal arena. It will probably encourage the large firms like Delong Investment to convert themselves into formal fund or trust companies, and then give them licences.

Insurance and pension funds

After the Insurance Law of 1995 and before October 1999, insurance companies were not allowed to invest in shares and were limited to investing their premium income in bank deposits and government bonds. Previously insurance funds had invested in real estate and there were even reports during 1996–97 that they were involved in share speculation. The government's position appeared rational: the share market was too volatile and poorly regulated for insurance and pension fund assets to be invested in it. However, in the long term, given the low returns on bank deposits and T-bonds, this situation was clearly unsustainable.

In 1999, therefore, the CSRC and the China Insurance Regulatory Commission (CIRC) began allowing insurance companies indirect access to equities. In October, a small number of authorised funds were allowed to invest 5% of their assets in investment funds. Then in March 2000 two insurers, Taikang Life and Huatai Property, were allowed to invest up to 10%. Others followed. According to the CIRC, during the first half of 2000, insurers invested Rmb9.6bn ($1.2bn) in the funds and in January 2001, five insurance companies, Pingan, Taikang, Huaan, AIA Shanghai and Jinsheng (Axa-Minmetals) were allowed to increase their investments to 15% of assets. The maximum was then increased to 30% for a number of firms, and in March 2001 the regulators allowed Pingan, New China Life and Manulife-Sinopec Life to invest all their premium incomes from unit-linked products in mutual funds. (Unit-linked products were introduced into China in 1999, and allow insurers to invest their premium income in securities and render the returns from this investment to policy holders.) By the end of 2001 insurance assets totalled Rmb459bn, about 5% of GDP. Around half of this figure was invested in bank deposits, 22% in T-bonds and 5.5%, Rmb25bn, in investment funds. The rest was held in cash. Allowing insurers to diversify their portfolios proved profitable, at least at first. In 2000 insurers made returns of 12% on their managed funds, compared with the 2.25% that the banks offered on deposits. A good deal of profits came from investment fund holdings. Ping'an Insurance did particularly well, reporting that its return on investment fund investments was 35% in 2000. However, the market's downturn in value in 2001 and 2002 has had a severe effect on all investors' results, including those of the insurance funds. Ping'an reported a 7.5% return in 2001; other firms probably had negative returns. This has damaged the prospects of them being allowed to invest more in equities.

However, in common with more developed stockmarkets, insurance funds can provide a long-term stable source of demand for shares. And so the CSRC is now working on extending the funds' access not only in terms of investment funds but also in shares directly. Within a few years, insurers should have the autonomy to invest in what they like, subject to standard prudential regulations. The expectation is that about 50% of insurance fund assets will be allowed to invest directly in shares over the next five years or so, although this is still subject to much debate among the regulators. In a crucial development in June 2001, the CSRC permitted insurers to establish their own fund management companies, a right previously limited to securities companies. Insurance firms are also keenly lobbying the government to allow them to develop industrial-asset funds and mortgage-backed securities and to make overseas investments.

Pension reform and the national pension fund

Another key to growth in the demand for equities will be the development of pension funds. Creating an effective system of old-age insurance is a challenge for any government. In much of Western Europe at present, the challenge for governments is to shift from publicly-funded pay-as-you-go (PAYG) systems (where there is no pension pot, but pensions are paid out of today's pension contributions) to systems where an individual pot is created, managed and then used to pay each individual's pension. The UK is the most advanced in reform, and has shifted the burden away from the state onto individuals and their employers. In their experience, the stockmarket has been a vital tool with which to manage pension assets. Shares are one of the best ways of achieving rates of return above the rate of wage growth over the long term. Thus, in the United States about 60% of pension assets are now invested in equities and the remainder is in fixed-income securities and cash.

The challenge for China is greater than that facing Western Europe for two reasons: demographics and the need for reorganisation. For one thing, because of the one-child policy implemented from the mid-1970s, the demographic profile is changing extremely rapidly: China's population is ageing. The old-age dependency ratio, the number of people aged over 65 to the number of 15–64-year-olds, will rise from 11% in 1999 to 36% in 2050. This will create a huge burden on those in work (since their taxes, at least at present, pay pensions). The one solace in the changing demographics is that, also because of the one-child policy, the number of children in China is declining rapidly. The 2000 census showed that the number of births were slowing at a considerably faster rate than had been expected. Since children are also dependent on working adults, a smaller number of them means a reduced burden. But in spite of this good news, the present pension system still looks unsustainable. Goldman Sachs estimates that some Rmb26.6trn will be required in pension assets by 2030 to provide sufficient income for 300m over-60s. Not much of that money has yet been seen. The World Bank estimates that total pension reserves in 1995 in China were worth less than 1% of GDP and China already had an implicit pension-related debt worth some 71% of GDP by 1997. Second, since the country is moving from a *danwei*-based system of welfare, where the factory or government unit provided all the welfare to its employees, including often a pension worth 80% of the final wage (in contrast to the 10–25% more common in the West), to a national system where pensions are paid out of pooled provincial funds, the institutional work required to make the transition a success is much greater.

To pay its pensioners, the government must first raise funds, and accumulate a vast amount of money. The three-pillar pension system currently being put into place raises its funds from employees, employers and the state through:

- a defined-benefit "public" pillar paid for by a payroll tax drawn from enterprise revenues;
- a mandatory-funded, defined-contribution pillar for each worker paid for by a payroll tax with contributions from both enterprise and employee;
- a voluntary supplementary scheme managed by the employer or an insurance company.

The scheme is being rolled out at a provincial level, but many of the poorer provinces, especially in the rust-belt of northeast China, are already running large deficits. At the provincial level pension funds totalled Rmb58.7bn in mid-1999, though many of these funds were being drawn down, rather than being built up, by increasing pay-outs and difficulties in collection. To meet these shortfalls, the central government established the National Social Security Fund (NSSF) in August 2001. The government intends to use the sale of state shares and bond issuance as well as direct contributions from the MOF to fund it. As of the end of 2002, the NSSF had accumulated Rmb80.5bn, all but Rmb1bn from the MOF.

Part of the challenge to boosting pension funds lies in constructing a system that allows both public and private financial assets to be profitably managed over the long term. Pension assets have to make real rates of return at least at the same rate as real wage growth. During 2001, although consumer price inflation was running close to zero, wage inflation was running higher, at 4–5% in urban areas. With returns on bank deposits and T-bonds of only 2–3%, government pension assets – restricted to these latter two investment options – were losing ground. In late 2001, therefore, the State Council announced that it would allow the NSSF to invest 40% of its funds in domestic equities. That would allow some Rmb32bn to be available for stockmarket investments at the end of 2002. However, there were reports that only NSSF funds raised through sales of state shares would be allowed into equities, in which case only some Rmb1bn would have been available. Half was marked off for T-bonds and a tenth for corporate bonds. The only direct investment by the fund was its Rmb12.7bn purchase of Sinopec shares in April 2001.

The development of a government-run pension scheme will increase the demand for equities over the long term and also bodes well for the quality of regulation. The NSSF and the provincial pension funds have a mandate to derive a steady income stream from their assets and conservatively manage their investment risks. They cannot afford to copy the high-risk speculative trading strategies of the securities companies, investment funds and informal institutions common in the 1990s. While previously the government has been only the seller of equity, now, in order to create an effective asset management system through which to meet its social liabilities, the government's own fund managers will have to become purchasers of, and investors in, equity. For this, the government will require the sort of things that any other investor requires: good-quality listed companies, tough regulatory enforcement practices, reliable financial accounts, more transparency in the regulatory process, a judiciary able to enforce ownership rights and, eventually, effective supervision of the regulator itself. In other words, pension development presages a shift in the incentives facing the government, and should also therefore mean a change in how the market is regulated (see also Chapter 7).

Asset management companies

In 1999 the MOF established four asset management companies (AMCs) to take on Rmb1.4trn ($169bn) worth of bad loans from the four large state-owned banks, about one-fifth of their total full NPLs (according to some unofficial estimates). It is the AMCs' official mission to get back as much cash as they can from the borrowers. They have generally settled for debt-equity swaps, a strategy imposed upon them by their political superiors, rather than filing for the borrower's bankruptcy. This results in AMCs taking minority stakes in poorly run companies whose managements remain unchanged. For the SOEs involved, it generally means business as usual, since the AMCs are too understaffed to be active in overseeing them, or to even turn up to their board meetings.

But putting aside the apparent failure of the AMCs in loan resolution, another question is what is to become of them in the future. Initially they were billed as temporary holding companies that would self-liquidate after having resolved their NPL portfolios, with an original target date of 2005. "When the Rmb250bn in unhealthy assets re-enters circulation," said Li Kangjin, on behalf of Cinda AMC in late 1999, "our historic task will be finished." But the AMCs are now backtracking: they want to become investment banks. In October 2000 the CSRC granted Cinda and Huarong AMCs underwriting licences, and two months later Huarong and Haitong Securities agreed to cooperate in underwriting, asset restructuring and fund management. In January 2002 Sichuan Dongfang Insulation Materials completed its preparations for a public listing, with Huarong sponsoring the firm through the approval process and then underwriting the issue. Several other listed firms have been underwritten by one of the AMCs.

In a number of ways the AMCs are well positioned to become investment banks. First, with Rmb10bn each in registered capital, the AMCs are huge, dwarfing even the largest securities firms. Galaxy Securities had only Rmb4.5bn in capital at the end of 2001. Second, they will have developed expertise in corporate restructuring and this will be in much demand in the future. Third, hundreds of debt-equity swaps have given them an enormous portfolio of assets to manage, on the basis of which they might issue investment funds. However, their transformation into investment banks will not be easy. Most of the AMCs' funds are currently tied up in NPLS, and even if they sustain their current high cash recovery rates of 25–30% they will not recoup the capital they spent on buying the loans at face value from the banks. Second, the AMCs are likely to be needed again to take on a second, probably larger, raft of NPLs from the four state-owned banks. Although official policy remains that the 1999 transfer was the last, the problem of the huge numbers of NPLs still present on the banks' balance sheets will have to be resolved somehow, and a transfer to the AMCs would be preferable to a simple write-off. Having to cope with a second tranche would severely cramp the AMCs' ambitions to develop other securities-related businesses. Third, it is doubtful whether much of the equity they now hold is worth much. Such stakes will likely be more a burden than the source of a revenue stream: the prospect of investment funds established on the basis of equities in SOEs whose loans were too bad for even the state banks to keep on their books is truly terrifying.

The development of financial conglomerates

The next decade should see a huge diversification in the types of firms that offer financial services in China. Many of the barriers that segmented the industry in the 1990s will fall. Insurers will be keen to branch out into asset management, securities companies into venture-capital activities and retail banks into investment banking. At the same time, a small number of firms will evolve into things resembling financial services conglomerates – China's answer to Citibank. The forerunners in this trend will be Hong Kong-based firms like CITIC and Everbright, and those Mainland firms with a presence in the HKSAR, like the Bank of China.

The Commercial Bank Law of July 1995 ordered China's retail banks out of the securities business, with the aim of controlling the spread of risk between different financial businesses, and banks were forced to sell their stakes in the securities firms they had founded and nurtured. Banks and securities companies were further separated in August 1997 when the banks were ordered off the SHGSE and forced to trade bonds between themselves on a new interbank market. Securities companies continued trading bonds on the exchange. And then in October 1997 the three financial sectors – banking, securities and insurance – were each given their own regulator; the PBOC, the CSRC and the CIRC, respectively. In early 2003 a new bank regulator looked likely to be established, with the PBOC retaining control of monetary policy.

China in the 1990s echoed the experience of the United States in the 1930s. After the Wall Street Crash in 1929, congressmen turned on the bankers, blaming them for corruption and establishing the first federal securities regulator, the Securities and Exchange Commission (SEC), where previously there had only been state statutes and much (ineffective) self-regulation. Congress also passed the Glass-Steagall Act which banned banks doing both retail (deposit-taking) and investment (securities) banking business, a separation that was further entrenched in the Bank Holding Company Act of 1956. The justification was, as in the case of China in the 1990s, to minimise apparent conflicts of interest and to limit the possibility of any crisis jumping from investment to retail banking or vice versa. Such segmentation did not, however, last for long. Although Glass-Steagall was only formally abolished in November 1999 courtesy of the Gramm-Leach-Bliley Act, America's banks had begun engaging in both retail and investment banking, as well as much else besides, in the 1980s. Authorised by the Federal Reserve, banks established holding companies through which they established subsidiaries that engaged in other financial services, including underwriting. Such financial groups were initially limited to deriving no more than 5% of their pre-tax revenues from their securities business, a limit that was later raised more than once.

The Federal Reserve, and later Congress, decided that the logic behind Glass-Steagall had been flawed. At the time of its passage, its supporters had argued that investment banks had used their detailed knowledge of companies gleaned through their lending activities to engage in insider trading. Second, it was believed that banks sustaining large falls in the value of their shareholdings had threatened the loss of deposit savings. However, revisionist accounts of the 1920s have shown that banks were in fact well able to keep their investment and retail activities separate, both in terms of both the flow of funds and of information. In other words, Glass-Steagall would not have prevented the Wall Street crash. Moreover, as consolidation has taken place in the United States, the conglomerate model has been shown to have a number of important advantages. Perhaps most important from the regulatory point of view is the fact that when one part of a diversified financial firm suffers a loss, another can compensate, thus providing greater financial stability to the whole.

A similar breakdown in the formal barriers between the three financial sectors is gradually occurring now in China. All the major retail banks have signed cooperation agreements with securities companies for a service that allows bank customers to trade stocks from their current accounts. This service, known as *yinzhengtong* (bank-securities link), allows securities companies to expand their customer base and allows banks to derive income from intermediary services. It also means that more money will remain in the hands of banks, rather than in the accounts held at securities companies, which makes it less vulnerable to brokers "borrowing" it for their own needs. Another area of cooperation is in open-ended investment funds which a number of banks are now successfully selling through their branch networks.

The greatest challenge to the current structure of the industry, however, comes from the groups established by the State Council as finance-raising and investment vehicles in the 1980s in Hong Kong. These firms are now diversifying into securities and using the holding company structure to do so. In March 2002 the State Council authorised Hong Kong-based China International Trust and Investment Corporation (CITIC) to establish reform China's first financial holding company, CITIC Holding Corp. This company now controls CITIC Ka Wah Bank in Hong Kong, CITIC Industrial Bank, CITIC Securities and CITIC Prudential Life Insurance, a joint venture with Prudential, a British insurer. Through the holding structure, CITIC will be allowed to engage in banking, insurance and stock brokering, as well as provide trust, lease and even real-estate services in Mainland China. The Everbright Group appears likely to follow CITIC and restructure as a conglomerate. And other groups, not based in Hong Kong, apparently do not have to wait until Mainland legislation is changed to follow, as the case of Bank of China (BOC) suggests.

BOC is widely considered to be the strongest of China's four state-owned commercial banks, largely because of the considerable assets it holds overseas. Its main business is retail banking and managing foreign-exchange transactions, but it wants to go further and become a financial services conglomerate with global reach. To this end it established a subsidiary, Bank of China International (BOCI) in London in 1996, to engage in corporate finance, mostly underwriting and syndicating loans. The bank moved to Hong Kong in 1998 and opened representative offices in Beijing and Shanghai soon after, apparently in readiness for an assault on the Mainland securities market. However, its strategy appears to have been disrupted by management disputes and China's entry into the WTO. The equal treatment for all foreign companies that membership of the WTO mandates, means that if the government allowed BOCI, a foreign investment bank, to operate freely in the Mainland, American and European banks would clamour for equal treatment. So, in late 2001 BOCI announced it was setting up a Mainland joint venture in which it would take a minority (49%) stake. Five Mainland companies were to share the remainder of the equity. The firm, called BOCI (China), was established in March 2002 with registered capital of Rmb1.5bn ($181m) and absorbed Gang'ao Securities, the brokerage arm of Hainan-based Hong Kong-Macao TIC, to gain an instant securities business. Remove the charade of its "foreign" registration, however, and the result is clear: a subsidiary of one of China's four major retail banks is now active in the investment banking business.

China is still a long way from creating American-style financial conglomerates. Banks registered in the Mainland are prevented from following BOCI and engaging in securities business, or even owning a domestic subsidiary that does so. But the trend towards diversification will be impossible to resist. Although risk management was a priority in the early 1990s, with WTO entry and the prospect of the arrival en masse of foreign financial institutions, the government is interested in leveraging every possible advantage to support its domestic firms. Giving them the size and ability to derive revenues from a variety of businesses are important means of achieving this. And as the financial services market develops, successful firms in other sectors will seek to move in too. Haier, the white goods manufacturer, acquired 20% of Anshan, a failing TIC, in August 2001 and later that year set up a joint venture with New York Life Insurance. When Changjiang Securities issued shares, Haier bought aggressively and had become a controlling shareholder by January 2002. It also now controls 50% of Qingdao Commercial Bank. Other industrial groups such as Baosteel are also expected to branch out into financial services.

5 The listed companies

By the end of 2002, 1,224 companies had listed in Shanghai and Shenzhen. But contrary to appearances China's stockmarket, unlike those in the former Soviet Union and Eastern Europe, was not yet a vehicle for privatisation: whenever companies were listed the state retained large controlling stakes. As a result, the market has evolved into a dysfunctional halfway house, where neither public officials nor private shareholders enjoy effective control over most listed firms, and few in management have incentives to help their firms create value. This badly organised equity structure – in combination with a developing legal system and interference from government and party officials – has meant that most companies initially performed badly after they listed, and then did worse. The poor quality of listed companies is the cause of the market's most serious problems, and until corporate performance and governance standards improve, there will be no significant improvement in the market as a whole. This chapter examines the performance and practices of China's listed companies. It explains how incomplete privatisation is the source of the problem and maps out some of the ways matters could be improved.

The ownership problem

The vast majority of listed companies are restructured SOEs that remain owned and controlled by state entities (despite the fact that after having

Table 5.1 **Ownership of listed companies, year-end 2000**

Country	% of shares held by largest shareholder	% of largest shareholders who are the state
China	47.0	42.0
France	56.0	1.0
Germany	59.7	0.7
Indonesia	20.4	1.5
South Korea	48.2	-
United Kingdom	14.0	0.0
United States	22.8	-

Source: World Bank

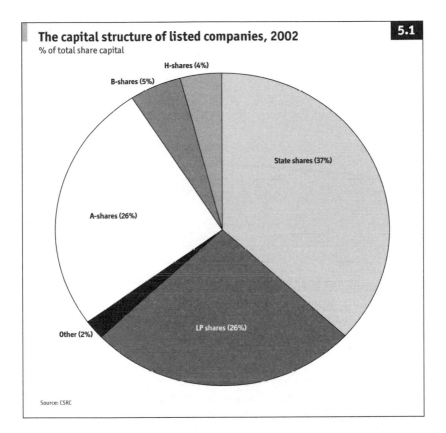

The capital structure of listed companies, 2002   5.1
% of total share capital

H-shares (4%)

B-shares (5%)

State shares (37%)

A-shares (26%)

Other (2%)

LP shares (26%)

Source: CSRC

been converted into "shareholding" enterprises they have lost their official classification as state-owned companies). Ownership is concentrated: the largest shareholder typically had a 47% stake at the end of 2000. Such concentration is not unusual compared with other countries, but the identity of the dominant shareholder is, as Table 5.1 shows. In 42% of listed companies in China the largest shareholders were state organs, and in most of the others it was SOEs who enjoyed control. These SOEs usually hold non-tradable legal person (LP) shares and represent the state.

Figure 5.1 shows how the market's share capital was divided in 2002. Non-tradable LP and state shares (categories explained in Chapter 2), typically make up 63% of a share capital. Neither type can be freely traded, although both can be transferred, the former with stock exchange approval, the latter with (much harder to obtain) MOF approval. Tradable individual shares, the private part of the market,

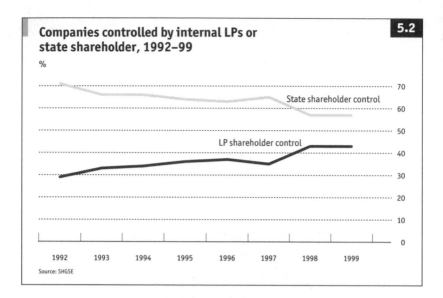

Companies controlled by internal LPs or state shareholder, 1992–99 | **5.2**

%

State shareholder control

LP shareholder control

1992 1993 1994 1995 1996 1997 1998 1999

Source: SHGSE

account for only 25–35% of a typical listed firm's equity capital. But many of these shares are held by other state-owned industrial enterprises, securities companies and investment funds.

It might have been expected, with the gradual withdrawal of the government from the economy over the 1990s, that the proportion of state and LP shares would have decreased during the decade. Figure 5.2, based on an SHGSE survey, shows just such a decline in the dominance of the state shareholder, from controlling 71% of listed companies in 1992 to only 57% of them in 1999. However, the graph also shows that the proportion of listed companies controlled by LPs increased from 29% to 43% between 1992 and 1999. Some of this shift was due to LPs buying state shares, and some was due to the fact that companies issuing shares later in the decade issued more shares to LPs (since they contributed more cash than state shareholders). It should also be noted that a growing number of LP shareholders are not state-owned companies, a topic dealt with later in this chapter.

State shareholders may appear to have significant control, but in practice their influence is limited. MOF bureau officials have neither the time nor the financial incentives to get involved much in the management of the firms in which they hold equity on behalf of the state. Rather, in practice, it is usually the LP shareholder who controls these companies, even those in which the state shareholder has a larger stake.

The LP shareholders do have the financial incentives and usually the political backing to take an active role. As a result, listed companies suffer from what is sometimes referred to as "one-shareholder dictatorship" (*yigu duda*) and the corporate governance problems that inevitably result. The cards are stacked in favour of the LP shareholder, which, if it is state-owned, often has the backing of local government; is often intimately knowledgeable about the listed company (having been involved in its administration pre-restructuring); and has unmatched power on the board. Given an inefficient regulator, deficient minority shareholder rights and the wider problems associated with a weak rule of law, it has been easy for LP shareholders to abuse their power and exploit their listed companies without regard for the interests of other shareholders. And so the purpose of restructuring and listing – to clarify ownership and create profit incentives, so that performance could be improved – has been betrayed by half-baked privatisation in which state-owned LP shareholders wield too much power.

So many of the problems of China's stockmarket come down to the bad behaviour of LP shareholders. This is, however, not surprising. For one, their firms have access to bountiful amounts of capital through IPOs and rights share issues, which creates incentives for theft. Second, these firms cannot be bankrupted, such is the political influence of their owners, so managements lack any incentive to use their funds efficiently. At the same time, while restructuring has increased the power of the LP shareholders, it has failed to introduce new institutions that effectively monitor and discipline them. LP shareholders generally have not been interested in their listed firm doing well over the long term since with weak regulation by the CSRC and help from local officials they can easily steal funds and assets from the company in the short run.

The board of directors

Stable majority shareholdings have meant that the board of directors is usually little more than the agent of the large state or LP shareholder(s). Weak legal protections mean that the board can usually ride roughshod over the interests of minority shareholders.

China's company law states that a board of directors must be made up of 5–19 people. By the end of the 1990s the average number of members of a board of a Mainland listed firm was 10.3, although this number was in gradual decline. Table 5.2 shows how directors were chosen at listed companies during 1996–99. The number of directors appointed by the largest two shareholders – those that held the state and LP shares –

Table 5.2 **How directors were appointed at listed companies, 1996–99**

Method by which new directors were appointed	——— Average no. of directors on board———			
	1996	1997	1998	1999
Chosen by shareholders	6.6	6.5	6.8	6.9
Chosen by largest shareholder	4.5	4.7	5.0	5.3
Chosen by second largest shareholder	1.4	1.4	1.4	1.6
Chosen by government bureau	1.3	1.0	0.7	0.6
Chosen by bank	1.3	1.2	1.1	0.8
Chosen by connected enterprise*	3.8	4.4	4.6	4.8
Chosen by non-connected enterprise	3.4	3.1	3.2	3.1

*A connected enterprise is one with an equity stake in the listed company.
Source: SHGSE

increased. In 1996 they chose an average of 5.9 directors, and in 1999 they effectively controlled 6.9 members of the board, well over half of its members on average. A more positive trend is the decreasing influence of the relevant government bureau (*zhuguan bumen*). By 1999 administrative officials were choosing only 0.6 members of the board, compared with 1.3 members in 1996.

The suspicion is that many companies, without effective shareholder discipline, overcompensate their senior managements. Table 5.3 shows the average compensation packages of some 160 firms: the other 320 firms surveyed refused to provide data to the SHGSE. Officially, at least, the average chairman received a remarkably modest Rmb53,646 ($6,463) in annual salary, the average CEO Rmb51,524 ($6,207).

Table 5.3 **Salaries of senior management, year-end 1999**

	Average salary (Rmb)
Yearly income of chairman	53,646
Value of shares held by chairman	533,719
Yearly income of CEO	51,524
Value of shares held by CEO	367,398
Senior manager's yearly income	69,088

Note: Only 30% of the 480 companies surveyed by the SHGSE provided salary data.
Source: SHGSE

But apart from salaries, senior managers enjoy many other benefits. According to a survey by the Ministry of Labour and Social Security in October 2001, the expense claims of executives at major SOEs averaged some ten times their official salaries; 86% of them had one company car, 23% had more than two cars and a handful had more than five cars. More than two-thirds of these cars were imported.

Share options are not yet officially used as part of salary packages in China, although numerous companies give phantom options to reward senior staff. China Telecom and Sinopec, for instance, by 2002 were offering top managers bonuses on the basis of the company's share price performance. Multinationals operating in China, unable to distribute options to their senior Mainland employees legally, are rumoured to organise alternative schemes, although few details are publicly available. The CSRC appeared keen to rule on the use of options during the 1999–2001 Internet boom, but since then the urgency has dissipated. When share prices are low, as they are now, options as a way of attracting and retaining staff have limited use.

Political interference

Given the ties that bind listed companies to the state, one huge problem is blatant political interference in their activities. According to a 2000 survey carried out by the SHGSE, 62% of listed enterprises – enterprises that are not classified as state-owned – said they had to report to an administrative bureau at the provincial, city or county level. Less than 10% of listed companies claimed they had no government superior. The same survey asked company representatives where the most frequent and serious disputes within the company took place. The largest group of respondents replied that it was between the board of directors and the company's Communist Party committee, as Table 5.4 shows.

There is frequent political interference in the operation of listed companies, often more so than before listing because of the additional funds available. Major business and investment decisions will often require the authorisation of the firm's party committee. Firms can be leaned on to buy and absorb other state-owned firms which are experiencing difficulties, or they can be persuaded to invest in projects that have political significance but little economic logic. Downsizing – sacking staff – is difficult when the party committee has a mandate to preserve jobs.

The case of Huaneng Power illustrates some of these problems. In April 2002 the New York-listed Huaneng announced that it was taking a 3% equity stake in China Three Gorges Electric Power (TGEP) at a cost of

Table 5.4 **Where do the most important and most frequent disputes take place?**

	% of enterprise respondents
Board of directors/party committee	22
Shareholders' meeting/board of directors	19
Shareholders' meeting/workers' representative group	17
Board of directors/workers' representative group	16
Board of directors/supervisory committee	12
Board of directors/union	5
Shareholders meeting/party committee	2

Note: Results based on enterprise responses
Source: SHGSE

Rmb253.6m. TGEP is a holding company that will absorb the assets of the Three Gorges dam project as it is built. Huaneng's investment valued TGEP at Rmb8.5bn. However, the Three Gorges project is not only a questionable investment in terms of its environmental and social costs, but also because of doubts over its viability as a profit-generating business. The project budget is already three times over the official figure of $25bn, according to some independent estimates. Even when its turbines begin turning in the summer of 2003, there are doubts about the marketability of the electricity they will produce. While demand for energy on China's eastern and southern seaboards will undoubtedly grow rapidly over the next 50 years, there are more cost-effective ways of meeting the demand. Gas-fuelled combine cycle plants, many of which have sprung up on the coast in recent years, are cheaper and quicker to build. Beijing will probably have to rely on administrative dictat to force provincial officials to use Three Gorges electricity rather than their own local power sources. According to an internal Goldman Sachs report obtained by the *South China Morning Post* in early 2002, it was suspected Huaneng had not carried out a proper financial analysis of the project. In addition, Goldman allegedly argued that "returns could be below [our] estimate of Huaneng's market-implied cost of capital (12.9%) and may be below 10%". Why would a power company with a great track record and a hard-won high reputation in Hong Kong want to get involved in Three Gorges? Analysts noted that Li Xiaopeng, Huaneng's chairman, was the son of Li Peng (at the time the leader of the NPC). Mr Li Senior is a Soviet-trained hydraulic engineer, and has been a keen supporter of the dam.

Performance of listed companies

One common saying among investors a few years ago was "First year profit, second year even, third year losses", such was the predictability of newly listed companies' performance. However, in recent years the speed of this decline from profit to loss has accelerated, making even this aphorism too optimistic. The Tailong Group, for example, listed in May 2000, and was already reporting losses by mid-2001. In 2000, 68 companies experienced dramatic declines in their financial results, 39 of which had recently issued rights and secondary shares (for which they would have had to report several years of good performance).

It is useful to think of the typical listed company as a machine – a capital-destroying machine. Bountiful capital, garnered from initial and rights issues, is funnelled into the company. And like a very efficient machine, all the capital disappears somewhere, either destroyed by inefficient operations or leaving by the back door. Local government keeps it going by providing preferential tax policies and bank loans. And, at least up until recently, regulatory bureaus have turned a blind eye to improprieties at listed companies, such as manipulating their own share prices or, more innocently, delaying important disclosures to allow insiders to position themselves. Listed companies did not even have to pay dividends. Guy Liu Shaojia, an academic at Brunel University in the UK, has examined the efficiency with which listed companies use their funds. To be productive, a company must use these funds in such a way as to produce returns that are above the rate that would be gained if the funds were simply parked in a risk-free savings account. However, Liu's analysis suggests that most companies fail to achieve this: they destroy rather than create value. While companies may report profits, some 70% of listed companies were actually destroying value in the late 1990s. According to Liu, in 2001 the average listed company destroyed some Rmb360.2m ($43.4m) worth of value.

Financial performance

One recent positive trend in their performance has been in companies' main business income (MBI), which increased on average some 37% in 2001. This type of revenue is important. To understand why, consider the different sources from where companies derive their income.

- ◪ Main business income (MBI) (*jingying*), be that paper manufacturing or retail banking. Another name for this is operating profits, a net figure that includes all operating revenues minus costs.

◪ Raised capital (*chouzi*): things like bank loans and IPO funds. A net figure would include all dividend and interest payments on this capital.

◪ Returns on investments (*touzi*). This includes income from investments in fixed assets and securities, etc, as well as any revenues derived from their sale, and a net figure would include the initial outgoings and costs of this capital.

MBI is the only one that says anything useful about the long-term viability of the business. If the main business is losing money, the company is living on borrowed time, whatever loans it obtains or assets it sells. Some investors already know this. Wei Xingyun, an analyst at Guotai Junan Securities, looked at share prices during 1996–2000 to see if they moved with company profits. He discovered three things. First, and no surprise here, government policy had a huge effect on prices, more so than profits. A local government-sponsored restructuring, for example, would usually have a huge impact on the share price. Second, companies' own future predictions of profit did not have much effect at all on prices, an indication that investors pay little attention to the (often exaggerated) claims of management. Third, investors do indeed respond to changes in reported profits, notably if those profits are based on MBI, and reward an increase in them with a higher share price.

Hu Bin at Huaxia Finance Securities looked at the 2001 results of listed firms in terms of the three types of income. On average companies' MBI increased, and the other two types of income fell. Why? MBI rose for at least two reasons. Listed companies got better, partly under pressure from the CSRC, at collecting receivables (money owed to them). Second, they appeared to have sold more goods during 2000, a year in which independent economists believe that growth in China picked up significantly from lows in 1998–99. The reasons for the decreases in their income from the investment and financing segments are slightly more complicated. During 2001, as the bear market took its toll, listed companies could not issue rights and secondary shares to raise additional capital as easily as before. So, they turned to the banks. Total bank lending to companies listed at the SHGSE increased from Rmb571m in 2000 to Rmb833m in 2001, which in turn led to an increase in interest payments. Greater outlays in financing costs decreased their income in this part of their accounts. At the same time, the CSRC cracked down on the common practice of companies not paying any dividends, forcing companies to pay out more cash to shareholders. And as if that

Table 5.5 **Listed companies' results, 2001**

	2001	2001 results compared to 2000 results
Weighted average earnings per share (Rmb)	0.14	-21.9
Average return on net assets (%)	5.56	-20.0
Weighted net asset value (Rmb)	2.46	-2.4
Average revenue from main business (Rmb)	1.34bn	+37.1
Average net profit (Rmb)	62.37m	+1.0

Note: 2001 results for 1,173 companies. Two listed companies had not published their results by April 30th 2002.
Source: Shanghai Securities Information

was not bad enough, companies' investment incomes also fell as their own investments in equities decreased in value.

The overall result was a deterioration in performance in 2001. Both average earnings per share (EPS) and return on equity (ROE) fell by some 20%, as Table 5.5 shows.

However, 2001 was just one year in a long line of increasingly dismal performances. Figure 5.3 shows the average EPS falling from Rmb0.37 in 1991 to Rmb0.14 in 2001. Look also at companies' returns on net assets, a ratio that indicates how efficiently assets are used and a critical pointer to a firm's ability to add value to inputs – in other words, to be productive. For listed companies, on average this ratio fell steadily from 74.69% in 1990 to 7.72% in 2000. In 2001 it fell further to just 5.56%. Changes to the accounting rules should be borne in mind in judging these results. There have been several significant revisions to the way companies account for bad debt, for instance, a change that has hit profits. Moreover, it is wise not to pay too much attention to the results before 1995, when the number of listed companies was small and the reliability of the data available is questionable. Zhang Xin, a professor of finance at Beijing University, argues that if changes in accounting standards are factored in and pre-1995 data ignored, then ROEs for listed companies have in fact held steady at around 8% since 1996. However, others dispute this claim, arguing that accounting changes do not eliminate a real decline in the performance of listed companies.

Earnings forecasts for 2002 appeared to show the first overall improvement in performance. In the first three quarters of 2002, the average EPS was Rmb0.13, compared with an EPS of Rmb0.14 for the whole of 2001. However, this rise, although welcome, appeared to be

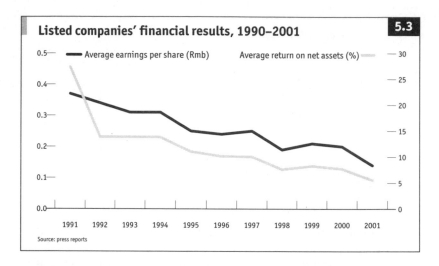

Listed companies' financial results, 1990–2001 5.3

Average earnings per share (Rmb) · · · · · · Average return on net assets (%)

Source: press reports

caused more by reduced losses at loss-making firms than a firming-up of profits across listed companies generally.

Another marker of the decline of listed companies' performance is the numbers reporting losses, of which there were 150 in 2001. Table 5.6 shows official figures for 1994–2001. Some of the increase can be accounted for by better accounting standards and tougher monitoring by the CSRC, but this is hardly good news. The suspicion is that many

Table 5.6 **Losses of listed companies, 1994–2001**

Year	No. of loss-making companies	% of total	Total losses (Rmb m)	Average loss per share (Rmb)
1994	2	0.7	33	0.13
1995	17	5.3	692	0.20
1996	31	5.9	2,075	0.37
1997	41	5.5	4,776	0.49
1998	77	9.2	11,965	0.36
1999*	–	–	–	–
2000	95	8.7	13,500	–
2001	150	12.9	21,500	–

* No figures available.
Sources: CSRC; press reports

more companies are hiding similar figures. Even Shenzhen Konka, China's second-largest television maker and previously a blue-chip firm, now appears among the loss-makers. Losses for all loss-making firms totalled Rmb21.5bn ($2.6bn) in 2001, an increase of 159% on 2000. Instead of being delisted, firms with two or three years' continuous losses are placed in the special treatment (ST) and particular transfer (PT) categories respectively. ST shares can only trade within a 5% daily band, while PT shares trade on a different system from the main board, and only on Fridays. They were limited to a daily 5% price change (in contrast to 10% for main board shares), though this extra restriction was abolished in 2000.

Rights issues, tax policy and dividends

Listed companies are often cash-rich, though poor performers. Two analysts at Guotai Junan Securities, Chen Xiangyong and Huang Xueli, have shown that while on average their operational performance has declined in recent years, their assets have in fact improved. Listed companies' average debt-equity ratio at the end of 1995 was 56.6%, but fell to 48.3% at the end of 2001, while average cash assets rose from Rmb167m to Rmb215m over the same period. By the end of September 2001, according to official figures, 173 listed companies had some Rmb22bn in liquid funds, an average of Rmb127m each, 5.4% of their total assets and 9.2% of their net assets. To put it another way, companies had the equivalent of 14.4% of all the capital raised from share issuance in 2000 in cash going spare. It is also worth noting that this figure excluded funds not reported to the CSRC, thought to be considerable since listed companies often "lend" surplus funds to their controlling shareholders.

One of the reasons for these large cash positions is that the CSRC has allowed listed companies liberal use of rights offerings (peigu) to raise capital. Common in Europe but not in the United States, rights involve a company issuing new shares to its existing shareholders, offering them the "right" to buy new shares at a 30–40% discount to the current market price. It can benefit both sides. The company raises additional funds, shareholders can maintain the relative weight of their holdings or can profit from the discounted price if they choose to sell the shares they buy. In China dominant shareholders also like rights offerings since they can gain access to additional funds and their control rights are scarcely affected. Table 5.7 shows initial and rights issues from 1993 to 2002.

Before 1995 rights issues were common – far too common. The

Table 5.7 **Capital raised in initial and rights A-share offerings, 1993–2002 (Rmb bn)**

	A-share IPOs	A-share rights issues	A-share rights issues as % of initial offerings
1993	19.5	8.2	42
1994	5.0	5.0	100
1995	2.3	6.3	274
1996	22.4	7.0	31
1997	65.5	19.8	30
1998	44.3	33.5	75
1999	57.3	32.1	56
2000	97.9	51.9	53
2001	75.1	43.1	57
2002	68.2	5.6	8

Source: CSRC

national quota system that operated for IPOs did not include rights offerings and provincial governments were keen to authorise companies under their control to issue as many rights shares as they wanted. This was, after all, a fabulously cheap means of raising additional funds. In 1994 IPOs raised Rmb5bn under the quota, and rights shares raised yet another Rmb5bn. Since this depressed prices, the CSRC moved to restrict rights issues, ruling in late 1994 that only companies with 10% ROE for three continuous years would be allowed to issue them. This ruling could not be implemented effectively in 1995, but during 1996–97 the volume of rights fell dramatically relative to IPOs, to around 30%, as Table 5.7 shows. Then in 1997, the government's policy changed again (see Chapter 2). Zhu Rongji, then vice-premier, decided that the stockmarket should be used to refinance the SOE sector on a much larger scale, and as a result the benchmark for rights issues was lowered. A company now needs an ROE of only 6% each year for three years, with an average of 10% over that period, in order to qualify. In 1998, Rmb33.5bn was raised through rights, 75% of the value of that raised through IPOs. During 1999–2001 rights issues accounted for about half the volume of money raised via IPOs, but then in 2002, the amount dropped dramatically, to only 8%.

In addition to having access to funds via rights share issues, most listed companies also benefit from direct financial assistance from the government, through tax relief, cheap bank loans, debt forgiveness and

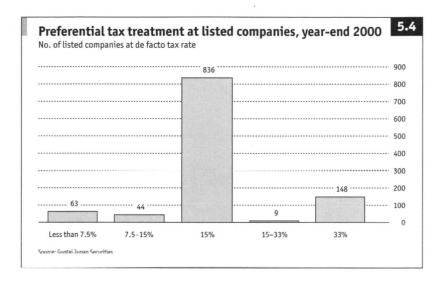

Preferential tax treatment at listed companies, year-end 2000 `5.4`

No. of listed companies at de facto tax rate

Source: Guotai Junan Securities

asset injections. Research by Hou Jixiong at Guotai Junan Securities suggests that at the end of 2000, some 87% of listed companies were benefiting from preferential tax treatment of one kind or another. Figure 5.4 shows de facto corporate income tax rates at a sample of 1,100 listed firms. Only 148 firms were paying the full 33% rate.

Of the remaining 952 companies, at least 290 were benefiting from "tax rebates", a practice by which local government levies corporate tax at the full rate, but then returns some of it to the company (this rebate is included in the tax rates in Figure 5.4). Changes to corporate income tax rules in 2002, however, will limit this practice. Corporate income tax, previously paid entirely to local government, from 2002 was shared with central government, initially on a 50:50 basis, and then on a 40:60 basis in 2003. That will make it harder for local governments to return funds to favoured firms, and will raise the corporate tax burden.

One of the most obvious indications of the poor quality of listed companies is their small dividend payments. Companies listed on the NYSE usually distribute 37–56% of each year's profits to their shareholders. As Figure 5.5 shows, the proportion of China's listed companies not issuing any kind of dividend (cash or free shares) rose from 17% in 1994 to 59% in 1999. By the end of that period, only 42 of the 800-odd listed companies had distributed cash dividends each year since their listing. One more positive sign was that the absolute size of cash dividends increased during the 1990s (see Table 5.8). By 1999 the average dividend-

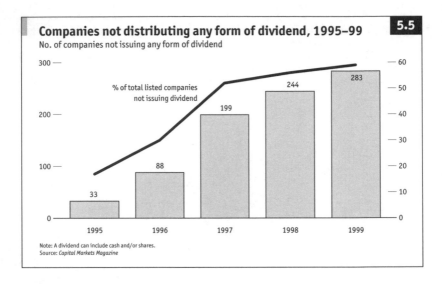

Companies not distributing any form of dividend, 1995–99 **5.5**

No. of companies not issuing any form of dividend

Note: A dividend can include cash and/or shares.
Source: *Capital Markets Magazine*

issuing company paid its shareholders in total some Rmb65m, as Table 5.8 shows.

In most other parts of the world, the dividend element of an investment is important. An exception is new companies from which investors hope to make their profit from capital gains. Does this hold true for China? Research by Zhu Baoxian, a securities analyst, says no. He found no relationship between the type of company and its dividend policy.

So what explains low dividend distribution in China? One reason is that small shareholders, the principal beneficiaries of dividends, have

Table 5.8 **Cash dividends, 1994–99**

	Total cash dividends (Rmb bn)	Average cash dividend (Rmb m)
1994	8.69	42.8
1995	7.94	40.7
1996	7.25	40.5
1997	11.0	52.1
1998	14.26	57.3
1999	18.84	65.2

Source: press reports

little power. They are easily outvoted at shareholders' meetings by the dominant shareholders and have little legal protection. Large shareholders do not usually worry about dividends since they benefit in more underhand ways (see below). Another reason is that there is little reason for companies to worry about losing investors. Given the limited supply of equities, the lack of alternative investment options and the amount of misinformation in the market, there are few incentives to attract long-term shareholders by paying dividends. In the West, small shareholders also wield little power. But they benefit from greater legal protection and the fact that institutional investors enjoy significant clout and will sell shares in a company if it does not maintain a healthy dividend policy. Indeed, many Western blue-chip companies listed in the United States and other developed markets pay cash dividends which increase on a year-on-year basis, whatever that year's profit figures, in an attempt to keep investors happy.

The CSRC has made various attempts to remedy the situation. For instance, in 2000 it ruled that a company had to pay a cash dividend if it wanted to make a rights share issue.

Asset stripping

Although capital does not often leave companies via dividend payments, it does have a habit of leaving quietly, and in large quantities, by the back door. Controlling shareholders frequently strip their companies of assets, financial and fixed. The main problem is that de facto authority over corporate assets has been devolved to managers and large shareholders, and none of the control mechanisms above these people, including an effective judicial system and regulatory bodies, have yet been put into place.

One popular method of disguising such theft is to call it a loan. Listed companies are half-jokingly referred to as loan-making machines (*tikuanji*) since they are all too frequently forced by dominant shareholders (often their parent companies) to lend their funds to the parent or affiliates of the group. The money is rarely seen again. A classic case is Jinan Qingqi Motorcycle. At the end of 2001 its largest shareholder had "borrowed" Rmb2.6bn of its funds. Table 5.9 shows companies that had made substantial loans to shareholders by the end of 2001. Investors should always pay close attention to the non-main-business-related receivables (NMBRR) section of the balance sheet. Known in accounting circles in China as the accountants' dustbin, this is where miscellaneous funds owed to the business are often parked. Another

Table 5.9 **Loans to major shareholders, year-end 2001**

Company	Total amount owed by shareholders (Rmb bn)
Jinan Qingqi Motorcycle	2.58
Shenma Industry	1.3
Beijing Shougang	1.7
Guangdong Kelon	1.3
Shenzhen Petrochemical	1.3
Sichuan Changhong Electric	1.4

Sources: *Caijing* magazine; Shenyin Wanguo Securities

common technique, slightly more ingenious than the loan, is for the listed company to guarantee a bank loan to its parent. When the parent defaults, the listed company has to assume liability for the repayment.

Even star performers are vulnerable to such tricks. Guangdong Kelon, an H-share company, was named by *Forbes* magazine as one of the world's 300 best small companies, the first Mainland company to appear on the list. But its shares were suspended in December 2001 after it was discovered that the group's former parent, Guangdong Kelon (Rongsheng) Group (GKG), had been "borrowing" the company's funds. Up to the end of 2000 loans from Guangdong Kelon to its parent totalled Rmb28.6m. In addition, Kelon Air-Con, a 60%-owned subsidiary of Guangdong Kelon, provided guarantees in May and June 2001 up to Rmb230m on loans granted to GKG. GKG went on to borrow Rmb210m from the Agricultural Bank of China (ABC), an amount that Guangdong Kelon in early 2002 was attempting to recover from GKG after the ABC had sued Guangdong Kelon as guarantor for the return of the funds. Guangdong Kelon was also discovered to have been paying its parent for non-existent advertising. As a result, in December 2001 GKG owed the listed company about Rmb1.3bn. Guangdong Kelon was forced to announce a Rmb1.6bn net loss in April 2002. The auditor commented that there was "material uncertainty" over the group's ability to continue trading. In April 2002 Guangdong Kelon was subject to another CSRC investigation, when its auditors claimed it had not set enough money aside to cover its losses: by the end of May it was still owed Rmb902m.

At the end of 2001 the CSRC ordered listed companies to release details of any loans owed to them by the majority shareholders and affiliates, all of which were to be immediately repaid. By March 2002, according to Shenyin Wanguo Securities, 115 listed companies had disclosed loans amounting to Rmb42.6bn, an average of Rmb370m each. However, only 14 companies announced that the loans had been repaid, and 34 of the majority shareholders had said that they intended to pay back non-cash assets. That should have set off alarm bells, since they were probably going to transfer assets which were worth considerably less than their official valuation, or which were wholly unsuitable to the listed firm. Sanjiu Medical, a listed subsidiary of one of China's largest drug firms, Sanjiu Enterprises, is a case in point. In September 2001 the CSRC announced that Sanjiu Medical's main shareholder had misappropriated Rmb2.5bn of its funds, a sum equal to 96% of the firm's net assets. After the scandal became public the board of Sanjiu Medical called on its shareholder to return the assets. Breaking its pledge to return all the monies by the end of September 2001, by March 2002 only some Rmb349m in cash had been returned. Sanjiu Enterprises then announced that it planned to transfer Rmb600m worth of fixed assets, including a biochemical project, a chain of pharmaceutical stores and the Guangzhou Brain Science Hospital, to its subsidiary in part payment. An even cheekier trick is for the parent to return intangible assets to cover a debt. In November 2000 Xiahua Electronics proudly announced that its parent Xiamen Overseas Chinese Electronics had sold it use of the "Xiahua" brand-name for Rmb320m. With a bit of cash thrown in, the parent's debt was covered.

False disclosures and the problem with accountants

The only way a value-destroying company can survive is if its managers, accountants and auditors fake its numbers. It is difficult – some would say impossible – to assess the real financial health of most listed companies in China since their accounts are so unreliable. One rule of thumb has long been to ignore their accounts completely, and assume that one-third of listed companies are insolvent; about a half more or less break even, and the remaining 15–20% are worthy of investment and a public listing. However, several analysts take an even more pessimistic view.

A number of recent surveys have provided substantive evidence of false disclosures. In a survey of 1999 annual reports, the SHGSE found problems with 38% of firms, the SHZSE 26%. The National Audit Office, in a random check of 32 audits of listed firms late in 2001, found 23 to be "gravely inaccurate". If this survey was representative, then 72% of

Table 5.10 **How believable are listed companies' reports?**

	Individual investors (%)	Institutional investors (%)
Completely believable	8.5	0.0
Basically believable	27.0	41.4
Partly believable	45.2	54.5
Basically unbelievable	16.1	3.0
Completely unbelievable	3.1	1.0

Source: Guotai Junan Securities, based on a 2001 survey of 2,100 individual investors and 100 institutions

China's listed firms had similarly problematic reports. Investors are, unsurprisingly, suspicious. A survey in 2001 by the Shanghai University of Finance and Economics found that 88% of investors interviewed believed that most listed firms provided inaccurate accounts. Another survey carried out in 2001 by Guotai Junan Securities, found only a slightly lower level of distrust. Asked how reliable they found company reports to be, individual and institutional investors had different responses, as Table 5.10 shows. Most institutional investors found that reports were only partly believable; none of them found reports to be completely believable. The responses of the individuals were more diverse, but still the largest group agreed: most company accounts were only partly believable. Asked if an audit by an accounting firm would enhance the reliability of a report, only 63.5% of institutional investors responded yes: one in three had such little faith in Mainland accountancy firms that they believed that it would have no impact on auditing standards. Asked if bringing in an international auditor would improve standards, 96.9% of institutional investors said it would.

It should be noted that China's accounting standards themselves tend to overstate profits. A survey of the year-end 1999 financial results of B-share companies by Tang Dingzhong of Guotai Junan Securities found that their total profits were Rmb5.3bn when calculated using the international standards, and Rmb7.1bn, a difference of 26%, when Chinese rules were used. For one thing, China's standards still tend to inflate the value of fixed assets. However, there have been some important improvements in recent years to China's standard, including increases in bad debt provisioning, which have narrowed the gap with the IAS.

The more important problem is that these standards are not often adhered to. This is because companies want their figures to show a ROE of over 10%, thus enabling them to qualify for a rights issue in the near future. If this is too tall an order, the important thing is to avoid recording a loss; otherwise the firm will be heading towards the ST (see above) category and hassle from the CSRC. There are, of course, a thousand and one means of manipulating accounts to give a good impression of a business, none unique to China. Here are some of the more common ones to watch out for.

Fake receivables

Receivables, income that is owed but has not yet been paid, are ripe for exploitation: they are included in the company's stock of liquid assets, are easy to fake and difficult to check up on. Suspiciously, many companies' receivables grew at a faster rate during 2001–02 than their cash income. Zhengzhou Baiwen, a chronically loss-making firm, was a great fan of receivables. One of the many tricks it used was fake sales to related companies. Baiwen and a friendly firm would sign a sale agreement, allowing Baiwen to log a receivable while neither side had any intention of carrying through the sale. The give-away was that according to the balance sheet Baiwen's receivables grew unusually rapidly, from Rmb49m in 1995 to Rmb911m in 1997, from 3.6% of MBI to 13.0%. Similar spurts in receivables as a proportion of turnover and/or inventory may indicate similar skulduggery.

Ignoring bad debts

Listed companies are usually positive that money owed to them will be paid. Ideally, provisioning should be made for possible bad debts and if the debt is over a year old, it should be written off. Many listed companies do not yet do this. Zhongji knew that one of its main debtors, Tianjin Boat Factory (TBF), was in trouble in 1998, but kept its Rmb50.2m debt on the books as a receivable. When TBF went bankrupt, Zhongji was finally obliged to write off the debt, causing the firm net losses of Rmb46.6m in 2000, and forcing it to move into the ST category.

Trading with relations and friends

Related-party sales, buying and selling among members of the same business group, are often little more than a mirage: the goods are falsely valued and may not even be wanted. But it is a convenient way of boosting profits. For instance, Susanshan, a chronic loss-making company, sold goods to its parent for Rmb160m in 1997, and went on to record net profits for the year of Rmb20m. A variation of this is for the listed company to buy goods at a low price from its controlling share-holder or a subsidiary, and then sell them at a much higher price to another company. In 2001 at least 593 listed companies were involved in such related-party trades. The deals were worth some Rmb499.7bn. For those firms trading in the ST and PT sections of the stock exchanges (reserved for two- and three-year loss-makers respectively), desperate to generate some revenues, this is common.

Deflecting attention away from the main business income

Profits derived from MBI are a good thing: as explained earlier, they indicate that the firm has a viable business. However, profit, wherever it comes from, is important. It keeps companies out of ST/PT purgatory and is necessary for plans to issue more shares. Some sophisticated investors concentrate on MBI, but many investors still do not distinguish between different sources of profits. If managers believe that their MBI is going to be poor, they will attempt to maximise other revenues in time for the mid-year and annual reports. Selling fixed assets is one option. Facing difficulties in 1999, Eastern Airlines received Rmb670m for several planes it sold, saving the company from having to record a loss. Alternatively, reworking the strategy of trading with relations and friends, companies can buy and sell assets, fixed or otherwise, from related parties. For example, in 2000 Shaanxi Long Mountain bought 10m shares from its parent company in one of the parent's high-tech subsidiaries. Having bought for Rmb1 a share, it then sold the stock to Meiying Glass for Rmb8 a share. The profit of Rmb70m made up 53% of Long Mountain's year-end profits. The way to avoid being taken in by this trick is to compare the company's returns on investments with the gross profit. If the former dominates the latter, get suspicious.

Large-scale fraud

There are, of course, other ways to manipulate accounts. The value of inventory and fixed assets can be inflated. Costs can be put through the accounts of the parent company. Lantian, another loss-maker, launched a major television advertising campaign in 2000, but none of the costs appeared in its accounts. Its parent picked up the tab.

Many firms massage their accounts in these ways. But a few engage in spectacular fraud. In recent years, due to investigations by both the CSRC and the media, a large number of so-called *baozhuang* (packaged) companies have come to light. These firms cooperated with their accountants, underwriters, lawyers and local regulatory officials to create extravagantly false accounts for their listing applications. Over 8,000 small investors lost money falling for the lies of Hongguang Industries, a Chengdu-based manufacturer of electrical goods. Issuing shares in June 1997, it raised Rmb410m. But to pass the approval process, the company faked, apparently with the assistance of local regulators, its profit records for the previous three years. For 1996, for example, it reported a profit of Rmb54m, when it had made a loss of Rmb100m. The company also made a rights issue worth Rmb400m in mid-1998. After a tip-off, the CSRC started investigating and delivered its findings in November 1998. As a result, Hongguang's chairman, He Xingyi, and general manager, Yan Zhancui, were jailed and several fines and administrative warnings were issued. By the end of 2000, the company had a disclosed debt of Rmb1.3bn, about half of which was owed to banks in Sichuan. Hongguang also owed Rmb130m in interest on bonds, many of which were "sold" to workers in lieu of wages.

Such cases have turned the spotlight on the accounting standards, a part of the soft infrastructure that will have to improve if the stockmarket is to mature. In October 2001 Premier Zhu Rongji called fraudulent accounting a "malignant tumour" that threatened China's nascent market economy. It is not lost on the country's leaders that reliable accounts are essential for further capital market development. Zhu's comments were triggered by the 2000 case of Zhongtianqin Accountants and the accounts they prepared for Yinguangxia, a firm, according to its literature, involved in agriculture and life sciences. This was the first time that an accountancy firm was the focus of a major scandal. It marked a turning point in the government's treatment of the issue.

With an annual income of around Rmb60m in 2000, Zhongtianqin was the most successful accountancy firm in Shenzhen, and one of the top five nationwide. It had over 80 companies, more than 60 of which were publicly listed, as regular audit clients. Its troubles began, however, when one of them, Guangxia (Yinchuan) Industry, commonly known as Yinguangxia, was revealed to have faked its profits to the tune of Rmb745m during 1999–2000. The fraud was huge: senior managers had signed off on false contracts, export documents, VAT invoices and tax rebate slips. Analysts suspected that the auditor had been bought off.

The government's response to the scandal was mixed. After an investigation, the CSRC and MOF fined Zhongtianqin Rmb2m and revoked its business licence, as well as the qualifications of the two partners involved in the Yinguangxia audit. It reported them, as well as four managers at Yinguangxia and its parent company Guangxia, to the

Public Security Bureau for criminal investigation. However, while Zhongtianqin was a highly public scandal and thus received tough treatment, lesser known accountancies caught cooking the books generally receive lighter punishments. In December 2001, for example, the CSRC fined Fujian Huaxing for inflating the profits of Fujian Jiuzhou during 1993–99. It fined the accountancy firm Rmb250,000 and confiscated a similar amount of illegal profits. However, such fines are not large compared with the revenues that such fake accounting services attract. A single listed company audit brings in fees of Rmb200,000–500,000, plus backhanders paid for any creative work. Moreover, the accountant involved in the Huaxing case was suspended for only one year, instead of being prosecuted or banned from the profession for life.

It should be remembered that 20 years ago China did not have an accounting industry. Much of the legal infrastructure now in place, especially the rules governing listed-company disclosure, is comprehensive, detailed and of high quality. However, as Stoyan Tenev and Zhang Chunlin, economists with the IFC and World Bank, argue in a recent report, it continues to suffer from many of the legacies of the central-planning era.

First, accountancy firms remain state-owned, and although they have been separated from day-to-day administrative control of the government (at least in theory), this status creates numerous conflicts of interest. Listed companies, their accountants and auditors are often owned by the same local government.

Second, there are a multitude of standards in use. Some Mainland firms use IAS, the international norm, some use GAAP rules developed for the United States, and some still use PRC standards, although in this case different industries often have different standards. As well as the lack of common standards, firms do not systematically identify the risks facing the firms they audit.

Third, audit is a highly competitive business. Intense competition between immature firms makes them try to nurture a comparative advantage in their willingness to disguise bad numbers. Moreover, accountants are allowed to consult on things such as tax for the companies they audit, as in most Western countries, but there is no effective monitoring of such activities.

Fourth, accountancy rules are still dominated by tax concerns. The MOF, the tax collector, still enjoys vast sway over accounting standards. A number of prudent accounting practices, such as increasing allowable deductions and income deferral, are not implemented because they would reduce taxable income. Also, in many cases the government continues to evaluate the performance of its firms on the basis of their total profits (and thus total tax contribution), rather than on their efficiency, measured by things such as ROE. Predictably enough, many companies thus maximise investment rather than the efficiency with which they use their funds.

The CSRC is making strenuous efforts to improve the quality of audit, but it is not easy. For example, at the end of 2001, it ruled that when an auditor disagreed with a listed company's accounts it would launch its own investigation, whereas previously disagreements had been allowed to stand. The CSRC is also fighting entrenched interests. In an embarrassing reversal in 2002, it was forced to water down rules announced in late 2001 that would have required any firm applying for a public listing in China to have both a domestic and an international audit. While firms like PricewaterhouseCoopers thought Christmas had come early, the country's domestic firms, fearing a loss of business and a very public loss of face, launched an aggressive rearguard action. Their lobbying succeeded: only a few of China's firms will now need both audits and most will continue to need just the domestic one. Tenev and Zhang argue that in terms of sustained reforms of the accountancy industry, accountancy companies need to be privatised, their operations and norms standardised and their non-audit activities more closely regulated. A professional association, rather than the tax-obsessed MOF, should be allowed to set accounting rules.

Improving listed companies

Asset restructuring

Many of the companies listed in the early and mid-1990s were of a poor quality and once they were listed, they got worse, as the basic inefficiency of operations took its toll and as majority shareholders plundered their assets. Strip away the false accounts, preferential tax treatment and subsidies, and the majority of listed companies are probably loss-making. Nevertheless, however bad they become, these firms still provide an important financing resource for local authorities, who are therefore loath to have any of their firms delisted. As a result, although the CSRC has attempted to seriously clean up the market (a process which really began in 1998), it has encouraged asset restructuring (*zichan chongzu*) instead of forcing companies to delist.

Asset restructuring is a broad category that denotes a reorganisation of a firm's assets (and liabilities) with the (at least formal) aim of restoring the firm to health. The company's liabilities may be transferred to

Table 5.11 **Asset restructuring of listed companies, 1997–2001**

	No. of listed companies	No. of asset restructurings	No. of companies involved in asset restructurings
1997	745	341	246
1998	851	647	226
1999	949	1,100	312
2000	1,086	1,051	531
2001	1,161	1,457	680

Source: Changjiang Securities

other entities or restructured (into equity, say); healthy assets will often be inserted, and the management of the failing firm may even be changed. One increasingly popular method – which raises additional capital, can improve management and almost always decreases the local government's involvement and exposure to the company – is the sale of LP shares (often a controlling stake) to an outside, usually private, investor (see below), while the local government retains a significant stake with its state shares.

Many forms of asset restructuring have become hugely popular, as Table 5.11 shows. In 2001 well over half of China's listed firms underwent some form of restructuring and it is common for firms to organise two or more restructuring deals in a single year.

An Zhaohong, an analyst at Changjiang Securities, has examined the various forms of asset restructurings. They are particularly popular among ST and PT firms that are desperate to get their shares back to trading normally. But such firms present particular challenges. The average PT firm has some Rmb300m–400m in debt on its books, and the suspicion usually is that much more hidden. Few buyers are willing to take that on. So the listed company, the old shareholders, the new shareholders and the creditors (mostly banks and local SOEs) must all share the debt burden. Local government is therefore essential in organising such deals, forcing all the different stakeholders to shoulder some of the debt. Its backing is also needed if the PT firm's often frozen assets are to be made liquid again. And in some cases, if a restructuring turns out to be impossible (or just takes time to organise), a straight subsidy from local government is paid, though this is becoming less common. For instance, PT Kaidi received Rmb40m from its local government to allow it to make a profit for 2001.

One straightforward restructuring method involves the listed firm selling fixed assets and using the cash received to pay off some its debts. This, however, is rare, since decent assets are hard to come by for firms in such desperate straits. It helps, though, if their major shareholders are buying – and are willing to overpay. For instance, PT Kaidi's largest shareholder bought fixed assets from PT Kaidi's subsidiary, Kaidi Sichan Zhuangchan. The assets had a book value of Rmb3.4m, but the shareholder paid Rmb18m. In 2000 it also bought out PT Kaidi's 84% stake in Zhejiang Kaidi Real Estate for Rmb19m, even though the company's total assets were only valued at Rmb6m.

Alternatively, a listed firm can sell the non-tradable shares it owns. These are actually often more valuable than their book value. For instance, Yongjiu sold its LP shares in three firms, Shanggong Shareholding, Guangdian Shareholding and Yuanshui Shareholding, raising Rmb67m during 1999–2001. The book (net asset) value of the shares was only Rmb27m. Land is another option, though it is rarely the only constituent of a deal since land-use rights are notoriously hard to define and protect in practice. In addition, there is tax. If fixed assets or land-use rights are transferred, then a considerable business tax (*yingye fei*) will have to be paid. If the asset transfer just involves shares, then only a (smaller) stamp tax is paid.

If there are no fixed assets, shares or even land to be sold, then at least debts can be rescheduled. Wangdian, for instance, owed its bank some Rmb400m, but was able to persuade Tongji Technology and Zhongjiang High-Tech to guarantee the loan and was thus able to reschedule the debt. Alternatively, the listed firm's bad assets can be swapped, usually with better assets provided by the parent. As the public face of a conglomerate group (and often its major cash-raising vehicle), a parent has an interest in improving the listed subsidiary (which it controls) even to its own detriment. If the price of the assets being inserted into the enterprise exceeds that of those coming out, the large shareholder usually forgives the difference.

Acquisition activity
If state ownership is the root of the problems of listed companies, asset restructuring alone will not help. The only way to improve them is to modify their ownership structure: China's stockmarket needs to become a vehicle for privatisation. In June 2002 Zhou Xiaochuan, then chairman of the CSRC, made a speech in which he stated that 200 of Mainland China's 1,100-odd listed firms were privately owned. This came as a

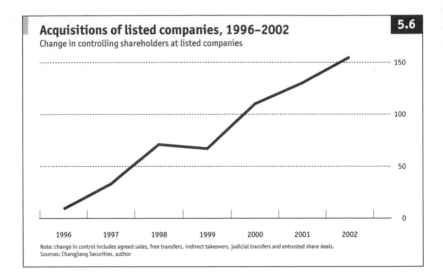

Acquisitions of listed companies, 1996–2002   `5.6`

Change in controlling shareholders at listed companies

Note: change in control includes agreed sales, free transfers, indirect takeovers, judicial transfers and entrusted share deals.
Sources: Changjiang Securities, author

shock to many, but as analysts took a closer look they discovered that under their noses an M&A market for listed SOEs was booming and that a surprisingly large number of private firms had gained backdoor listings (see below). The most common route for private companies to gain access to the market is by taking over defunct listed companies.

The first known instance of an M&A deal involving LP shares was in June 1996 when the privately-owned Zunrong Group bought shares in the SHZSE-listed company, Shenzhen Zhonghao. LP shares are not tradable on the market, but they can be transferred with local government and stock-exchange approval. Since 1997 these approvals have been much easier to obtain and the M&A market for listed companies has grown fast, as Figure 5.6 shows. Or rather, the acquisition (*shougou*) market, where a target firm is bought and absorbed, is growing fast. Mergers (*hebing*), where two or more firms combine to form a new entity, are much rarer, as is the case in the West. In 2001, 130 companies, some 11% of the total, experienced a change in their controlling shareholder. It appears that in 2002 this number grew to over 150. Most of these sales occur in tandem with one of the other forms of asset restructuring outlined above.

Targets frequently have poorly performing businesses, large debts and regulatory issues with the CSRC. As Table 5.12 shows, the income per share of the majority in 2001 was in the Rmb0–0.1 range, below the average income per share of all listed companies of Rmb0.14. Over a

Table 5.12 **Income per share of companies undergoing a change in the controlling shareholder, 2001**

Per share income	More than Rmb0.3	Rmb0.2–0.3	Rmb01–0.2	Rmb0–0.1	Less than Rmb0
No. of companies	2	8	17	85	28
% of companies	1.5	6.2	13.0	57.7	21.6

Source: Changjiang Securities

fifth of targets had negative earnings per share, that is, they were making losses. The purchaser, usually a private firm, might be buying an awful company, but much more importantly it is buying a listing place. With bank financing still off limits to all but the most successful private firms, a listing remains a valuable commodity.

However, it takes more than poor performance for a listed company to become a viable takeover target. Even a poorly-performing company may have an unusually high share price (see Chapter 2). While P/ES for most developed markets have historically fallen between 10 and 20, for most of the 1990s P/ES in Mainland China were above 40. With these valuations, any acquisition attempted via the open market would have been a prohibitively expensive venture. Target firms are cheap for another reason: buyers do not buy control via the listed individual shares, but instead via the non-tradable LP, and sometimes state, shares. These are much cheaper and can be bought in one lot from the current holder. The price of the LP shares depends very much on the firm's NAV, its book value. Government regulations require that state-owned shares (both LP and state shares) cannot be sold for less than the NAV (with exceptions for companies with very large debts). For listed firms with poor businesses, it is likely that the business's book value considerably overstates its actual value. However, on top of the official NAV, a premium of some 20–30% is usually paid for LP shares, still well below the price of the trading shares. And there is evidence that local governments may offer other inducements to buyers (tax breaks, access to bank credit, etc.)

Commercial sales of LP shares from one entity to another accounted for some two-thirds of the changes in controlling shareholders in 2001, according to analysis by Changjiang Securities. There are other ways by which control of listed companies can change hands, as Table 5.13 shows, some of which involve privatisation.

Table 5.13 **How control at listed companies changed in 2001**

	Agreed sale	Free transfer	Indirect takeover	Judicial transfer	Shares entrusted
No. of companies	88	27	4	11	4
%	66	20	3	8	3

Source: Changjiang Securities

- ◪ Free transfer. About one-fifth of the changes in corporate control – less than in previous years – in 2000 and in 2001 involved the transfer of state shares from one government organ to another, usually as the result of a reorganisation of the responsibilities of various parts of the bureaucracy, or as the result of a ministry being forced to cut its links with business. No cash is involved nor, obviously, any privatisation.
- ◪ Indirect takeover. Company A, which has a controlling LP share stake in Company B, is taken over by Company C. Company C thus assumes control of Company B. This process can involve privatisation if Company C is a non-state concern.
- ◪ Judicial transfer. Here an (often insolvent) LP shareholder is forced by a court judgment to transfer its stake in a listed firm to a creditor or sell these assets at auction to other parties (the revenues going to the creditor). This can also involve privatisation since the recipient is often a non-state entity.
- ◪ Entrusted shares. This is a useful and increasingly popular halfway house to a full sale of LP shares. Buying a listed company is a complicated and risky business. But if the shares can be borrowed for a while (for a fee), rather than bought, then the buyer has an opportunity to get to know the company (and check its books for inaccuracies). For example, Xinan Pharmaceuticals took a controlling stake in the Taiji Group on this trust basis first, and when satisfied with the company (and its accounts), moved to take over the group properly.

Does M&A make sense?

Some analysts have doubts about the real gains that a transfer of ownership via an LP share sale entails. For one thing, the identity of the targets – the listed firms – is a little odd: why would anyone want to acquire these value-destroying companies? Taking over a listed firm, especially one trading in the ST or PT categories, will rarely allow a purchaser to extend its product lines, expand into related businesses or enhance its technology. Instead, listed companies are usually bought for their one real asset: their listing place. Does this rationale undermine the utility of these acquisitions? The answer rather depends on what happens after the acquisition. In many instances, acquisitions have been little more than short-term scams. *Zhuangjia* buy control of a defunct listed company, inject a few assets into it to create a buzz about its future (but never intending to actually engage in any substantive restructuring), wait for the price to rise and then sell out. Zhongke Chuangye is an infamous and complex example of this.

Although phoney M&As are quite common, there are signs that many acquisitions, especially in recent years, are leading to more productive outcomes. Research by Dongfang Gaosheng Gaolei (DGG), a consultancy, suggests that purchasers are becoming more serious about improving the companies into which they buy. Its analysts looked at 26 listed companies whose controlling shareholders had changed twice since 1996. The first time round the firms' average ROE doubled from 5.4% before the acquisition to 10.0% in the year immediately afterwards. But ROEs declined rapidly soon afterwards, indicating that nothing substantive had changed. Assets had been inserted and debts transferred out, leading to an instant improvement in the balance sheet, but no fundamental change in the operations or management had occurred. The new assets sometimes turned out to be useless or were quietly removed soon after. By the time of the second takeover, the average ROE among these firms had declined to 2.1%. After the second acquisition, however, ROEs rose to an average of 11.2% in the first year and then stabilised. DGG argues that the second wave of new shareholders were more interested in turning these companies round than their predecessors.

A growing number of purchasers are companies with substantive businesses. Previously, investment companies were the dominant type of purchaser and appeared to be generally less committed to serious restructuring. These new purchasers are more likely to insert real assets (or sometimes their entire firm), remove inefficient management and use the listing to raise investment capital for their real, and profitable, ongoing businesses. Of course, M&As in more developed markets are notoriously unreliable ways of adding value to either side. The scale of the restructuring that is demanded, the scope for debilitating clashes of corporate cultures and the difficulties involved in properly absorbing new products, functions and expertise mean that more often than not the value of a firm will not be enhanced by taking over another firm. Firms that announce acquisitions are usually punished with a falling share price. However, since the deals in China involve such huge asset restructurings and are priced so cheaply, it appears that it is much more economically useful.

Research by Zhang Xin, a professor at Beijing University, supports this argument. He has looked at profit rates at a large number of companies that experienced a change in their controlling shareholder and found that they rose from an average of 23% in the year of the deal to 26% two years later, though they fell in the third year. He argues that this suggests that most M&As in China have a beneficial impact on the performance of a listed firm. If he is right, the future looks much brighter for China's stockmarket. A two-stage approach to privatisation is evolving: stage one – restructuring into a shareholding company and doing an IPO; stage two – having one's LP shares sold to a private investor. This may not be the most efficient means of improving the performance of SOEs, but it is certainly better than a no-privatisation at all policy.

M&A regulation

The CSRC has attempted to create a regulatory environment that supports legitimate M&As and discourages fake deals. The first national regulations that included rules on M&A were issued by the newly established CSRC in April 1993. First, they imposed a 0.5% limit on individuals' holdings of any one listed company (a crude measure designed to prevent privatisation and that was abolished in 1998). Second, the regulations attempted to create a fair and open mechanism for takeovers, although the effect was to stop takeovers all but entirely.

When an LP purchased 5% of the shares of a company there was an obligation to report this to the stock exchange and the CSRC, and then to report again at each 2% change in the holding. This gave minority shareholders better information about possible ownership changes. When the new shareholder had got a stake of 30% there was an obligation to make a tender offer for all outstanding shares to all the other shareholders, the so-called mandatory offer (*shougou yaoyue*). However, the cost of buying up sufficient shares on the open market with these regulations in place was prohibitive: the announcements alerted others to the potential takeover and attracted buyers, pushing up prices. Moreover, few listed companies had more than 30% of their total shares trading openly, making such a takeover all but impossible.

For these reasons, few M&As took place until the new craze for asset restructuring hit listed companies in 1997. In Shanghai the government decided that the only way to revive its listed companies was to insert new assets, forgive old debts and bring in new management. Since officials usually lacked the resources to do this themselves (and wanted to limit their vulnerability to these loss-making machines), they were often willing to sell controlling stakes to private companies, while retaining state shares. These transfers usually took the form of an agreed off-exchange transfer of non-tradable legal person (LP) shares (*xieyi shougou*). In some circumstances, they also sold off state shares. Most involved ownership stakes of 25–29.98%. However, when a stake of over 30% was transferred, the CSRC appears to have allowed all companies that applied an exemption on the need to make a tender offer for the other shares. As the deals have flowed since 1997, the CSRC has been forced to add detail to its regulatory framework. In 1998 it announced that if a restructuring resulted in the main business of a company changing, then it should be treated as a new listing, requiring CSRC authorisation. However, the CSRC, faced with the large volume of deals and the desire to encourage M&As (with the aim of saving listed firms), changed the rules in June 2000 to post-hoc reporting, whereby the deal could simply be reported after it had been done. It also stated that one year after the restructure the company could apply to make a secondary or rights share issue (one of the prime goals of the purchasing firm). Then in December 2001 the authorisation system was reintroduced in order to prevent fake M&As. Any major restructuring (defined as any restructuring, whether involving a change in ownership or not, that affected 50% or more of the assets of a company) was considered a new listing and had to be authorised by the CSRC. In May 2002 the CSRC established a Restructuring Authorisation Committee to process these applications.

In October 2002 the CSRC issued comprehensive regulations on the takeover of listed companies. The rules maintained the need for CSRC approval and tweaked the tender offer system: any entity, once it had acquired a 30% stake in a listed company and then still wanted to increase its holding, was now obliged to make an offer to all the other shareholders to buy their shares. The CSRC may still issue an exemption if, for example, it believes that the purchaser will spend all of its money on restructuring the listed company (and would not go through with the deal if it were forced to spend millions buying others' shares). The new rules also boosted the disclosure requirements and laid out the technical details of share transfer.

But the regulatory framework still requires some work if the M&A market is to work better. Take financing, for instance. A typical M&A deal requires a lot of capital. In more developed markets it is common for firm A to buy firm B using its own shares. If cash is needed, then firm A can turn to its bank for a loan. However, in China, a firm cannot borrow from the bank to finance such a deal, and until the October regulations was not able to use its shares. Banks are forbidden to be involved in securities-related transactions. As a result, firms have relied on cash raised internally or lent to them by other investors. This has restricted both the number and the size of the deals done. Then there are the legal restraints on ownership. While LP shares, usually held by state-owned firms, can now be transferred fairly easily, state shares, held by local bureaus of the MOF, still require MOF authorisation to be sold. This is harder to obtain. Relaxation here would deepen the market in corporate ownership, and would be another step forward in reducing the scope of administrative officials to intervene in company operations.

Hostile takeovers

Acquisitions of China's listed companies are almost entirely friendly, since approval from numerous government bureaus are required for them to take place, and are often organised with the help of the CSRC and local government. But there have already been a small number of hostile acquisitions. The first, and most famous, was the takeover of SHGSE-listed Yanzhong Industries Baoan, a SHZSE-listed company. Shanghai Yanzhong was the first company in reform China to openly issue and list shares, in 1986. Almost 90% of Yanzhong's shares – the company originally being a collective rather than an SOE – were tradable. On September 30th 1993 Baoan gained a 17.1% stake in Yanzhong, but neglected both to report its position and stop buying shares after it had gained a 5% stake, as required by the regulations. After carrying out an investigation and levying a Rmb1m fine on Baoan, the CSRC allowed the takeover to go ahead.

However, there have been few hostile takeover attempts since; they are extremely difficult to achieve through buying individual listed shares. Here, again, Yanzhong is illustrative. Yuxing InfoTech, a VCD player and set-top box manufacturer, was the first private company to list on Hong Kong's GEM market. Using some HK$400m ($51m), six of Yuxing's affiliates bought a 5.41% stake in Shanghai Founder Yanzhong (SFY) in April and May 2001. (Following an investment by Beijing University, Yanzhong had changed its name and concentrated on computer manufacturing. Most of its shares were still tradable.) Yuxing's chairman, Zhu Weisha, thought the purchase gave him control, but Beijing University's Founder Group, owner of a 5.01% stake in SFY, had other ideas. At a shareholders' meeting in June 2001, Zhu attempted to have his men voted on to the board. But after a fight had broken out and the police had re-established control, Yuxing's takeover was voted on by the shareholders and rebuffed. This appeared to be the first time since 1949 that a privately-owned listed company had attempted to take over another privately-owned listed company.

Listing of private companies

Private companies now technically enjoy equal treatment with restructured SOEs in their search for a stockmarket listing in Shanghai (the Shenzhen exchange ceased taking new A-share listings in 2000). In 2000 the old quota system for IPO applications – which had favoured state-owned firms – was abandoned. However, the CSRC did not adopt a registration system, like that used in the United States where a firm only needs to fulfil certain disclosure standards and is then free to publicly list. Instead the quota was replaced with an approval system managed by the CSRC, which retains the authority to accept or decline a firm's application for issuance. A firm can now apply to the CSRC for a listing and, assuming it fits with the industrial plan of the State Development and Planning Commission (SDPC), the CSRC sends its application to a semi-independent CSRC listing committee that then decides whether it can go ahead. Its ownership structure is not explicitly taken into account in the process.

In practice, however, non-state concerns are still discriminated against. There are a number of reasons. First, there is a basic timing issue. Many hundreds of SOEs applied to list in the late 1990s, before the process was officially opened up to non-state firms, and have not yet had the opportunity to go forward. The recent bear market has further stacked the cards against private firms. Low demand for shares is restricting the CSRC's ability to allow IPOs to proceed. According to the CSRC, in August 2002 about 300 firms had already received permission to list, but could not do so because of the lack of demand. The vast majority of these firms were former SOEs. Of the 1,000 or so firms undergoing "coaching", a one-year process that supposedly trains company managements in the art of good corporate governance, the vast majority, perhaps some 90%, were also state-owned.

There are political and regulatory barriers as well. Political pressure to favour former SOEs is still present at every stage of the issuance process. The company law requires any firm applying for public issuance to have been in existence for at least three years, with an ROE of 10% or more for the three most recent years. Many large private companies previously flew under the regulatory radar to avoid taxes and other administrative interference and have had difficulties in getting their financial documents in order. Others attached themselves to SOEs, paying a fee to use their name, stationery and bank accounts. Such "hang-on enterprises" (guahu qiye) were very common. In some areas of Wenzhou in Zhejiang province, an area which is famous for its private-sector activity, over 90% of firms used this disguise. Other firms registered as collectives (jiti qiye) with neighbourhood and village committees. These were the so-called red-hat (hong maozi) firms that not only profited from lower taxes and less administrative interference, but also gained access to bank finance and stockmarket listings. Many only restructured into shareholding companies in the late 1990s, that is, they joined the line of IPO applicants late.

If the competition were to be free and fair, there is little doubt that non-state firms would win most of the issuance places. Research by Gary Jefferson of Brandeis University and colleagues has examined the productivity of different types of firms in recent years (Table 5.14).

One finding was that while unrestructured SOEs performed badly, shareholding firms (former SOEs listed in Shanghai and Shenzhen) did even worse. Both recorded serious declines in productivity during 1993–96. Non-state firms did the best, with positive productivity growth over the period. This analysis not only points to the need for more non-state companies to be allowed to list, but is an indictment of the current policy on shareholding and listing.

There are exceptions, however. According to research by New Finance magazine, some 57 of the 1,160 listed companies at the end of 2001 were non-state companies that had won a listing in their own right. Indeed, three of the five richest private citizens (in terms of their shareholdings) won approval for an IPO for their companies from the CSRC. Taitai Pharmaceuticals, Guanghui and Yongyou Software (the first company to receive listing approval after the elimination of the quota system in 2000) were all private (minying) companies when they applied for their listings. Such enterprises are often supported by their local governments. The Fuxing Group, a Shanghai-based pharmaceuticals company, for example, listed in 1998 with strong Shanghai government backing, raising Rmb348m. Local governments are increasingly

Table 5.14 **Average annual growth of total factor productivity, 1988–96**

Year	SOE	Collectives	FIEs*	Shareholding	Other
1988–92	2.11	3.13	1.11	–	2.11
1993–96	-2.91	0.43	-3.14	-7.96	0.64

*Foreign-invested enterprises.
Note: "Other" refers to officially registered private firms employing more than eight workers, as well as shareholding co-operatives that are not part of the collective sector.
Source: Gary Jefferson

championing large private firms under their jurisdiction: the tax revenues are beneficial and a successful private concern is a useful symbol of modernisation. Foreign visitors are often taken on a tour round Fuxing as an example of Shanghai's vibrant private, high-tech economy, before visiting the super-modern stock exchange building in Pudong.

6 The regulatory framework

One of the oldest jokes about China's stockmarket is that it is the only place in the People's Republic where it is legal to gamble. The real money, of course, is not made by the gamblers but by those who rig the game. In the early 1990s they were called *dahu*, large investors. Later in the decade they became known as *zhuangjia*, a word used in imperial times to denote the landlords. *Zhuangjia* control the stockmarket like feudal estates, ruthlessly exploiting everyone for their own profit with scant regard for the law. Much has been done to improve regulation since the early days, especially since 2001, and the CSRC should be congratulated for its enormous efforts and considerable successes. However, corruption is still rife and it breeds cynicism about the market among both foreign and domestic observers. This chapter provides a brief history of the development of regulation and describes the rules that now define transactions in the primary and secondary markets.

Local government regulation, 1990–97

China's stockmarket was established as an "experiment" in the mid-1980s. Using this label was a useful way for Deng Xiaoping and others to drive economic reforms forward while circumventing conservative opposition within Beijing. Who, after all, could oppose an experiment? But with such experiments in which the central government was not directly involved, the power to make and enforce policy and regulation was usually devolved to local authorities. The Shanghai and Shenzhen municipal governments were given extensive powers to develop and regulate the new stockmarket. The exchanges themselves were established in late 1990 under their control. And after 1992 provincial leaders throughout China were given the authority to nominate and select SOEs to restructure and list. Central government defined the big issues, but had little impact on how the markets were actually run.

The problem with this set-up was that local leaders had powerful incentives for rapidly developing the market and listing their most financially desperate firms. In Shanghai and Shenzhen the new market brought in investment funds for local firms; and for the local authorities stamp tax revenues from trading activity and the business taxes levied on securities firms' profits were both very welcome. Local government coffers also benefited from all the profits of the financial institutions they owned. The upside was almost limitless for these local governments and they were isolated from the risks of fast development because in the event of any financial crisis the PBOC and MOF would have to step in. In addition, good *guanxi* with leaders in Beijing could protect local political leaders from any political or legal trouble. Thus local leaders lacked incentives to ensure that regulation developed at a suitable pace and as a result the two exchanges grew quickly but suffered from poor regulation. As a result, hundreds of poor-quality firms were listed. Local power also undermined the quality of regulation of the secondary market because securities administration bureaus (*zhengguanban*) operated under local control, and not only supervised the listing process but bore responsibility for the ongoing regulation of listed companies, securities companies and TIC securities operations. This was the theory: in practice they largely ignored their regulatory duties.

The securities trading centres

One of the most radical acts of independence on the part of provincial governments during the 1990s was the creation of the securities trading centres (*zhengquan jiaoyi zhongxin*, STCs). In April 1990 the central government gave its approval to the SHGSE. Officials around the country took note; some also applied to set up stock exchanges to allow local companies to raise funds. Black markets in bonds and shares had already sprung up in many places. Then, emboldened by Deng's comments in favour of a stockmarket in early 1992, provincial officials started designing their own exchanges and applying to Beijing for permission to open them. Legislators in the NPC were also keen on the idea. Li Yining, an economist, made a public plea for the immediate opening of new exchanges in Guangzhou, Xiamen and Hainan. He also suggested that Tianjin, Chengdu, Wuhan and Shenyang should be allowed to open them at some point in the future. Zhu Rongji, newly arrived in Beijing in early 1993, had other ideas. He wanted the equity experiment tightly quarantined to two cities. An order went out from the State Council that only Shanghai and Shenzhen would be allowed to operate public markets in shares.

In quiet defiance, provincial governments went ahead anyway and called their exchanges securities trading centres instead. In September 1991 the Sichuan government set up the Chengdu STC. Hainan, Wuhan, Shenyang, Tianjin and Chongqing followed in 1992, and by the end of 1996 China had 25 STCs dotted all over the country. They were exchanges in all but name, complete with trading floors filled with computers and brokers' agents and boards displaying real-time prices. In addition to these local centres, there were also the two national computer-based trading systems for shares, STAQS and NETS. These mostly listed T-bonds and LP shares, were run from Beijing by the SCORES and PBOC respectively, and, unlike the STCs, did not prosper after 1993 because of the State Council's ban on further listings.

The main business of the STCs was to trade securities listed on the SHGSE, together with some listed on the SHZSE. By providing a site at which brokers' orders could be easily communicated with the Shanghai exchange (they were linked via fibre-optic cables and satellite), the centres operated rather like sophisticated brokerage offices. Shanghai, interested in increasing its own trading volumes, subsidised their membership fees and helped with technology. Many of the more daring STCs also listed securities of their own; T-bonds, local investment funds, and at least 12 of them listed the shares of local companies. In total 500–1,000 companies were listed, providing an important source of investment capital for companies that could not get a place on the national issuance quota.

Since the trading centres never officially existed (the State Council never authorised their existence), sorting out regulation for them was tricky. No national regulations were ever passed for trading or conditions for listing. This lack of regulation led to problems, notably in the repo market. Repos are deals in which bondholders borrow money, usually from banks, using their bonds as collateral. As such they allow financial institutions to cover their short-term liquidity needs. However, many of the STCs allowed brokers to trade repos without having the bonds on deposit. When the borrower defaulted, the lender and/or the trading centre assumed the debt. Many STCs thus became hugely indebted.

In 1997 the financial crisis in Asia panicked China's senior leadership into cracking down, and the CSRC was ordered to close all the STCs down. Most of the listed shares were bought back by the issuing companies or converted into debt. Some of the centres turned themselves into securities companies; others, including the large operation at Wuhan, simply closed. But the continuing difficulties firms face in accessing finance has meant that demand for local stock exchanges has not diminished. In spring 2000 the central government unveiled the "Develop the West" policy which was aimed at fostering development in the poor western provinces. Almost immediately there came calls for a stock exchange or two to be established in Chongqing or Xian to help raise funds. The central government ignored the pleas but the idea is not likely to die.

Crisis and the rise of the CSRC

At three intervals, in 1992, 1995 and late 1996/early1997, scandals involving poor regulation by local-government officials destabilised the stockmarket and undermined the wider financial system. As the market and the impact of such scandals grew over the decade, the central government became more interested in asserting its control. Set up in late 1992 after rioting in Shenzhen in August, the CSRC was meant to facilitate this. At the same time, a State Council-level committee of ministers was established to oversee stockmarket policy, instead of the PBOC which had overseen the market until late 1992 and the 8.10 riots. However, the State Council Securities Commission (SCSC) was uncoordinated and the CSRC was initially ineffective. The regulator lacked authority, it was understaffed and it suffered from competition from other government bureaus, most notably the PBOC and the SPC. Most seriously, as explained above, it was undermined by provincial officials. The CSRC could not appoint the presidents of the stock exchanges or even of local securities offices, all of which remained managed by local government. Local officials controlled the issuance process. This led to a number of dangerous regulatory deficiencies. After the T-bond futures scandal involving Wanguo Securities sent tremors through the market in February 1995 (see Chapter 2), the State Council banned T-bond futures and endowed the CSRC with more powers, but these were still inadequate.

In late 1996 and early 1997 competition between Shanghai and Shenzhen for listings and trading volume got out of hand. Investors rushed into the market as prices rose, there was enormous speculation, and an estimated Rmb1bn worth of bank funds went into shares, illegally, through the repo market. There was suspicion that senior leaders in both cities had encouraged local banks to become involved. These activities, bolstered by fears among the party's senior policy-makers that the financial crisis in Asia could spread, destabilise China's entire financial sector and trigger political instability, forged a new consensus: stockmarket regulation had to be overhauled. Many changes were announced at the National Financial Work Conference, a joint party and government event, in October 1997. Commercial banks were banned from trading bonds on the stock exchanges and moved to a new bond market on the interbank market, thus preventing securities companies from borrowing funds from banks via repo contracts. More importantly, regulatory powers were concentrated in the CSRC and local governments were sidelined. The CSRC gained the right to appoint the heads of the two stock exchanges. The SHGSE got a new president, Tu Guangshao, who had previously worked at the CSRC (and was a CSRC vice-chairman at the time this book went to press). Gui Minjie, another CSRC staffer, was posted to the SHZSE. Local securities administration offices were also brought under CSRC administration (which allowed issuance approval powers to be fully wrenched back from the provinces) and the PBOC, which had previously enjoyed a measure of authority over securities companies, was forced to hand over its powers to the CSRC. This left the local governments without formal influence and the other ministries with significantly less sway. In 1998 the CSRC was upgraded to the rank of "an organ operating directly under the State Council", and Zhou Zhenqing, a senior ally of Premier Zhu Rongji, was appointed its chairman. China's new Securities Law passed in late 1998 put many of these institutional changes on a legislative footing.

The Odyssey of China's Securities Law, 1992–98

Bismarck is supposed to have advised a friend that if he liked laws and sausages then he should never watch either of them being made. In December 1998 the NPC passed the law that it had been drafting and arguing over since the summer of 1992. The drafting process was indeed a huge mess, and it also revealed much about the vying forces that are trying to shape regulation in reform China.

Li Yining, a professor of economics at Beijing University, assembled a group of economists in August 1993 to draft the law under the auspices of the NPC's Financial and Economics Committee (FEC). All laws related to the economy had previously been drafted by officials in the State Council's Legislative Affairs Commission or a State Council bureau, so this marked a significant change. The FEC drafters were given unusual autonomy. No government bureau or party organ told them what to write, and influenced by their Western economics training, they advocated a market-oriented agenda. For instance, they proposed a regulatory structure like that of the United States, with a national dedicated securities regulator. At the time in China regulatory powers were spread thinly between local governments, the CSRC and PBOC and other ministries. The drafters also supported selling off state shares and wanted the law to include (and thereby encourage the emergence of) all manner of new financial instruments, such as futures, which did not yet exist in China.

After the FEC had finished, its draft was passed to the NPC's Commission of Legislative Affairs (CLA). The CLA's formal role is to bring its legal expertise to bear on the technicalities of drafts. But a mixture of duty (the commission was mandated to ensure that legislation was in line with State Council policy) and bloody-mindedness led the commission to completely rewrite the FEC's draft of the Securities Law. By early 1994 they had removed most of the progressive articles, had reorganised the regulatory structure to re-empower local governments and the PBOC, and had limited the law to cover only corporate debt and equity. When the FEC drafters found out, they accused the CLA of wrecking the draft. The CLA responded by saying that the FEC had been hopelessly idealistic. Instructed to resolve their differences by the NPC leadership, the two groups fought for their respective policies and came up with a number of unworkable compromise drafts during 1994-95. Meanwhile, the SCSC, as well as State Council bureaus, simply issued their own rules with which to regulate the market. This was made possible by a notice passed by the NPC in 1982 that enabled State Council bureaus to issue regulations on economic matters with full legislative authority. After the 1995 T-bond futures scandal, the stockmarket's future was thrown into doubt and the party leadership instructed the NPC to stop drafting completely.

The political logjam was unblocked in 1997 by two things. First, the financial crisis in Asia deeply scared Zhu and his advisers. They immediately prioritised the improvement of regulation in an attempt to prevent the crisis spreading into China. Second, there was new blood at the top of the NPC. Li Peng, fresh from two terms as premier, took over as chairman of the NPC's standing committee in March 1998. (The previous incumbent, Qiao Shi, had made a nuisance of himself within the party by calling for increased supervision of the executive and party by the NPC which, after all, is the ultimate source of authority in the constitution. Qiao had, however, shown little interest in the Securities Law.) Li ordered the FEC and CLA to resolve their differences and told them to have a draft ready by the end of the year. Most of the key regulatory decisions (the structure of the regulator, the instruments to be included, etc) had already been made by the party's own Finance and Economics Committee by this time. The Securities Law was passed in December 1998, and came into effect on July 1st 1999. However, despite the media hoopla, its impact was minimal. By mid-1998 almost all the regulatory structures were already in place, mostly introduced through State Council rules. The significance of the Securities Law was rather that it forced government officials to resolve their differences and sent out a clear signal to local officials that the central government now had a policy for the stockmarket and was ready to enforce its will.

The CSRC in charge, 1998–

Since 1998 the CSRC has had authority over the stock exchanges and local securities administration offices, a large budget derived from fees levied on trading, and an array of administrative powers with which to punish offenders. Its empowerment has led to a number of positive changes in regulation. With the withdrawal of local governments from the issuance process, the quality of companies coming to market is widely agreed to have improved. In the past the stock exchanges often turned a blind eye to trading violations. This does not happen so much now, since the exchanges are micro-managed by the regulator. Exchange staff take instructions from and report to CSRC staff daily. All important decisions about the listing and delisting of stocks, the disciplining of exchange members and policy decisions are taken by the CSRC. Previously, companies benefited from lacklustre regulation by the PBOC and poor coordination between that organ and the CSRC, but since responsibility in this area has been clarified it is more difficult for securities companies to hide their bad practices. However, despite the changes that have been put in place since 1998, serious deficiencies in regulation remain.

Regulation of the primary market

The primary market, where firms first issue their shares, suffered from three problems during the 1990s: political control of share issuance; the quota system; and administrative pricing. Improvements have been made in all three areas.

Political control of the issuance process

The CSRC has improved the issuance process by de-politicising it. In June 1993 it established an Issuance Examination and Approval Committee (IEAC) of about 20 people to vet issuance applications and secretly vote on them. However, the committee did not have much power. Up until 1997 local government, the SPC and other senior leaders decided which firms should be approved. But when the Securities Law was implemented in 1998, the IEAC came into its own. Now expanded to some 80 professionals drawn from the legal, accountancy and financial industries, as well as from academia and the CSRC itself, the committee is divided into ad hoc subcommittees of eight people (whose identities are supposedly secret). Officially they have the final say on all applications. It is generally accepted that the use of these committees has cut down on the corruption in the listing process and has also reduced pressure on the CSRC leadership from other officials. However, the identities of committee members are well known to many and there are stories of pay-offs to some of them.

The quota system

The quota system operated from 1993 to 2000. The SPC determined each year's volume of equity issuance and the CSRC would then divide this up among the provinces and ministries. It is, of course, worth remembering that the quota system did have a number of useful functions. Without it the stockmarket would have been swamped with shares, such was firms' pent-up demand for investment capital. The quota also allowed funds to be channelled towards important sectors such as natural resources, utilities, heavy industry and manufacturing SOEs, and away from light industry, real estate and finance. This bias has lived on well past the end of the quota system in 2000, as Table 6.1 shows, thanks to the CSRC's ability to screen applicant firms.

The quota system was damaging in at least two ways. First, the government regularly used it to manipulate market sentiment. For example, in late 1996, with the market hitting new highs daily, Zhu announced an enormous increase in the following year's quota in an effort to deflate what he believed to be a speculative bubble. Second, the whole process was inevitably vulnerable to lobbying and corruption. In June 2002, for instance, Chinese media reported that at least 12 companies from Jiangsu province, including the SHGSE-listed Jiangsu Sunshine and the SHZSE-listed Wuxi Little Swan, had bribed regulators to gain market listings during the 1990s. Such stories do little to raise the eyebrows these days. What was special about this scam was that these companies had not simply bribed local officials to get on to the Jiangsu quota list (more or less standard practice) but had avoided the provincial quota altogether by apparently paying bribes to national officials.

The quota system was eliminated in 2000, although the CSRC has continued to operate an approval system rather than the registration system common in more developed markets. Enterprises must seek CSRC approval rather than simply register their intention to issue shares and fulfil a comprehensive set of disclosure requirements. America's SEC makes no consideration of the quality of any domestic issue as long

Table 6.1 **Industry breakdown of issuance to firms, 2001**

Industry code	Industry type	Total capital raised (%)
A	Agriculture	0.5
B	Mining	25.3
C	Manufacturing	48.1
C0	Food and beverages	6.0
C1	Textiles	1.4
C2	Wood products	0.0
C3	Paper and printing	0.7
C4	Chemicals	5.3
C5	Electrical equipment	1.5
C6	Metals	12.0
C7	Machinery	10.3
C8	Medicine	10.9
C9	Other manufacturing	0.0
D	Utilities	6.5
E	Construction	2.0
F	Transport, logistics	5.1
G	IT	5.2
H	Wholesale and retail trade	1.6
I	Financial services	0.0
J	Real estate	3.5
K	Social services	0.0
L	Broadcasting and culture	2.3
M	Conglomerate	0.0

Source: CSRC

as all the risks it entails are disclosed (though where the shares trade is a decision partly based on the quality of the issuer). The CSRC, in contrast, remains concerned not only about the veracity of firms' accounts, but also about the quality of the company, which industry it operates in and its ownership structure.

The IPO process and administrative pricing

As well as controlling the volume of issuance and the types of companies that could come to market, the government also controlled the IPO price. During 1993–99, the CSRC set a P/E ratio of about 15 as its standard

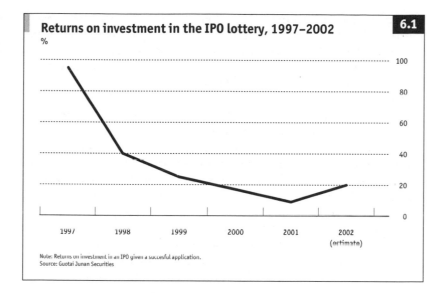

Returns on investment in the IPO lottery, 1997–2002 `6.1`

%

Note: Returns on investment in an IPO given a successful application.
Source: Guotai Junan Securities

for all new issues, no matter in what industry the firm was operating, its growth prospects or the value of its projected cash flows. Since secondary market P/ES were commonly four times or more higher, share prices would usually rocket on the first day of trading. This created huge incentives for the take-up of IPOs and thus fulfilled the government's need to sell all its IPO shares.

Such was the huge demand for these instant riches that an IPO lottery system was established soon after the 8.10 riots in August 1992 to choose who could subscribe to new shares. (The 8.10 riots in Shenzhen were triggered by investors frustrated by local-government corruption in an IPO.) Funds had to be deposited in a trading account and if the account was chosen in a lottery by the CSRC, the account owner would then buy the IPO shares. If not, the money was returned. However, the system was open to corruption since if an institutional investor had enough funds, and could open enough share accounts, it had a much better chance of winning the lottery, several times over. Figure 6.1 shows the returns an investor could expect from a successful bid to buy into an IPO between 1997 and 2002. Before 1997, the average return was above 100%. Even at its lowest return of 9% in 2001, it was still an attractive option for a two-month risk-free investment.

In Western markets IPOs are also priced to leave some money on the table, that is to price the IPO so that there will be a moderate price rise on the first day. According to Jay Ritter at the University of Florida, in the United States the average underpricing of IPOs – the difference in the opening and closing price on the first day of trading – was 8% in the 1980s and 15% during 1990–98. This systematic underpricing is designed to attract investors who would otherwise, because of their lack of information about the company, be too risk-averse to buy. In China, such a huge discount in the IPO could be seen to reflect the government's chronic lack of confidence in the companies it was allowing to issue. Why would anyone want to buy into such awful companies without the guarantee of some serious upside on the first day?

However, this way of pricing IPOs has changed and since 1998 the CSRC has relaxed the rules for IPO pricing. It now allows underwriters, in co-ordination with the listing company, to set the price themselves. This has led to a rise in P/ES in the primary market, and some prices during the bull market of 2000–01 were up to 60-times earnings. This has meant more profits for underwriters (since their fee is set at 2.5% of the value of issuance), but also more risk. After the July 2001 bear market began, IPO P/ES fell and a number of rights issues were under-subscribed, leaving several underwriters obligated to buy up large volumes of shares.

The CSRC attempted to improve the lottery system in early 2000 when it required that a subscriber to an IPO issue must already own at least Rmb10,000 worth of shares. This move was designed to force lottery subscribers to participate in the share market over the long term, instead of just playing the risk-free IPO lottery game. It was also designed to increase the costs of those investors who used false accounts. However, the plan could not be implemented since securities companies and the stock exchanges could not create a system by which applicant accounts holding the requisite value of shares could be accurately identified, communicated to the exchanges and entered into the lottery. In April 2002, however, work on the software had progressed, and the scheme was rolled out.

Regulation of the secondary market

China's stockmarket is a notoriously corrupt place. Securities firms, investment funds, finance companies and rich individuals all manipulate prices and spread prodigious amounts of false information. Barely a day now passes without a story of how a *zhuangjia*, a manipulator or a group of manipulators, has bought up a stock, created rumours of asset injections or high-tech business plans and then sold the shares at

Table 6.2 **What hurts you most?** (% of respondents)

	Individual investors	Institutional investors
Insider dealing	35.2	30.1
Manipulators (zhuangjia) spreading false information	31.9	19.4
Company delaying disclosures	15.9	11.8
Company issuing false reports	11.5	38.7

Source: Guotai Junan Securities, based on a 2001 survey of 2,100 individual and 100 institutional investors

their peak to naïve investors. Asked by Guotai Junan, a securities firm, in a 2001 survey, individual and institutional investors ranked the things that they believed most hurt them. The results are shown in Table 6.2.

The results are interesting. False company reports were rated the most damaging to institutions but least damaging to individuals. Institutions were less worried about *zhuangjia*. There are a number of possible explanations. First, institutions can more easily recognise when *zhuangjia* are manipulating a share: they can spot the tell-tale signs through their technical analysis of price movements and trading models. However, they do pay closer attention to accounts. Individuals are more vulnerable to insider trading and *zhuangjia* manipulation since they rely more on rumours in their trading. They rarely read company reports, let alone rely upon them to make their investment decisions.

Regulators privately admitted in 2000 that at least 30% of stocks were being actively manipulated at any one time. But it is of course another thing to talk about such issues publicly: while some problems are admitted, the true scale of corruption is rarely publicised. When it is, there is trouble. In January 2001 Wu Jinglian, head of the State Council's Development Research Council, condemned China's share market on television for being "worse than a casino" (*buru duchang*) – at least in a casino there were rules, Wu observed wryly. He argued that individual investors were not adequately protected and that the market had little economic utility. Wu is one of China's most senior economists, and was involved in pushing through market reforms during the 1980s and 1990s. He has long been critical of the stockmarket, but these comments triggered a remarkable reaction. In the four days following his appearance on TV, prices fell sharply and on February 11th a group of other eminent economists, including Li Yining, Dong Fureng, Xiao Zhuoji, Wu Xiaoqui and Han Zhiguo appeared together on TV to dispute Wu's claims. Li Yining said that while there were problems "they should not blur our eyes to the achievement of the stockmarket". He continued: "All countries have similar problems in the early stage of their stockmarket and they should not be exaggerated." Of course, making a scientifically credible comparison of stockmarket corruption across countries would be very difficult. What can be safely assumed, though, is that most people watching the dispute agreed more with Professor Wu than with Li and friends. And it is scandals like Zhongke Chuangye that makes them feel this way.

Scandal of the century: Zhongke Chuangye

Zhongke Chuangye, otherwise known as China Venture Capital, was the leader of a new wave of high-tech stocks that took the Shenzhen index to new heights in the summer of 2000. However, over the space of a few days in December 2000 and January 2001 its share price fell over 90% as revelations of a huge price manipulation scam swept the market. The case involved at least 120 securities companies and other financial institutions from more than 20 provinces and cities, as well as some Rmb5.4bn ($650m) worth of funds. The scandal revealed much about who is involved in stockmarket corruption and how the game works.

By early 1998, using some 1,000 trading accounts, Zhu Huanliang, a Shenzhen *zhuangjia*, had under his control about 90% of the floating shares of Kangdaer, a poultry-breeding firm listed on the SHZSE. The firm was a disaster: most of its assets had been secretly sold off and there were few operating revenues left to sustain it. Zhu offered Lu Liang, a Beijing "investor", half of his shares in the company in exchange for additional financing and the chance to be involved in "reinventing" the company. Lu sought the backing of a number of firms, including many of the big-name securities companies and TICs. China Coal Trust and Investment Company, Nanfang (Southern) Securities, Haitong Securities and CITIC, among others, got involved. Securities companies provided 80% of the 1,565 securities accounts used in the scam, selling them for about Rmb190 each. The Hainan operation of Southern Securities and Shenyin Wanguo's Lujiabang branch in Shanghai provided the most accounts. Lu raised additional funds from institutions in Beijing and elsewhere and bought half of Zhu's stake and 35% of Kangdaer's state shares for Rmb700m. Zhu and Lu then inserted some new assets and converted Kangdaer, at least in theory, into a high-tech company. Under the pseudonym "Mr K", Lu got busy writing investment advice columns in the Chinese media, plugging high-tech stocks in general and Kangdaer in particular. In August 1999 a report about Kangdaer appeared in the *China Securities News*, announcing its imminent restructuring into a high-tech giant involved in genetic medicine research, Internet service provision, e-commerce and venture capital. Investors could not believe their luck. From Rmb17 in 1998, Kangdaer's stock had risen to Rmb40 by the end of 1999. On December 13th 1999 came the *coup de grace* when Kangdaer changed its name to become Zhongke Chuangye, China Technology Enterprises, a perfect draw for investors made about the "new economy". On February 21st 2000, the company's shares hit Rmb84.

The scam then started unravelling. In July 2000 Zhu decided it was time to make his move and he starting selling off Zhongke shares. Caught off guard, and with the share price under pressure, Lu and his backers attempted to buy the shares, but they lacked the funds. Then in October, the CSRC began investigating illegal share dealing at Beijing Zhongke, another company established by Lu, but could not uncover sufficient evidence of wrongdoing. But rumours of investigations into the company and of the scam leaked out in late December and investors fled. Zhongke's stock fell by its 10% daily limit for ten days in a row, soon wiping out Rmb5bn of its market value.

Zhu fled to Hong Kong, if rumours are to be believed, with Rmb500m in cash stashed away on his speedboat. On January 10th 2001 the CSRC announced they were investigating insider dealing and price manipulation at Zhongke, as well as at Yian Keji, another successful high-tech stock. Lu was brought in for questioning at the CSRC but released. However, he had other problems: many of the firms and rich individuals who had lent him money had lost millions, and Zhu was suddenly not a popular man. (The chairman of a firm closely connected with Lu was attacked in the street in the summer of 2002 and hospitalised.) With the CSRC apparently refusing or unable to offer him protection, Zhu walked into the offices of *Caijing* magazine and told his story. His idea appears to have been to use the publicity his story created to make himself untouchable. A few weeks later, he was put under house arrest. But embarrassingly for the government, he then escaped (there are rumours of him bribing the Public Security officials guarding him). Neither Zhu or Lu have since been found.

That did not stop the CSRC and Public Security Bureau pursuing criminal charges against others involved in the scam. In June 2002 the case was heard at the No. 2 Beijing Municipal Intermediate People's Court, the first time a secondary market scam had made it into a criminal court. The trial was expected to last only three days with the verdict a foregone conclusion. Seven defendants, the lieutenants of Zhu and Lu, pleaded guilty and asked for their sentences – which could have been for up to five years in prison – to be mitigated because they were only accessories to the crime. Everyone was surprised when, after four days, the judges announced that they would postpone their decision on the case, citing the complexity of the crime and their inexperience in such matters as reasons for seeking further advice. In early 2003 there were rumours that the judges were finally ready to give their judgment.

Why is regulation so poor?

Much improvement has occurred in the quality of regulation since 1998, especially since 2001, a subject discussed further in Chapter 7. However, it still leaves much to be desired. No one engaged in price manipulation or insider trading has yet been imprisoned. Usually those breaking regulations receive no more than a (non-public) warning issued by the CSRC. Only in serious cases are public censure, fines and bans used. However, even fines, which rarely exceed a few thousand renminbi, are usually no threat since several million renminbi can be made in profit in a typical scam.

Why has enforcement remained so weak for so long? Of course, this is common in all emerging markets and there are a number of factors common to all of them. Young stockmarkets are often poorly regulated because of officials' lack of expertise in regulation and the limited resources available. Most importantly, the rule of law is generally weak.

However, an important additional factor in the Chinese context is the conflict between the CSRC's two mandates. Since 1998 the CSRC has been the national regulator, charged with enforcing rules, maintaining order and generally protecting investors, especially small ones. Yet the regulator is also a government agency, operating under party direction, and as such it has also been mandated to support the government's industrial policy. As Chapter 2 explained, this has primarily involved supporting former SOEs. So in addition to ensuring that SOEs have access to equity capital, the CSRC came under considerable pressure in the 1990s to ensure that demand for these shares was maintained. A bullish secondary market has been required to maintain positive primary market sentiment. At least up until mid-2001, the government appeared resigned to allowing speculation to go on more or less unhindered since a clampdown in the secondary market would have reduced liquidity and destroyed demand for shares. The problem was one of policy priorities and political will. However, as Chapter 7 explains, there are important changes taking place in the economy and in the priorities of the State Council, which have meant that this strategy is changing. The rationale that sustained poor regulation is disappearing.

7 Re-regulation and the future of China's stockmarket

The CSRC leadership under Zhou Xiaochuan between 2000 and 2002, and now under Shang Fulin, the new chairman, is not only regulating the market better but is also giving serious consideration to liberalisation. Since 2000 a series of new, market-oriented policies have been rolled out which have begun to lay the foundations of a more efficient market. This process might be called re-regulation: changing the rules of the equity game to allow market forces greater sway and to place greater limits on the government's ability to intervene. Implementation of long-standing rules has improved; new instruments have been introduced; foreign institutions are being allowed entry; and ad hoc administrative interference is giving way to regulation. Most importantly, it appears that the wisdom of using the stockmarket as a tool of industrial policy is now in question.

Change has been evident in all areas of the market. The severe crackdown on price manipulation and insider dealing that began in the summer of 2001 apparently indicated the senior leadership's intention to protect small investors, even if this meant adversely affecting investors' confidence and thus SOE financing. Fines became heavier, offenders now face the possibility of going to prison and the Supreme People's Court has even allowed private suits against listed companies to proceed. The CSRC has worked hard to develop new instruments which will deepen and mature the market: not only investment funds, but also convertible bonds and index futures. The system for IPOs was liberalised, which led to competitive pricing, and in early 2002 the rules governing brokerage commissions were loosened, triggering intense competition in the sector and encouraging further consolidation. Efforts were even made to resolve the problem of non-tradable shares, a move that should help improve corporate governance at listed firms. It will take time to implement these policies, but it all points to a government heading in the direction of Western norms and away from "Chinese characteristics".

These reforms are not happening because of the good intentions of the senior leadership, or because a small group of Western-trained lawyers, accountants and economists have gained influence at the

CSRC, although such factors may help. The key reason for these changes, and for the changes that will continue to occur over the next decade, is that the government's industrial, welfare and budgetary priorities are shifting. During the 1990s the stockmarket was used to finance the SOE sector and regulation was subordinated to the role of protecting these firms; protecting investors and ensuring the market worked efficiently were lower priorities. However, during the decade of 2000s this strategy is set to change as the government becomes more interested in privatising state-owned firms, selling its industrial assets to raise much-needed funds and creating a modern pension system. As the government pursues these new policies, the role of the stockmarket will evolve significantly. The result will be a larger, better regulated market populated by a growing number of non-state firms and institutional investors (including some foreign ones), in which standards of disclosure, fairness and transparency will be better than at present. However, this transition will not be painless and will be resisted by elements of the bureaucracy.

Why China's stockmarket will improve

Why are markets well regulated? Why is the capital market in the United States better regulated – and despite recent scandals still is – than the one in China? Regulation is effective when it successfully tackles the information asymmetries in the market. For example, companies selling securities often know far more about their quality than the purchaser, and large, well-resourced institutions are bound to be better informed about the goods on offer than the small investor. It is difficult for many participants in the market to make a full and objective assessment of the securities on offer. Without some form of regulation that guarantees the truthfulness and timeliness of the disclosures, sellers of shares and large institutions will attempt to cheat and purchasers, understandably, will not be trusting enough to part with their cash.

Although a strong and independent regulator might help matters, it is by no means sufficient. Other things are needed to ensure trading occurs on a fair basis. Firms must police themselves, motivated not only by the stick of prosecution but also by the carrot of retaining their reputation. Of course, sometimes reputation is not enough, as most of the world's major investment banks proved during the 1998–2000 boom years of the Internet bubble, but it remains an important consideration nonetheless. Pressure from civil society expressed through independent courts and an independent media is vital. Both relieve pressure on the regulator by enforcing the law and monitoring behaviour. Political institutions such as the legislature, full of members ambitious to be seen to protect their constituents' rights, help to provide the necessary legal basis for regulation and diminish the executive's ability to intervene in the market. Many of these institutions (free press, independent courts, a legislature independent of the executive) are best nurtured in a liberal democracy. Of course, none of these institutions ever work perfectly: regulatory agencies can be captured by the business interests they are supposed to police; the courts can be costly places to pursue justice; and the media may become bored by unspectacular and complicated financial fraud. But on the whole these factors usually come together to provide good regulation in developed markets. Many of the problems faced by emerging markets stem from the fact that this wider institutional environment is lacking.

It comes as no surprise, therefore, that many of the institutions necessary to provide decent regulation are not yet in place in China. The Party Central Committee and State Council dominate economic and political development. While financial institutions remain state-owned, they will continue to rely, in part at least, on government support (rather than their reputations) for growth, and government officials will continue to be able to interfere in their operations. Despite recent improvements, the legal system, the press and the regulator are not independent and there are clear limits to their influence. This all leads to an overwhelming question: in the absence of liberal democracy what will drive the improvement of stockmarket regulation in China?

The haiguipai and their enemies

Searching for the source of change, many observers have noted the growing influence of the overseas returnees, the *haiguipai*. By 2002 the CSRC was recognised as the most professional, sophisticated and market-oriented of China's financial regulators (with the CIRC, the insurance body, a poor third). Part of the reason was that no other government agency in China was so stuffed full of economists, lawyers and accountants who had worked and/or trained overseas. Most of the CSRC's departments are now headed by returnees, and they also dominate a special committee established within the CSRC to develop strategic plans for the future of the market.

Anthony Neoh was a highly visible example of this trend when he joined the CSRC as a senior consultant in 1998 at the express wish of Premier Zhu Rongji. As the chairman of the Hong Kong Securities and

Futures Commission (HKSFC) he had advised the CSRC throughout the 1990s. As well as becoming an informal spokesman for the CSRC during 2000–01, Neoh is credited with pushing forward a number of important policies, including the sale of state shares, opening the market up to foreign investment and an American-style compliance and registration system for listing companies. He has also worked on proposals to set up a shareholders' foundation. Based on a model that worked well in Taiwan, such a foundation would buy a few shares in every listed company and could thereby act as the representative of all shareholders in suits against companies accused of fraudulent behaviour. An insurance system for investors who lose money through such frauds has also been suggested (companies themselves being unlikely to pay up), though it is unlikely that the government would fund this, such would be the size of demand from wronged investors.

Continuing Neoh's work, but in a fully operational role, is Laura Cha, who became a CSRC deputy chairman in 2001 and who was the first non-Mainlander to be appointed a deputy minister in post-1949 China, even though she is not a party member and cannot attend CSRC party committee meetings. Cha, like Neoh, also worked previously at the HKSFC. Most of her HK$5.4m salary – a similar figure as her salary at the HKSFC, but at least six times that of her CSRC colleagues – is donated to a foundation to send CSRC officials overseas for training. Cha, who has a reputation as a tough operator, has been credited with pushing corporate governance reform, for instance strongly backing moves to appoint more independent directors.

During 2002, as the bear market continued to tear at investors' nerves, the returnees attracted much criticism from small investors, as well as others in government, and economists who should have known better. The general line of attack was that the returnees' support for things like the sale of state shares (described below) showed that they did not understand China. They stood accused of using Western concepts in a Chinese context. This line of criticism underpinned much of the media coverage, but also spilled out in more dramatic forms. Shawn Xu, the head of research at China International Capital Corporation (CICC, a joint-venture investment bank), and also a returnee, is reported to have a received a death threat after he predicted in early 2002 that prices had further to fall before they could be considered fair value. He had apparently failed to realise that in the Chinese context, P/ES could remain above 40 forever. Much of the criticism of the *haiguipai* is nothing more than a strange form of racism: the accusation is that the returnees had somehow lost their "Chineseness". The criticism springs from ignorance, from the jealousy of economists trained in China of those who had received training abroad and from the understandable anger of those who lost a lot of money as share prices fell.

The fact is that there is nothing peculiarly "Chinese" about China's stockmarket. Its problems are tied up with the transition from a socialist to a market economy and the continued influence of an authoritarian political system: nothing more, nothing less. It is these institutions that create the challenges: Chinese culture – whatever that is – has nothing to do with it. Hong Kong, Taiwan and Singapore, all with rich Chinese traditions, host vibrant capitalist economies and well-developed capital markets. Institutions – not culture – are the issue here, and institutions, fortunately, can be reformed, given sufficient political will. Attacking speculation, reducing public ownership, limiting administrative interference and entrenching the rule of law are good strategies for improving China's stockmarket, just as they are useful in every other emerging stockmarket context, although the style and timing of application may vary from market to market. For the most part, the *haiguipai* understand this and are in the best position to develop policies that will support the healthy, long-term development of the market.

But the *haiguipai* operate within the bounds of the politically possible. They face much opposition to what they are doing from other government bureaus, and not only on ideological grounds. Since their agenda, broadly defined, is to delink the stockmarket from industrial policy, they also face hostility from those who would lose economically from such a change. They have lost several battles since 2000, including over the state share issue and the need to import international accounting standards, because of this. Ultimately, whether the market improves and the agenda of the *haiguipai* is supported is a political decision for the senior leadership. Since 1996 their dominant policy has been supporting the SOEs above everything else. If that does not change, the quality of regulation will stay much as it is. But it appears that this policy is being questioned, and that new priorities are beginning to influence the State Council's attitude to the stockmarket.

The end of industrial policy

The industrial policy plank on which stockmarket policy was based through much of the 1990s is slipping. Increasing numbers of senior officials recognise that state ownership has failed. Government support for the SOEs and other state-controlled firms is being eroded, constrained and eliminated on a scale unimaginable even five years ago. Hundreds of SOEs have been closed or sold off. According to the State Economic and Trade Commission (SETC), by August 2001 81% of 63,490 small and medium-sized SOEs in existence at the end of 1996 had undergone "structural reform", most involving buy outs by employees. According to the World Bank, China had an average of 277 company bankruptcies each year from 1989 to 1993, 2,100 a year during 1994–95, and 5,640 during 1996–97. Most of these involved SOEs. As Chapter 5 noted, productivity is declining in the state-owned sector as a whole, and particularly quickly in the listed shareholding companies.

If the economic imperative for the government to decrease its ownership of industry were not strong enough, China's WTO commitments severely limit its ability to practise an interventionist industrial policy. The government has agreed to strict limits on its use of subsidies (even when they are used to facilitate privatisation): any subsidies that predominantly benefit SOEs will now be actionable by WTO members. Although by August 2002 the government had not yet signed the WTO's Government Procurement Agreement, it did commit itself to abide by its principles and to sign it in the near future. When it does, it will not be allowed to award contracts to state-owned firms without a competitive, transparent and fair bidding process. By promising a raft of market-opening commitments and tariff reductions, the government weakened the crutches that keep most SOEs standing. Most SOEs will now have to move towards international standards of efficiency and best practice, sell out or go out of business. Even the most important indirect subsidy for state firms left out of the WTO entry accords – cheap financing through state-owned banks – is now being constrained. State banks are now under pressure to reduce NPLs and so are becoming reluctant to lend to SOEs.

The government's retreat from the market is not unlimited. The senior leadership is still committed, at least in theory, to actively supporting a group of 500 or so major state-owned conglomerates operating in sectors such as telecommunications, transport, utilities and financial services. Only a third of these firms have been listed so far, which means that the stockmarket may well continue to be used to support them. However, even this strategy looks set to shift as the government recognises its limits. Peter Nolan at Cambridge University has examined the development of these conglomerates over the 1990s and has benchmarked them against their global peers. Nolan shows that the policy has failed. It has resulted in firms becoming over-staffed, unfocused, bureaucratic and highly uncompetitive.

There are three main reasons. The first is intense domestic competition. One way for China's SOEs to grow strong would be for them to sell into a huge, protected domestic market. Standing on this foundation, the argument goes, they could then go global. Unfortunately, thousands of non-state SMEs, some supported by local governments, some completely private, undercut them on price and have more flexible labour policies. Shougang, a leading steel manufacturer, competes with hundreds of smaller firms, many of whom produce low-grade steel more cheaply. The intellectual property of Sanjiu, a listed pharmaceutical firm set up by the PLA (but now thought to be free of military control), is abused just as easily as that of GlaxoSmithKline. Second, these conglomerates have been prevented from pursuing expansion either via M&As or through organic growth. Provincial leaders have protected local firms by preventing takeovers by firms from other provinces, and some ministers in the central government have feared that they may lose influence if SOEs grow too big. Third, the government needs to sustain employment. Conglomerates find it hard to fire workers and so cannot follow their multinational competitors in downsizing and outsourcing. Instead of downsizing, they have had to absorb smaller, loss-making SOEs, some 2,000 during 1994–97. Rather than nurturing a focus on a core business, this encourages diversification. Given these problems and the constraints of WTO membership, it seems likely that it will only be a matter of time before China, like Japan and South Korea before it, questions the benefits of using statist means to pursue industrial development.

With the passing of traditional industrial policy, the way will be open to significant improvements in the stockmarket. This will be a gradual process, not least because the privatisation of listed SOEs will take some time. However, it will introduce a new dynamic to regulation as the CSRC will lose its mandate to protect and nurture listed firms. The regulator will have a much freer hand in regulating the market since the political imperative to protect listed SOEs from market forces will be eliminated and resistance from local government owners reduced. In contrast to state shareholders, private shareholders will have more incentives to maximise the value of their firms. Moreover, if securities companies are privatised as well, there will be fewer political obstacles to improving behaviour in the market, since the CSRC will be able to punish wrongdoers with impunity.

Government debt

The government is spending more than it collects in tax revenues, and is running a deficit of some 3% of GDP, which it funds through issuing bonds to domestic investors. Official liabilities, mostly T-bond debt, are currently worth some 16% of GDP. This is not a problem: it is well below the generally accepted 40% of GDP danger level. However, as Nicholas Lardy at the Brookings Institution has pointed out, this official debt figure is misleading. Instead, the government's implicit financial commitments should be considered. For one thing, the government will have to recapitalise the four state-owned banks. The sums involved are huge, however. The official estimate for NPLs at the end of 2001 was Rmb2trn, 30% of total loans at the four state banks, some 25% of GDP. The PBOC has since claimed that NPLs at the four banks fell by Rmb59.7bn during the first eight months of 2002, and have continued to fall. Independent analysts, though encouraged by the banks' increased transparency, are concerned that the figures still understate the bad debt problem. Most estimate NPLs to be worth 30–60% of total loans, a heavy long-term burden on the state's finances. A mid-range estimate of 40% of GDP is used in Figure 7.1. The government will also have to pay pensions, for which the World Bank estimated an unmet liability of around 70% of GDP in 1997. The current pension liability of the government is difficult to calculate since it is still unclear how the new pension system will be funded. But that is part of the problem: there is still no viable plan on how to move from the current pay-as-you-go (PAYG) system to a funded system.

Total government debt, for which a rough breakdown is provided in Figure 7.1, most probably now exceeds 140% of GDP. It could well be greater than Japan's, which stood at 140% of GDP in 2002.

If the economy does not continue to grow, if the generation of NPLs in the banking sector is not stemmed and tax revenues are not boosted, in 5–10 years' time the government will experience severe difficulties in meeting all its financial obligations. Comparison with other economies that have faced financial distress in recent years highlights the size of China's potential crisis. China's debt is nearing that of Indonesia's at the height of the Asian financial crisis. As Table 7.1 shows, NPLs there

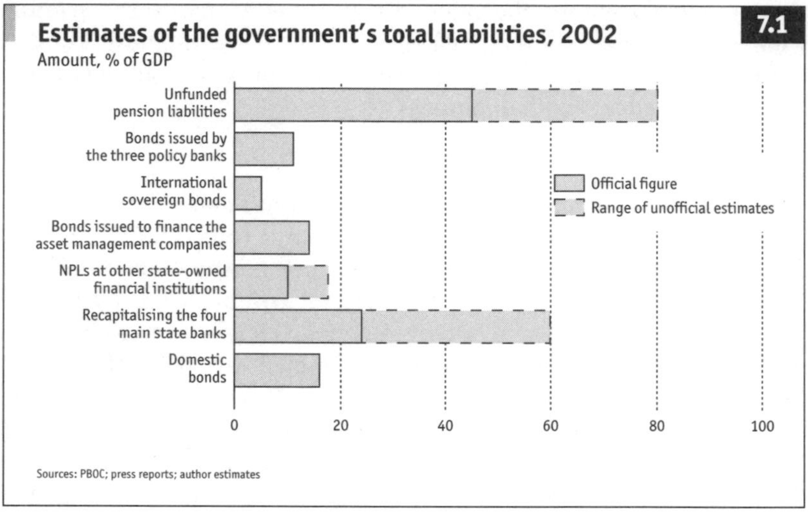
7.1
Estimates of the government's total liabilities, 2002
Amount, % of GDP
Unfunded pension liabilities
Bonds issued by the three policy banks
International sovereign bonds
Bonds issued to finance the asset management companies
NPLs at other state-owned financial institutions
Recapitalising the four main state banks
Domestic bonds
Official figure
Range of unofficial estimates
0
20
40
60
80
100
Sources: PBOC; press reports; author estimates

totalled 64% of GDP, and the fiscal costs of rescuing the financial sector amounted to 45% of GDP. China's advantages are that it is not facing a financial crisis, it is mostly insulated from financial events overseas, and that public confidence in the banking system – and in the government's ability to sort it out – is surprisingly resilient. The comparison with Indonesia, however, does reveal the seriousness of the problem.

There are a number of ways of dealing with them. A number of Chinese economists liken the situation to the movie *Speed*, in which a bomb would be detonated if the speed of a bus dropped below a certain level. Their argument is that if economic growth can be kept above a certain level, an explosion in the financial system can be avoided. Indeed, if the economy grows, and the debt stops growing, then the stock of debt as a proportion of GDP will gradually fall – even without any direct action. It would then probably just remain an accounting issue, and would be solved by mild inflation (that would deflate the real value of the debt) and improved tax collection.

The nightmare scenario, however, involves economic growth slowing and debt expanding. If this occurs, what will the government do? One response would be to print money. This would rapidly deflate the debt, but it would cause inflation to rise and would most likely trigger social instability. As many in the party remember, inflation of 20–25% a year in the urban centres was one of the factors behind the student-worker protests in Tiananmen Square and throughout China in 1989.

Table 7.1 **NPLs and the fiscal cost of restructuring the financial sector in financial crisis**

Country	Date	Fiscal costs (% of GDP)	Peak in NPLs (%)
Argentina	1980–82	13–55	9
Brazil	1994–96	4–10	9
Colombia	1982–87	5-6	25
Indonesia	1997–	45	64
Malaysia	1997–	12	24
Mexico	1994–95	12–15	11
South Korea	1997–	15	19
United States	1984–91	5-7	4

Sources: "Financial sector crisis and restructuring: Lessons from Asia", IMF, September 1999; *World Economic Outlook*, IMF, 1998; Lehman Brothers

Another equally unsavoury option for the government would be to cut back on spending: pensions would be the obvious target, as would SOE subsidies, but this would also be problematic in terms of its social impact. The one solution that would dovetail nicely with the shift already apparent in industrial policy would be for the government to speed up its sale of assets. There are signs that this is already occurring. As Chapter 5 explained, listed companies' LP shareholdings are already being sold and the sale of state shares is now a technical issue rather than an ideological one. The SETC and SDPC have drafted articles on foreign investment in large SOEs, Shenzhen has already started an experimental scheme of major SOE asset sales and the CSRC has released reform China's first M&A code. The direction appears to be set. Zhu Rongji has reportedly already taken to calling the selling off of state assets "privatisation" rather than "diversification of ownership", the official CCP term. His successor, Wen Jiabao, may make Margaret Thatcher look positively Maoist in her approach to public ownership.

What impact will privatisation have on the stockmarket? For one thing, it will have many of the long-term implications identified above; the government will have less cause to protect and nurture market players and more cause to provide a level playing field. But privatisation also augurs a massive surge in the supply of equity, and this means that the government will have to carefully nurture demand. The current ability of the market to absorb new shares is limited. Table 7.2 shows A-share

Table 7.2 **The capacity of the market: IPOs as a proportion of GDP, 1997–2002**
Rmb bn

Year	GDP	Total A-share issuance	A-share issuance as % of GDP
1997	7,477.2	85.3	1.1
1998	7,955.3	77.8	1.0
1999	8,205.4	89.4	1.1
2000	8,940.4	152.7	1.7
2001	9,593.3	118.2	1.2
2002	10,360.4*	73.9	0.7

Note: includes both IPOs, rights and secondary issues.
*Estimate
Source: CSRC

issuance as a proportion of GDP during 1997–2001. Even at its peak in 2000, the stockmarket could supply only the equivalent of 1.7% of GDP in funds. As the market slumped in 2002, A-shares only raised 0.7% of GDP.

Before the year began, Guotai Junan Securities analysed the potential dynamics of supply and demand for equities in 2002. Table 7.3 shows its estimate for demand during the year: in total the market needed to attract some Rmb220bn. Table 7.4 shows estimates for funds that Guotai Junan thought might become available in 2002, some Rmb140bn–210bn. This figure was highly dependent upon more private savings coming into the market via Rmb40bn–70bn in investment funds and on rule changes that did not happen. Insurance funds, for example, remained

Table 7.3 **Estimates for demand for stockmarket funds, 2002**
Rmb bn

	Estimated amount
Share issues (IPOs, rights and secondary issues)	110
Convertible bond issues	10
State share sales	30
Trading costs (stamp tax, commissions, etc)	70–80
Total	220–30

Source: Guotai Junan Securities

Table 7.4 **Estimates for funds becoming available in 2002**

Source of capital	Estimated funds becoming available
New investment funds and old ones increasing their capital	30–50
Insurance funds	20–30
Social insurance funds	20–30
Joint venture fund management companies	10–20
Securities companies increasing their own capital	10–20
New private company investments	50–60
Total	140–210

Source: Guotai Junan Securities

banned from making direct investments in shares and the bear market put off many private companies from investing funds. No joint venture funds got off the ground. In addition, the government's stance on selling off state shares caused funds to exit the market.

In 2002 the government clearly failed in its bid to nurture sufficient demand. Due to lack of demand, the A-share issuance programme had to be sharply cut back. It is clear then that in order to privatise on any significant scale the government needs to do much more if it is to attract anything like these funds into equities. It will need to attract small investors into the share market on a larger scale than ever before, as traders in their own right and through institutional funds. This requires huge improvements in regulation to restore public trust in the market, and is another reason to be hopeful for government action in this area in the near future. There is certainly money out there. According to a recent McKinsey survey, there are 30m urban households with an annual income of more than $4,300. This number is doubling in size every two years, and 4% of them, currently some 1.2m households, have deposits of over $100,000. But not enough of these assets are being committed to stocks. By March 2002 urban households were committing less than 10% of their financial assets to shares, down from 14% during 1998–2000. If the market were better regulated, that figure could rise to 20–30%, providing huge support for the government's privatisation programme.

Creating a pension asset management system
China is currently establishing a modern pensions system. With an

ageing population, this will be one of the government's most important tasks over the next decade. But apart from the manifold problems involved in collecting funds, there is also the issue of how to invest the funds that are raised. Pension assets are thought likely to grow to Rmb2.5trn by 2012, and Rmb8.3trn by 2022, up from Rmb125bn at the end of 2001. Some of these funds will be privately managed, some publicly. In December 2002 the government selected six fund management companies – Boshi, Penghua, Harvest, Changsheng, Southern and China – to help it invest its national pension fund. The only way pension, mutual and insurance funds will be able to provide returns above the rate of wage growth will be if they are invested in a well-regulated stockmarket. China's stockmarket now offers quick profits for big risk takers, and is therefore ill suited to the task of managing pensions. The clear imperative is for the government to work to turn the market into a safe enough place for pension funds.

Improvements in regulation, 2001-02

In mid-2001 there were clear signs that these new macro-policy objectives were starting to bite. Indeed, the CSRC announced 2001 was to be "regulation year" and launched its most aggressive enforcement campaign yet. Market confidence and prices collapsed, but despite criticism from many within and outside party and government, the CSRC stuck to its guns. In March its chairman, Zhou Xiaochuan, talked euphemistically of the struggles going on. "There are often conflicts between long term goals and short-term gains when new policies are launched," he said, "but we should have a long-term perspective." Sustaining the focus on the long term will be tough, but Zhou was correct: there will be no gain without substantial pain. Gains were made across a wide range of areas during 2001–02. They included capacity building at the CSRC; improving listed company governance and performance; expanding the role of the courts in regulation; attempting to introduce supervision of the CSRC; easing restrictions on LP share trading and organising the sale of state-owned shares. All these pointed to a regulator getting to grips with the key issues.

Capacity building at the CSRC

In order to strengthen the CSRC's ability to investigate and punish crimes, in July 2001 a second Enforcement Bureau was established by the CSRC and the Ministry of Public Security (MOPS). Unlike the CSRC's in-house Enforcement Bureau, this office enjoys important extra powers, including the ability to access details of bank accounts and to freeze them, both powers long denied a frustrated CSRC. Each of the nine regional offices of the CSRC is reported to have established such a bureau, staffed with some 260 personnel in total, mostly from the MOPS.

The State Council appeared to loosen its tight grip on the CSRC in the second half of 2001, allowing it to investigate and punish badly behaving firms with greater impunity. Incomplete statistics show that between July and October 2001, 11 listed companies were investigated and punished by the CSRC for false disclosures at the time of listing. In September 2001 the CSRC announced punishments for five securities companies: Guotai Junan, Southern, Haitong, Guosen and Everbright. Firms which Guosen and Everbright had brought to market made much worse than expected profits (which cast doubt on the quality of their due diligence) and several firms helped by Guotai and Southern were found to have falsified their accounts. Punishments for nine other securities companies were also announced. The Sanlian Group, Jiangsu Securities (since absorbed by Huatai Securities), Heilongjiang International Investment and Wuhan Securities were found guilty of trading stocks through individual share accounts. Their illegal gains were confiscated, and the three firms were fined Rmb300,000–737,000; several general managers were also fined. For their part, the Shenzhen branches of Qinghai Securities and Zhongjingkai were accused of illegally lending funds to clients and fined. In August 2002, the first brokerage was closed down by the CSRC. Anshan Securities' transgressions were, however, not made public. The breadth of these investigations and the toughness of the regulator's response was unprecedented.

As well as clamping down on firms, the CSRC also moved to consolidate its control over the stock exchanges by appointing a new chairman at each. Previously, stock exchange chairmen had been local appointees who lacked any real influence: it was the two presidents (zong jingli, also translated as general managers) who ran the show. Since 1997 they had been appointed (and were sackable) by the CSRC, rather than the local governments as before. However, the two new chairmen, Geng Liang at the SHGSE and Feng Fuxiang at the SHZSE, since their appointment have assumed overall control from the presidents, Zhu Congjiu and Zhang Yujun respectively. The latter remain in charge of day-to-day operations, and the chairmen oversee development and negotiate with local and central government bureaus. What seems to have motivated this move was that the bureau-level ranking of the two presidents had put them at a disadvantage when negotiating with local officials. The exchanges are both ranked as bureau – *ju* in Chinese – which means that their leaders rank well below many municipal officials. The Shanghai mayor, for example, is ranked the same as a minister, putting him two notches above the exchange presidents. Deputy mayors could also easily pull rank. But having previously worked as vice-chairmen of the CSRC and having the rank of deputy minister, Geng and Feng could give the stock exchanges more influence within the local bureaucracy. In the summer of 2002, there was also talk of the two exchanges, technically still independent of the government, being made into state bureaus. This would be only a formal move, since the exchanges are already fully integrated into the CSRC bureaucracy as they are.

Improving listed companies

The CSRC has also succeeded in improving corporate governance at listed companies. For instance, it has introduced since 1998 new disclosure regulations, accounting standards and other rules that are slowly having a beneficial effect. One of these required former SOEs to have operated in their final, restructured form for at least one year before listing. This was an attempt to prevent hidden debts suddenly coming to light once the firm had listed, as has often happened. In addition, underwriters also now have to spend one year coaching each applicant enterprise about good corporate governance and the behaviour befitting a public-listed company (although those involved say that in most cases these activities have little effect).

Another area that the CSRC has attempted to intervene in is the use of capital raised in the stockmarket. When a cash-starved firm receives its IPO windfall, many of the promises made in its prospectus are often forgotten. There have been many cases of IPO funds being diverted away from the core business to real estate, share speculation and the pockets of managers and large shareholders. The CSRC has tried to clamp down, with some success. In November 2001 it banned companies' LP shareholders from using proceeds from the IPO and demanded that they open a separate bank account for these funds, and that the company and bank should issue quarterly reports on how the funds are being used. According to its rules, if 20% of the funds are used for different purposes from those set out in the prospectus without the shareholders' approval, the firm would be judged to have broken the law. In addition, the rules stated that if the IPO revenues were not used within two years of the issue, then a shareholder vote would be needed to approve a new plan for their use. The CSRC also moved in July 2002 to force any listed company wanting to issue new shares worth more than 20% of its total capital to gain the agreement of half of its shareholders.

Boards of directors

One of the most important moves to decrease the control that LP shareholders have over listed companies has been increasing the number of non-executive directors on their boards. A study by the SHGSE in 2000 found only eight independent (that is, non-executive) directors among some 3,000 surveyed. The few non-executives who did serve were often little more than names on the company's letterhead. Some admitted openly that they "lent" their names to the company to give it additional credibility but had little idea of what management did. In an attempt to improve this, the CSRC ruled in late 2001 that each listed firm should recruit at least three non-executives by 2005 and laid out their responsibilities. The move was publicised as a huge leap forward in governance standards.

There is a question of whether China has the requisite number of suitably qualified people. After initial doubts, there are indications that the CSRC will in fact meet its goal, partly by setting up month-long training courses in Beijing and Shanghai and partly because of the salaries on offer. A number of qualified professionals, fearing that they might be caught up in sleaze, decline offers of directorships. However, the majority do not. Some companies can afford to pay more and hire famous names to enhance their reputation. Li Yining, economics professor at Beijing University, is thought to have five independent directorships, the maximum one individual can acquire. A famous name can attract a payment of some Rmb250,000 a year. Less famous names can expect to make around Rmb24,000-36,000 a year, or more if they are experienced. One member of the CSRC noted in 2002 that he often found that independent directors were better paid than executives within the company.

A more pressing question is whether these new arrivals will have any impact. There are reasons to be doubtful. According to CSRC rules, a 5% equity stake is necessary for a shareholder to nominate an independent director. Since often only state-controlled LP shareholders have a large enough stake to do this, there exists a serious question over to whom independent directors will owe allegiance. If it is indeed left to the LP shareholder, then nothing much will probably change. Second, research into the impact of independents in the United States is ambiguous, to say the least. Although boards with more independents generally fire underperforming CEOs faster than boards dominated by insiders, Sanjay Bhagat and Bernard Black, two academics, have found an adverse relationship between the number of independents and performance among American companies. Stoyan Tenev and Zhang Chunlin, economists at the IFC and World Bank, argue that the CSRC runs the danger of putting more emphasis on the provenance of directors than their responsibilities and liabilities. They recommend a number of measures.

- Boosting all directors' legal liability. In late 2001 an independent director, Lu Jiahao, of Zhengzhou Baiwen, a firm infamous for cooking its books, was fined Rmb100,000 by the CSRC and briefly held in custody. Since Lu received no payment for his services and had no say in decisions, he sued the regulator. He lost the case on a technicality (though it seemed the law and common sense was against him, since as a director he had a clear responsibility to know what was going on within his company). But at present it is unclear whether directors can be held personally liable for their actions and if they can be criminally prosecuted for their actions. They should be. However, they also need protection from malicious actions. In other countries, the business judgement rule, which holds that legal decisions by directors taken in good faith cannot be subject to legal action, is used to good effect.
- Easier procedures for removing directors. At present they cannot be sacked before the end of their term without just cause. This protects the poorly performing ones.
- Greater transparency. Most reports prepared by and for the board should be published. All relationships between directors and the company should be divulged: too often directors take profitable consultancy work with the firm, which prejudices their ability to oversee management effectively.

Restructuring and delisting

There have also been important improvements in the CSRC's attitude to loss-making companies. As Chapter 5 explained, the favoured method for dealing with them has been to place them in separate categories of the exchanges, Special Treatment (ST) and Particular Transfer (PT), and wait for them to be rescued by their local government sponsors. The ST category was created in 1998 for firms with two years of continuous losses or other problems; they were subject to a 5% daily price limit (later removed). In July 1999 the two exchanges, under CSRC instructions, created the PT category, to which ST firms with three years' losses were transferred. PT firms trade only on Fridays and are also subject to a 5% limit. At the end of 2000 there were 61 ST companies (23 at the SHGSE and 38 at the SHZSE) and ten PT companies (seven at the SHGSE and three at the SHZSE).

Once transferred, the local government owner of the firm was on notice that it should restructure it. The incentives to do so quickly and effectively have been steadily increasing as the CSRC's threat of actual delisting became more credible. A successful restructuring would involve assets being injected, debt being restructured and removed and, often, a private company buying control of the company through a sale of LP shares (as Chapter 5 explained). The average PT firm has some Rmb300m–400m in debt, and no revenues to speak of: it is often only the listing place itself that attracts buyers and keeps government officials interested in keeping the value-destroying machines alive.

The attempted redemption of Hongguang Industries illustrates some of the difficulties involved. In late 1998 Hongguang was transferred to the PT section of the SHGSE. The firm had huge debts, there were suspicions that more were hidden, and the company was continuing to haemorrhage cash. But in May 1999 the Chengdu government, Hongguang's owner, announced that the Fortune Scientific and Technological Group from Guangdong province had agreed to invest up to Rmb260m in Hongguang and restructure the firm. Hongguang was split in two to limit the new owner's liabilities. Rmb954m worth of debt (together with the laid-off workers who demanded continuing benefit payments) was put into the Hongguang Group (which remained owned by the Chengdu authorities), and Hongguang Industries, with Rmb250m worth of debt and Rmb250m worth of assets, was separated off and renamed Chengdu Fortune Science and Technology (CFST). The Chengdu government then transferred its 35% stake in CFST to Fortune for no charge and the Fortune group injected additional assets into the firm. Although Hongguang had recorded a loss of Rmb70.6m in 2000, CFST made a profit of Rmb8.1m in 2001 and was relisted in May 2002, the first company to leave PT to return to the main board of the stockmarket. However, the jury is still out on the quality of the restructured entity and whether the company can become a viable business.

Such restructuring may sound like a good idea. However, the ST/PT framework is harmful in a number of ways. First, there is the huge waste of time and financial resources spent on saving these firms. In truth, it is usually only the listing place itself which inspires all this effort and makes the loss-making firm valuable. Bankruptcy followed by asset sales would be more efficient. Second, the weak bankruptcy regime itself creates incentive problems. With soft budget constraints, managers have less incentive to manage well and owners have no reason to oversee managers properly. Whatever they do, they know that they will be rescued eventually. Third, the impossibility of delistings has led to bizarre incentives being created in the secondary market. Because investors have expected ST and PT firms to be restructured and rescued, their share prices often trade at higher prices than when they were on the main board. Moreover, speculation is rampant despite the tighter trading limits. A 2001 survey by the SHZSE Research Institute found that 61% of investors purchased ST/PT category shares because they hoped that a restructuring plan would result in a huge price jump.

In 2001 the CSRC seemed to be at least half committed to solving these problems. In January 2001 the regulator announced a new regime in which shares of companies recording three years of losses would be automatically suspended (instead of going into the PT category). Within 45 days of this announcement the firm could file an application with the stock exchange for a 12-month extension to its listing. Otherwise, or if the exchange declined the application, the CSRC would then order the firm to be delisted. In December 2001 the CSRC revised the rules again: after three years' losses, a firm was to be automatically delisted rather than suspended, though it could still gain an extension if it successfully explained how it intended to return to profitability. This new framework in effect eliminated the PT category (but it is worth noting that, unlike most other countries, it was the regulator, not the stock exchange, that had the ultimate power to delist a firm). The SHGSE was soon allowed to delist PT Shanghai Narcissus, and the SHZSE delisted Guangdong Kingman and Shenzhen Zhonghao in 2001. By the time of writing a dozen firms had been delisted.

However, these rulings were undermined by a compromise. After being delisted, a firm could apply for its shares to be traded on an OTC basis at the branches of a number of large securities firms. In other words, the listing was transferred. The Securities Industry Association (SIA), the industry grouping managed by the CSRC, is organising this new OTC market and the SHZSE is providing the trading facilities. The hope is that by forcing investors to open special trading accounts, speculation in these stocks will be reduced even while the companies are allowed yet another chance to restructure and improve. But it is a dangerous precedent to set, and it seems likely that speculation will simply move with the shares to the new market. The reason for the compromise was political. Local governments strenuously oppose the delisting of "their" firms, since while listed they are great cash-raising vehicles. Second, there are clearly fears over how investors will react. After all, the government signed off on these firms' books and authorised their listings in the first place. Small protests at delistings now take place regularly outside the CSRC offices just off Beijing's Finance Street (*Jinrong Jie*) and in July 2001 the president of the SHZSE received a bomb threat after the delisting of Guangdong Kingman. Other death threats have been received since.

Allowing the courts to play a role in regulation

The government seems to be willing to support the development of a role for the courts in stockmarket regulation. First, the government may allow the courts to rule on private suits brought by investors; up to the present only the CSRC has been empowered to punish illegal behaviour. Second, it may also increasingly use the courts to prosecute wrongdoers, whereas previously the CSRC has been content with using its own administrative powers to warn and fine.

Hundreds of private suits had been brought against listed companies for false disclosures by the end of 2002. The first involved Jiang Mou's complaint against Hongguang Industries, heard in a Shanghai court in December 1998. She claimed that their false disclosures at the time of the IPO had robbed her of the Rmb3,136 she had paid for their shares. The court found that there was not enough evidence to link Hongguang's lies with Jiang's losses, and that in any case it was up to the CSRC to decide all such matters. This was an unsatisfactory judgment. The considerable benefits of the CSRC sharing some of the regulatory burden with the courts were lost. Given the right incentives, investors (and their lawyers) can also monitor fraud and take action against it, freeing resources for the CSRC to do other things. Second, allowing the courts to hear cases brought by private citizens creates disincentives for company employees and others to engage in fraudulent behaviour in the first place.

Undeterred by the Hongguang judgment, a trickle of similar suits were filed during 1999–2000. And as word spread in 2001 about the possibility of gaining revenge through the courts, and more scandals came to light, this trickle turned to a torrent. By December 2001 some 363 investors had instructed Zhonglun, a law firm, to sue the management of Yian Keji (Yorkpoint Technology) for Rmb24.6m. More than 100 investors brought a similar suit against Yinguangxia. In January 2002 Song Yixin, a lawyer with Wenda Law Firm in Shanghai, advertised for clients in his bid to sue two listed firms, Heilongjiang Sun Field Science and Technology and Shanghai Jiabao Industry and Commerce. This was reform China's first such advert. He received 500 telephone calls, and in August 2002 was proceeding with some 80 claims against the companies for false disclosures. But these suits did not only affect listed companies. Shenyin Wanguo Securities, for instance, was sued for its part in underwriting Daqing Lianyi, a notorious *baozhuang* firm in north-eastern China, and accountants and lawyers also faced litigation.

Lower courts were overwhelmed with the onslaught of angry investors and their offices had no idea how to deal with them. Central government officials worried that if the suits were allowed to go forward, many listed firms might have to pay huge damages, more than enough to bankrupt them. It came then as no surprise when in December 2001 the Supreme Court banned such private suits. However, facing pressure from investors and supported by reformers inside the government, the Supreme People's Court relented in early 2002 and allowed investors to sue firms, but only those whose disclosures had already been judged to be false by the CSRC. Later that year 11 small shareholders in Hongguang Industries won the first compensation ever, of Rmb225,000, in an out-of-court settlement from Guotai Junan Securities. In January 2003 a new regulation required all litigants to band together in a group action (which, in contrast to a class action, only allows a judgment to be effective for a group of named litigants). Daqing Lianyi had been hit by at least 80 separate suits by August 2002, a number that would mean some 3 tonnes of paper being delivered to the court. In addition, the new regulation set out how compensation should be judged.

As these cases wind their way through the courts, a number of questions will have to be answered, such as what the personal liability of those found guilty is. And what additional changes to the law are required to facilitate small investors' suits? Class actions, where a lawsuit is pursued on behalf of a number of persons with identical grounds for action, and where any judgment holds for all those affected by the wrongdoing, were not possible. The Supreme Court disallowed their use late in 2001. Without the benefit of joining in a class action, the costs to individual investors of mounting a suit are high.

But when a company is fined, there is the matter of payment. Companies that fake their results are usually in poor financial health and will have few liquid assets with which to pay fines. Even if they did, enforcing the judgments would be tough. Song Yixin, the Werda lawyer, suggests that the firms' local government backers could be made liable, but this would be extremely hard to do, both in law and in practice. There are calls from the NPC and some sections of the CSRC for some kind of compensation fund to be established that would reimburse small investors in the event of a court finding in favour of them. There would still be, of course, the issue of how such a scheme would be funded, but a small, hypothecated tax on trading might work.

The second way courts can get involved in regulation is through increasing the severity of the punishments of those involved in securities-related crimes. In Western markets, company directors are usually held personally liable for any false disclosures they might make. Indeed, the United States Sarbanes-Oxley Act, the legislation passed in July 2002 in the wake of the corporate scandals, toughened up this framework and even extended the reach of American criminal law to the executives and auditors of foreign firms listed in the United States. About 50 Chinese firms fall under the auspices of Sarbanes-Oxley and will be required to comply with new reporting rules. (There is also the intriguing possibility of the directors of Chinese firms facing criminal charges in American courts if problems appear in their accounts.)

In China it has traditionally been the company that is hit with the fine. This simply punishes small shareholders and leaves management unscathed. The CSRC has recently started levying large personal fines on company directors – a good change. The fines of the chairman and two senior managers of Zhengzhou Baiwen show the way ahead. The company was fined Rmb2m, the chairman Rmb300,000 and the two managers Rmb200,200 each. Levying fines without pushing for criminal convictions has been standard practice for a number of years. But in early 2002 they were charged with false accounting, a crime which carried a maximum penalty of three years in prison, and fined Rmb200,000 each. In November 2002 the three were given suspended jail sentences of between two and five years, the first time the managers of a listed company had been successfully prosecuted. In 2001 some 80 criminal cases were launched against individuals involved in crimes connected with the stockmarket. In 2003 they will start coming to trial en masse, in an entirely welcome, if rather late, development.

Improving oversight of the regulator

Power tends to corrupt, and absolute power corrupts absolutely. So said Lord Acton, a British historian and member of parliament. Although the CSRC is certainly one of the most professional ministries at the level of the State Council (though it is not a State Council member), it still needs to be overseen. Currently, this is the responsibility of the Communist Party through its Financial and Economic Committee and Financial Work Commission. If the market is to mature, this will need to change. The courts, the parliament and the media all have a role to play in monitoring the CSRC and encouraging it to do its job better. However, there are few signs that the party is ready to relinquish its control.

For one, it seems unlikely that the courts will be used in the foreseeable future to supervise the CSRC, though there will certainly be the odd case. There will certainly be nothing comparable with the United States, where Eliot Spitzer, the New York City attorney-general, set much of the agenda for investment bank reform by aggressively prosecuting the banks in the wake of the Enron scandal. It was he who forced the industry to restructure its research operations and who pushed the SEC into organising more radical regulatory reform. Lawyers from China looked on aghast: they have little influence over the CSRC. There are only a small number of exceptions. In May 2002 Zhejiang Securities filed a suit in the Beijing People's High Court disputing a CSRC judgment that had removed its trading licence and levied a fine of Rmb503m. In 2001 the same court had found in favour of a lower court ruling against the CSRC in the case of Hainan Kali Central Development and Construction. Kali had disputed the CSRC's handling of its IPO application. The CSRC was forced by the court to reconsider the application after the judges decided that it had not followed its own procedures correctly. Such cases, unheard of till recently, are likely to remain rare. The CSRC still wields extensive powers and there are many ways in which it can punish firms that make its life difficult, not least through rationing licences for asset management, and venture-capital and other activities. Zhejiang itself had few other options since the fine and the ban on trading made it insolvent. Other firms are less likely to take action against the CSRC.

There is also a role for the NPC to play in stockmarket regulation, if the party and State Council are willing to allow it a little more room for manoeuvre. In the United States congressional committees oversee the activities of the SEC and have the right to call commissioners to account for their rules and their rulings. The congress also had considerable autonomy to draft and pass legislation which defines regulation, the

Sarbanes-Oxley Act being the most recent example. For their part, delegates from the NPC and the Chinese People's Political Consultative Conference now regularly criticise the CSRC for weak enforcement, but have no institutionalised means through which to oversee its activities or call its leaders to account. At its March 2002 meeting the NPC criticised the CSRC for "listing unqualified companies, [and for failing to stop] the falsification of financial statements by listed companies, insider trading of listed companies with their controlling shareholders, excessive speculation and manipulation". Many within the NPC have been actively involved in attempting to improve regulation since the early 1990s. But in this official statement it was obvious that insufficient notice had been taken of the steps taken by the CSRC during 2001–02 to remedy many of these problems. It is possible that under an enlightened political leadership, the role of the NPC as a monitor of State Council activities could be nurtured.

As the market grows, the demand for intelligent, accurate, investigative journalism will increase. There is already a massive media industry devoted to the market, including dozens of newspapers, journals and television and radio shows. Three newspapers have been accorded the rank of official publications and are thus qualified to carry CSRC notices and listed-company reports and disclosures. However, in recent years these papers and the other unofficial organs have had a nasty tendency to carry advertising and misinformation in the guise of "factual" stories. There is a deepseated suspicion among investors about their reliability. Many journalists have become rich through talking up companies in coordination with *zhuangjia*. However, there are exceptions to this rule. For its part, *Caijing* (Finance and Economics) magazine has campaigned for better regulation and has broken a series of major stories (including the Zhongke Chuangye scandal) that have forced a reaction from the CSRC. *Xin Caifu* (New Finance) magazine is another high-quality magazine published in Shenzhen. One senior CSRC official, when asked by the author what the CSRC thought of *Caijing*, replied "We love it", and then, smiling and lowering his voice, "and we hate it too". If *Caijing* and others keep forcing the government into investigating, all the better. But there are limits to what the new media can do. Stories about corruption within central government, including within the CSRC, are not yet allowed.

Making non-tradable shares tradable

For all the recent talk about corporate governance in China, you would have thought that the concept was invented there. Since the Asian financial crisis, corporate governance – the art of running a firm in the interests of its owners – has become hugely popular and the stock exchanges and the CSRC have devoted enormous energies to understanding it and creating rules to improve it. But as previous chapters have shown, the current abuses by the management and the dominant shareholders of listed firms are too gross and the mechanisms of corporate governance – such as independent directors and more frequent reporting – too weak to solve them. Only when ownership is transferred into private hands will there be a real incentive to improve the standards of corporate governance.

It is therefore good news that listed companies are now being quietly privatised through the sale of LP and state shares. Ideological opposition to privatisation within the party is now far weaker than when state and LP shares were invented in 1992. A number of officials have stated that the government is willing to reduce its holding in most listed firms to 50%. Some have even suggested that it would accept even lower stakes as long as it retained control-rights. This is an important and welcome shift. However, there are considerable difficulties in how the elimination of LP and state shares, even on a gradual basis, can be achieved. One challenge is to ensure that adequate demand exists. A second issue is pricing. How can all this non-tradable equity be valued? In recent years several sale methods have been tried: strategic one-to-one sales of LP shares (those examined in Chapter 5); auctions for LP shares; and sales of state shares organised along the same lines as rights and initial offerings. While LP share sales have, in general, been successful, state share sales have experienced some problems. The lesson may be to use the LP sale method for the sales of state shares too.

LP share auctions

Whereas the sale of state shares is a high-profile issue, and relies on senior policymakers to design and implement a hugely-publicised sell-off scheme, the trading of LP shares at auction, which sprang up on a large scale in late 2000, is organised by market players themselves and has been almost unnoticed by the general public. LP share auctions had their origins in a speculative play on the part of *zhuangjia*, some of whom in early 2000 came to the conclusion that the State Council would soon allow LP shares to be converted into normal individual shares and be listed. Their suspicions were raised by a number of changes in the regulatory framework. In March 2000 the CSRC allowed the listing of any state and LP shares issued during a rights offering that had ended up in the hands of individuals. In August it relaxed rules on the conversion of state shares into LP shares, and in September it allowed LP B-shares to be listed. Many had heard rumours of these moves earlier in the year, and had positioned themselves by travelling around the country and buying up tens of thousands of LP shares, usually for less than 10% of the price of the listed shares. They then started organising auctions for these LP shares, mostly in Shanghai, but also in Beijing and Shenzhen.

Nearly all the buyers and sellers at these auctions were large investors who set up small private companies to facilitate their ownership of LP shares (individuals being banned from owning them). Shares were initially traded at close to NAV, but then rose in price, although to levels still well below market prices. According to the *China Economic News*, Shanghai hosted auction trade worth Rmb500m in the first five months of 2001. Another report claimed that in the first four months of the year auction firms nationwide received close to Rmb30m in commission fees. The market got even hotter when in May 2001 Anthony Neoh was reported as saying that an easier way of making non-tradable shares tradable was by using the principle of first in, first out. In other words, the LP shares of companies that had been listed first should be the first to become tradable. LP share prices rose some 30% after these comments.

However, prices soon dropped, and the number of auctions had declined by 2002, as it became obvious that the CSRC was not going to make LP shares tradable anytime soon. The lack of a clear government line on the legal status of the market was also damaging. The Securities Law (Art. 32) states that any securities "approved for trading shall be quoted and traded on stock exchanges". If an auction counts as trading, then LP auctions were clearly illegal. Their legality is still unclear. Sales of LP shares still continue, but the bulk of them not at auction; instead, the CSRC has backed the development of one-to-one commercial sales, as Chapter 5 explained. These have been relatively successful, in contrast to the CSRC's attempts to sell state shares.

Attempts at selling state shares

The CSRC has had two attempts at selling the government's state shareholdings. The first was in December 1999 and involved two A-share listed firms, China Jialing Industry, a 75% state-owned motorbike maker, and Guizhou Tyre, which was 58% state-owned. Another ten firms were earmarked to follow. Jialing intended to sell 33% of its state shares and Guizhou Tyre 10%. The CSRC announced that the sale price would be set above the net asset value, but that the P/E ratio of the shares would be less than one-tenth of the market P/E. This pricing technique did not take account of market demand. However, it should still have produced a low enough price for the market to absorb. Although it is unclear what then happened, it appears that the listed companies and their underwriters elected to go for higher prices than recommended by the CSRC. For Jialing the price was Rmb4.5, a P/E ratio of about 13, and Guizhou Tyre was priced at Rmb4.8, a P/E of 17. Faced with such high prices, investors did not subscribe in anywhere near sufficient numbers and the underwriters had to buy 18% of the shares offered by Jialing and 26% of those of Guizhou Tyre. Other share prices fell too as the failure of the experiment became clear. Its fingers burnt, the CSRC postponed all further sales of state shares.

Thinking it had learnt its lesson, the CSRC plunged into the field again in July 2001. This time the plan was for companies to sell off enough state shares when they made an IPO or secondary offering so as to raise additional funds worth 10% of the funds already raised. The state shares would then become tradable, and the extra funds would go to the government's pension fund. Fourteen companies went ahead with IPOS or secondary issues, and Huafang Shareholding, Fenghuo Communications, Beisheng Pharmaceutical and Jiangqi Shareholding were first on July 26th. Many other companies were lined up to follow. Shenyin Wanguo Securities estimated that up to Rmb7bn worth of state shares could be sold in 2001.

However, this scheme was also flawed in at least two ways. First, the pricing method was unrealistic: state shares were being sold off at the same price as the individual IPO and rights shares. And by this time IPO prices had been allowed to rise to high levels. No account was made for the fact that with the massive extra supply of equity on the horizon, investors were looking for a significant discount. No account was taken of the artificially high valuation of listed company shares (which, as Chapter 2 explained, is at least partially explained by the restricted supply of equity). Analysis of the first attempt at selling state shares and experience from the LP auction market suggest that non-tradable equity is only valued at 20–30% of the market price. This pricing issue has enormous implications. Estimates in the official press that state share sales could raise some Rmb1.7trn, some 16% of GDP, for the pensions fund were based on these vastly overinflated prices.

According to a back-of-the-envelope calculation, using the estimate of state shares being worth 20–30% of individual shares, a more reasonable estimate of the funds that can be raised from state shares – and this over an extended period of time – is some Rmb330bn, only 3% of GDP. Just as in the former socialist block in the 1990s, there was an unrealistically optimistic expectation of the revenues that could be raised via state asset sales.

The second obvious problem with the July 2001 scheme was that it failed to lay down reliable guidelines for when, and in what quantities, state shares would be sold. With plans for future sales unclear, investors were left to fear the worst: a sudden tidal wave of equity that would destroy the value of their portfolios. A credible timetable was required.

With market confidence shattered, the market lost 30% of its value from its peak in March 2001 to the end of the year. The losses were worth some Rmb600bn. This hurt small investors, but more importantly it threatened a significant interest group: securities and fund management firms. Many became dangerously exposed as prices slid, and this was all the more worrying for the CSRC because many of the securities firms had previously "borrowed" customer funds illegally to finance their own positions. Many became unable to meet their liabilities. Investment funds and SOEs with money in the market also lobbied hard. The CSRC was barraged with calls to suspend the sell-off, as was the senior leadership. There were also reports of brokerages in Shanghai being attacked. One rumour claims that Jiang Zemin ordered the sales stopped himself, fearing for social stability. For his part, Premier Zhu Rongji was thought to be more supportive of the sell-off, at least in theory, since he, like many officials, recognised the imperative of building up a pool of money to fund future pensions. However, when the announcement that the sales would be suspended was made in October 2001, the CSRC made it clear that they would continue at some point in the future. Faced with uncertainty over when this would be or what shape the sales would then take, investors just kept selling. It was a real mess. Even the *People's Daily*, a party mouthpiece, took the regulator to task, opining that "the hasty introduction and suspension of the scheme, though both well-intended, are indications of the CSRC's inconsistent governance of the market".

Credit should be given to the CSRC for its attempt to improve transparency in the aftermath of the debacle. In November 2001 it asked the public for suggestions on how to go about organising future state share sales. It received several thousand letters and emails, and in December it published an edited list of the proposals and asked the research departments of nine securities companies to examine seven of them in detail. A month later, it convened a consultation meeting to discuss the two most popular methods. The first involved a form of administrative pricing. State shares would have their sale price set on the basis of a formula linking their NAV with annual earnings. The shares would then be sold through private placements, repurchased by the firm itself or converted into debt – depending on a shareholders' vote. The second option, a better one, involved market-based pricing above a set floor. An auction would be held for the state shares of selected companies, and if the winning bid's price was above the NAV then the sale would be authorised. Since it encouraged the market itself to value firms (even above an artificially high floor), it was a better solution allowing for greater transparency, and more flexibility. The State Council Development Research Centre supported the second scheme as, apparently, did many in the CSRC. The MOF, however, reportedly backed the first since it led to higher prices, and, it thought, more revenues. With leaders divided, the meeting broke up without consensus. Having been suspended for several months and with the market still nervous, on June 23rd 2002 the State Council announced that the sell-off scheme was to be permanently stopped. However, the announcement appeared to relate only to the method used in July 2001 and the door was apparently left open for other schemes, including the direct transfer of state shares to the national pension fund and to private investors. With the creation in March 2003 of a new central government commission to manage the state's asset holdings, which presumably will include state shares, the question of if, and how, sales might progress became further clouded.

8 Foreign investors' entry: the prospects and the dangers

Since joining the WTO in December 2001, China's financial sector has at last started to open up on a significant scale to foreign involvement. Indeed, WTO membership portends China's eventual integration into the world financial system. However, although foreign retail banks are guaranteed treatment equal with national banks by 2006, the speed of the opening of the stockmarket will be much slower. The government will keep the capital account closed for the foreseeable future, meaning that unrestricted foreign investment in the A-share market is not on the horizon. Only minority foreign stakes are allowed in joint-venture firms: 33% in joint-venture securities firms (JVSFS), and 33% in joint-venture fund management firms (JVFMFS) rising to 49% by 2004. No timetable for wholly owned operations has been set. Beijing is anxious to protect its wannabe investment banks from foreign competition, and its economy from the potentially destabilising effects of global portfolio capital flows.

But looking past the limited concessions made to gain WTO membership, the prospects are much better. The dynamics of China's reforms will create further incentives for the government to broaden the scope of foreign firms' activities in the capital market. It needs their funds, dynamism, expertise and global networks. Although its WTO accords do not contain binding commitments to do so, the government will still probably experiment and move forward on an ad hoc basis. For example, in 2003 the CSRC is introducing small amounts of foreign funds into the stockmarket through the QFII scheme. Though restricted at first, these funds could become significant in a very short time. Sales of non-tradable LP shares to foreign investors are also likely to start in 2003. Such sales could result in foreign takeovers and restructurings for listed companies. It will not be long before a JVFMF raises capital domestically, and then is given management of government pension funds.

The implications for foreign investors of WTO membership

After the initial excitement in late 1991 about Shanghai Vacuum, the first B-share issue, China's stockmarket soon disappeared from the radar screen of the major international banks. They still (in 2003) could not underwrite, broker or own A-shares, investment funds or domestic bonds. Most players have representative offices in Shanghai and Beijing, but most of the business – underwriting international Chinese issues – is done from their offices in Hong Kong.

Although the bilateral trade and investment agreement signed with the United States in November 1999 did not presage huge change, it did go some way to liberalise entry conditions. The key provisions of the agreement, detailed in CSRC regulations issued in June 2002, are as follows.

- ◪ Joint-venture securities firms (JVSFs). A foreign party may own up to 33% of the stock capital of a JVSF. These companies may, without hiring Chinese intermediaries, underwrite A-shares, and underwrite and trade B-shares, H-shares and government and corporate bonds. They cannot, however, broker or deal in A-shares on a proprietary basis. No timetable has been agreed for increasing the 33% ownership limit. JVSFs will need Rmb500m in registered capital, a relatively large sum, and at least 50 qualified employees, to receive a licence.
- ◪ Joint-venture fund management firms (JVFMFs). The foreign party may, again, initially own 33% of the company, a percentage which will be allowed to rise to 49% after 2004, subject to the approval of both shareholders and the CSRC. Such firms may manage funds raised in China, and must raise Rmb200m within three months of launch. The foreign party will need paid-up capital of Rmb300m, though the rules are silent on whether JVFMFs can be set up by multiple foreign parties. Management fees are set at 2.5% or below; quite a generous rate compared with Western markets.
- ◪ Registered foreign securities companies may directly engage in B-share trading without using Chinese intermediaries. Their representative offices may become "special members" of the stock exchanges.

The bilateral agreement does not state how many licences will be granted to JVSFs or JVFMFs or provide a timetable for when these licences will be granted. The prospects for the two types of joint ventures are examined below.

Joint-venture securities firms

A few foreign firms are intent on setting up JVSFs. In March 2002 BNP Paribas became the first foreign bank to gain permission from the CSRC to establish one. Its partners are Wuhan-based Changjiang Securities and Haier, a white goods and electronics manufacturer that wants to move into financial services. CLSA, a subsidiary of Credit Lyonnais, had also signed an agreement with Xiangcai Securities, a mid-sized firm based in Hunan province. Citibank has signed a broad co-operation agreement with Galaxy Securities, and there were reports of HSBC negotiating a stake in an existing concern in mid-2002 (although these were followed by reports that HSBC had withdrawn from negotiations).

However, in general, neither side, foreign or Chinese, appears to be particularly keen on the JVSF idea. Big international players – like Merrill Lynch and Goldman Sachs – have kept quiet (Morgan Stanley already having established a JVSF in 1995, CICC, on which more below). Indeed, Wall Street investment banks did not, unlike European insurers, push hard for concessions in this area when the United States and China were negotiating the latter's entry into the WTO. This, at first, appears strange since the size and rapid development of China's financial sector should make it an attractive target for international players. The reasons for their reluctance are threefold.

First, the market is still small in absolute terms: as Chapter 1 explained, China's stockmarket is less than 2% the size of that of the United States. Since it is also overpopulated in terms of securities companies, the likelihood is that JVSFs will not be very profitable. Low margins will be exacerbated by CSRC rules that restrict things like the fees that can be charged on underwriting services. Second, the major international banks will continue to be involved in, and profit from, deals round the edges of the sector. Money and reputation is to be made underwriting the international IPOs of major Chinese companies, which foreign firms can handle just as well from their Hong Kong offices. In addition to traditional banking, some of the banks will also get involved in other areas. Goldman Sachs, for instance, has been uncharacteristically aggressive in its approach to China, making a series of large direct investments in several real estate and high-tech ventures, with somewhat questionable results. Both it and Morgan Stanley are also dipping their toes into the bad-debt market. Third, it is likely that the foreign banks could only have won concessions for joint ventures, a corporate form that is fraught with difficulties. There are two risks with a JVSF: one is that it will be a disaster; the other is that it will be a success. The majority of joint ventures fail because of clashes between the two shareholders because of differences in culture or aims. Given that local firms are undercapitalised, inexperienced and often guilty of suspect behaviour, the risks to an international investment bank's reputation are legion. And if, like CICC, the joint venture becomes successful, it then becomes a competitor.

In August 1995 Morgan Stanley established China's first joint-venture investment bank, China International Capital Corporation (CICC). The state-owned China Construction Bank and Morgan were the dominant shareholders. After initial teething problems (and internecine fighting between the American and Chinese managers), the firm has become the vehicle of choice for major firms issuing shares abroad. In 2000, for instance, the firm led the underwriting for China Unicom and Sinopec on the international markets, raising a total of $8.29bn, making it the largest book runner in Asia outside Japan that year. CICC also lead underwrites domestic issues, taking the largest domestic issuer ever, Baoshan Steel, public in December 2000.

As well as a team which received extensive training from Morgan and a base in Beijing, one crucial competitive advantage that CICC boasts is the presence of Levin Zhu Yunlai, Zhu Rongji's son, on the senior management team. Another, of course, is its chairman (the Construction Bank president), who also has a direct line to the premier. This allows it to win the best IPO deals. Although its success for the Chinese owners is obvious, analysts are divided on how successful CICC has been for Morgan. On the one hand, the American firm has taken part in creating what is now widely regarded as China's best investment bank. Experience has been gained and some good relations fostered. On the other hand, CICC has failed to live up to Morgan's initial hopes of being an entry-vehicle into the Mainland market. Instead, the Americans have lost any effective control over management of the venture and, even worse, appear to have created a successful rival. Ironically, with WTO entry, such are the rules governing joint ventures that Morgan was actually forced to reduce its stake in the bank in February 2002 from 35% to 34.2%, allowing the domestic owners majority control. CICC therefore acts as a salutary reminder of the dangers of establishing a joint venture in this sector.

Foreign banks also might want to consider the political risks involved in operating in China. These come from all sides. Morgan itself regularly receives bad international press for CICC's involvement in such projects as the Three Gorges Dam. Groups such as the International River Network are targeting Morgan Stanley for its underwriting of bonds by the China Development Bank, most of whose revenues are channelled into the Three Gorges project. Goldman Sachs acted as lead manager in the IPO of PetroChina in April 2000, and was criticised because of the involvement of the parent company, China National Petroleum Corporation, in Sudan and in resource extraction in Tibet and Xinjiang. Morgan was also criticised for its involvement through CICC in the IPO. In addition, several US congressmen expressed opposition to the issue because of human rights concerns. If it had not been for BP Amoco buying a 2.2% stake, the IPO might not have gone ahead. And it is not only the NGOs and US congressmen who can get angry. In August 2001 Credit Suisse Group was temporarily banned from doing business in the Mainland because CSFB, its investment banking arm, organised a Hong Kong conference at which ministers from Taiwan, the "rebel province", participated. The bank also organised a Taiwan-government backed roadshow to Europe. The CSRC chairman, Zhou Xiaochuan, warned that banks guilty of "political misconduct", by which he meant treating the Taiwanese government as if it were a sovereign entity, would be met with "dissatisfaction" in Beijing. CSFB was then reportedly dropped from the underwriting team for China Unicom's and China Aluminium's IPOs. After John Mack, CSFB's legendarily tough CEO, had gone to Beijing to plead the firm's case in October 2001, Jin Liqun, the deputy finance minister, appeared to signal a relaxation of the ban, saying that he hoped CSFB could "continue to contribute to the peaceful unification of the motherland".

For their part, Chinese firms have also been reticent about getting involved in JVSFs. They, after all, understand this market, know how to make money in it, can raise additional capital from within China relatively easily and are not yet ready to extend overseas. They too would be creating potential rivals. It is therefore only the mid-sized firms who are currently keen on JVSFs.

Joint-venture fund management firms

Foreign firms are much more bullish on JVFMFs for a number of reasons.

First, China's fund sector is underdeveloped. The 15 or so firms operating in 2002 only accounted for some 10% of market capitalisation, meaning that there is ample space for additional firms to be established and to grow fast. The huge amount of bank savings, plus the prospects of enormous growth in pension and insurance fund assets, mean that demand for fund management is also sure to grow large fast. In late 2002 the State Council began contracting the management of public pension funds to fund management companies and JVFMFs will be in a good position to apply for these. In mid-2002 urban households were committing less than 10% of their financial assets to shares, down from 14% during 1998–2000. If the market were better regulated, that figure could rise to 20–30%, and most of the money could find its way into funds.

Second, the government is clearly behind the sector's development. As explained in Chapter 7, it needs professionally-run funds to buy and hold equity (to calm volatility and to manage the private sector's savings more efficiently), and to manage its own pension funds. For these reasons, foreign firms have the reasonable expectation that more licences and friendlier regulations in the fund sector will be granted to them in the near future.

In 2001 there was a rash of some 20 co-operation agreements signed between foreign and domestic firms, shown in Table 8.1. In August 2000 Jardine Fleming (now JPMorgan Fleming Asset Management, part of JP Morgan Chase) signed the first co-operation agreement with Hua'an Fund Management. This co-operation has involved training in managing open-ended funds, marketing and customer support, together with help in developing other products.

In 2002, however, much of the initial enthusiasm among the foreign firms faded. A number of them privately admitted that without management control of the JVFMFs, the risks were too great. Even outside China, some 80% of JVFMFs fail. For their part, many of the domestic fund firms questioned the logic of helping to establish a JVFMF that would compete with them. Neither do many see the rationale of selling equity in their own, successful businesses. INVESCO, a fund management firm based in the United States, found this out the hard way. It started working with Penghua Fund Management in May 2000 on establishing open-ended funds, the first of which Penghua issued in April 2002. Once that was over, INVESCO reportedly pushed for the two firms to set up a JVFMF over which it would have de facto control. (Even though the foreign investor can only own 33% of any venture, there are means by which a minority shareholder can enjoy de facto control, for instance by gaining the right to appoint senior management.) However, Penghua's chairman is reported to have angrily dismissed the demand and INVESCO was soon left looking for a new partner. In late 2002 INVESCO applied for approval to set up a JVFMC with Great Wall Secu-

Table 8.1 **Prospective joint-venture fund management partners, year-end 2001**

Chinese partner	Foreign partner
China Southern Fund Management	HSBC Asset Management
Hua'an Fund Management	JPMorgan Fleming Asset Management
Penghua Fund Management	INVESCO
Changsheng Fund Management	ABN AMRO Asset Management
Dacheng Fund Management	Deutsche Asset Management (Asia)
Fullgoal Fund Management	Bank of Montreal
China Everbright Securities	Prudential
Guotai Fund Management	UBS Asset Management
Galaxy Fund Management	Schroder Investment Management
Shenyin Wanguo Securities	BNP Paribas, IFC
Guotai Junan Securities	Dresdner Bank
Haitong Securities	Fortis Investment Management
China Southern Securities	Commerzbank
Guotong Securities	ING
Guangfa Securities	Franklin Templeton Investment Management
Xiangcai Securities	Credit Lyonnais Securities Asia (CLSA)
Everbright Securities	Prumerica Financial

Source: Zhongtianwang

rities. Other prospective partners, including Huaxia and Schroders, have also split up. But this experience is not universal. Firms like UBS Global Asset Management and Guotai Fund Management (GFM) are working for a future together. Other foreign companies are targeting securities companies and companies from other industries keen to diversify into asset management. Four JVFMFs were authorised in 2002: Allianz AG, a German financial services firm, and Guotai Junan Securities (the parent of GFM); SG Asset Management and Fortune TIC; Fortis NV and Haitong Securities; and ING Asset Management and China Merchant Securities. For their part, China's retail banks and insurance companies are still banned from having anything to do with shares, but that will soon change.

Some industry insiders initially believed that the CSRC would issue some 15 licences for JVFMFs before the end of 2002. But that target was too optimistic. Things will not move fast. If the CSRC authorises a handful more JVFMFs in 2003, and allows them to issue one or two funds each, then after between six months and one year a second, larger batch could be authorised. However, even with the possibility of increasing their stake to 49% by 2006, foreign players could face many of the problems that Morgan Stanley did in their CICC adventure. If the first batch runs into problems, more foreign firms will decide to wait until they can have full control before they commit to the Mainland.

Listing of foreign companies and acquisition of Mainland companies

Foreign involvement in China's share market will occur in the other direction as well. Firms with substantial foreign ownership stakes will soon be allowed to list, and the ban on foreign purchases of PRC equity (outside the B- and H-share markets) appears to be loosening.

There is likely to be an expansion of FIES and even wholly-owned foreign companies listing in Shanghai. The first official move in this area by the government came in November 2001 when the SETC and CSRC announced that FIES that were stock limited companies, were less than 50% foreign-owned and had independent operations in the Mainland would be allowed to apply for a public listing. These rules apparently excluded companies like HSBC whose operations in China were fully foreign-owned. Since then, however, there has been talk of the CSRC allowing majority-foreign owned companies to list as well. By late 2001 there were reports that the China-based ventures of some 14 foreign companies had applied for listing, but nothing was heard about these applications during 2002. These included a number of well-known companies such as Kodak, Unilever and HSBC. The Bank of East Asia wanted to be the first Hong Kong company to be listed in the Mainland. Others included domestic companies that had previously attracted foreign investment, such as Shanghai Guangming Dairy, which sold a 5% stake to Donoa, a leading French dairy firm.

An alternative method also being discussed is the China Depository Receipt (CDR), which like the American version, the ADR, would allow companies with shares listed outside Mainland China to be traded on the Shanghai exchange. This would involve the shares being deposited in a Mainland bank, which would then issue depository receipts in those shares, which would then be publicly traded. However, according to reports, this scheme would, initially at least, be reserved for red-chips and H-share companies, those Mainland companies based in Hong Kong. In April 2002 there were reports of four Hong Kong-listed companies readying themselves for issuing CDRs – China Mobile, China

Resources Enterprises, Shanghai Industrial Holdings and Beijing Enterprises. However, by August 2002 the proposal had apparently been blocked. There was opposition from several ministries to offering further preferential treatment to red-chips and H-share companies at the expense of domestic companies.

Foreign involvement in listed companies' M&A

As explained in Chapter 5, the M&A market for listed companies is already growing rapidly. The prospects are good for foreign investors to be soon allowed to join in. China attracts a lot of FDI, some $50bn a year. However, only some 5% of this investment is involved in cross-border acquisitions. The rest goes into starting new firms, either partly or wholly foreign-owned, so-called greenfield investments. In contrast, 40–60% of FDI going into Indonesia, Thailand and South Korea during 1998–99 went into acquisitions. However, as rules relax, the M&A component of China's FDI will inevitably rise.

There are several reasons for this. First, China still restricts foreign investment in a large number of sectors, notably services (where the acquisition of domestics firms is often the entry mode of choice for foreign investors). Second, many foreign investors want to use China for their mid- and high-tech manufacturing operations. But since, unlike in much of the rest of Asia, there is little in the way of such firms already established, the obvious choice is greenfield. Third, since China is not undergoing economic crisis, its companies are less desperate to sell themselves off.

By the end of 2002 foreign investors were not yet permitted to own A-shares, and LP shares were still off-limits too. However, during the 1990s, a number of foreign firms gained large stakes in listed companies. The story began in July 1995, when two Japanese firms, Isuzu and Itochu, purchased 40m LP shares in Beijing Lightbus, giving them a 25% stake and control. The deal received the CSRC's approval. But Li Peng, the then premier, was reportedly angry about the deal and amid fears of a flood of such sales to foreigners, banned them. Isuzu and Itochu later probably regretted their groundbreaking move: they sold their stake in 2000 after Lightbus failed to perform.

A few deals have gone through since, using LP B-shares which are issued by the listed company rather than purchased from another shareholder (thus apparently bypassing Li's 1995 ban). For instance, in September 1995, Ford spent $400m buying 138.6m newly issued LP B-shares in Jiangling Motor to become its second largest shareholder. In

March 1999 Huaxin Cement made a similar move, selling 770m new B-shares to Holchin BV, a subsidiary of Holcim, a Swiss construction materials firm, giving it a 23.5% stake.

Another permutation involves a foreign firm buying out its listed partner, or using a joint venture to do so. In March 2001 Michelin and China's largest tyre company, Shanghai Tyre and Rubber, a B-share listed firm, established a joint venture, Shanghai Michelin Warrior Tyres, in which Michelin took a 70% stake. The new venture then spent $320m of Michelin's money on buying most of the assets of the Chinese parent. The result is that Michelin has de facto control of the listed firm.

Lawyers can be even more imaginative. In October 2002 the world's largest brewer, Anheuser-Busch (AB), sealed a deal in which it agreed to buy convertible bonds in three instalments from Qingdao Beer. After seven years, this $182m deal will give AB a 27% stake (the bonds will be converted into H-shares) in Qingdao, making its the second largest shareholder after the city government. The deal awaits MOFTEC approval. However, the deal did not give AB control since the shares were given restricted voting rights.

Furthermore, rules issued by the CSRC in October 2002 seem to leave open the possibility that foreign firms may be allowed to buy controlling stakes in listed firms by purchases of standard LP shares. In late 2002, the first such deal appears to have been set up when the Shenzhen government announced its intention to sell its 22.6% LP share stake in Shenzhen Development Bank to Newbridge Capital, an American finance firm. The deal – if successful – would herald not only a ramping-up of the limits on foreign investment in PRC financial services (previously limited to 5% stakes), but also the possibility that the huge LP share market will be opened up to foreign involvement.

However, foreign investors who do take the plunge are getting into rough waters. They will have to tackle all the classic issues: overvaluations, huge debts and businesses which have seen better days. They might even have to face public hostility. In late 2002 public concern grew with the increasing awareness of the extent of LP share sales and the low prices involved. As chapter 5 explained, buyers of LP shares buy them at huge discounts to the prices of the A-shares that normal investors purchase. For instance, when Citigroup bought a 5% stake in the Shanghai Pudong Development Bank in December 2002 it paid Rmb3.3 per share, while listed shares were trading at Rmb9.3. Some investors cried foul. Some analysts defended the low price based on the fact that Citigroup's shares could not be traded. Even so, the system of differential pricing does seem unfair and could cause acrimony with investors.

It is important to note that this M&A market will be driven by interests different from the domestic M&A market. Domestic firms buy listed-company LP shares primarily in order to obtain a backdoor listing and gain access to finance, but foreign firms are interested in gaining control of companies with assets that will be useful to them in expanding into China. Their favourite targets will be firms with clear shareholding structures, few debts and strategic assets.

But although the CSRC is apparently keen to allow foreigners to purchase LP shares, other ministries are less enthusiastic – and they, more than the CSRC oftentimes, have the power to develop regulation. For instance, in October 2002 the Ministry of Foreign Trade and Economic Co-operation (MOFTEC) issued new draft anti-trust rules. Although trumpeted as China's first attempt to create a framework for preventing monopolies, the rules focused on controlling foreign investment. For instance, they ruled that any acquisition by a foreign entity worth more than $30m, or which raises the foreign stake in a venture to over $100m, or which constitutes the 11th foreign-invested project in the sector that year would be subject to administrative review. The $30m benchmark is too low and the rules pay little attention to consumers' interests. Most of the new rules simply increased the MOFTEC's ability to monitor and constrain sales to foreigners. In a number of ways they appeared to contravene WTO rules and principles. At the time of writing, it was unclear whether they would be implemented.

The qualified foreign institutional investor framework

China's WTO entry agreements make no mention of QFII. However, in November 2002 the CSRC announced that it would follow Taiwan and various other developing countries and implement the scheme. The decision presaged the opening up of China's capital market to the outside world. QFII will allow foreign investors, including banks, insurance companies, fund management institutions and any other institution meeting the criteria to import and export funds into the Mainland, even while China's capital-account controls are maintained. These funds will then be exchanged into renminbi, kept in a special account managed by the PBOC, and the foreign investor will be free to buy and sell A-shares within certain limits.

The rules governing the new QFII scheme are strict. A fund manager who wants to take part will need assets of more than $10bn.

Banks must rank in the world's top 100 in terms of asset value. Each QFII will be able to invest only $50m–800m and can buy no more than a 10% stake in a single listed company. The total permitted foreign stake in a listed company will not exceed 20%. The remittance rules are also tough: capital will be locked in for one year for qualified institutions, and three years for closed-ended investment funds (though this lock-up is on remitting money out of China, rather than on selling shares).

Despite the restrictions, the CSRC's move was historic. Most analysts had pencilled in China's introduction of QFII for 2005 or thereabouts. Officials within the PBOC and SAFE responsible for the renminbi were known to be strongly opposed to any move that might weaken their controls on the capital account. That the QFII scheme won approval from the senior leadership this early on – and in the run-up to the 16th Party Congress when all major policy decisions were supposed to be on hold – was an important indication of the CSRC's ability to push forward with reforms.

The rules were widely (and mistakenly) judged to be too restrictive. In fact, going slowly at first is a very wise policy. The magic of QFII is that the rules can be adjusted easily if things go well. In the early 1990s Taiwan instituted the QFII system and it turned out to be a very successful move. Ken Ho at JP Morgan Securities argues that Mainland China's scheme closely resembles that of Taiwan, and that there is good reason to believe that the CSRC will follow Taiwan's Securities and Futures Commission in relaxing the rules rapidly as the government's confidence with foreign investment grew. For instance, the limit for a single QFII's investment in a listed company rose from 10% to 15% in 1997 and 30% in 1998. By December 2000 the limit had more or less disappeared. Although individual institutions were initially limited to bringing in $5m–50m, by the end of 2001 many QFIIs were being allowed to bring in $3bn. This limit will soon be dropped completely.

As well as introducing modern investment techniques, QFII also supplied capital to Taiwan's firms. By the end of 2002 net inward remittance from all foreign investors in Taiwan's stockmarket exceeded $42bn. In the case of Taiwan, foreign investors benefited from their ability to take a direct stake in one of world's most important technology economies. In the case of China, foreign investors have long been limited to the restrictive H-shares and disastrous red-chips, and many will be keen to expand their exposure to China's growth. There may well be less than 100 listed firms that will provide credible investment propositions, but more will come, especially if the restructurings associated with recent M&As are successful.

Of course, Taiwan's successes have been accompanied by problems. One of the most serious has been remitting money out of Taiwan. For sums of over $50m, QFIIs had to seek central bank approval, a process that often took months. This in turn made investors vulnerable to the NT$/$ exchange rate, something which hit QFII profits during the Asian financial crisis of 1997-98 and beyond. Another problem has been the size of investments a QFII could make. The financial authorities have preferred to allow in capital in bite-sized chunks. Most major financial institutions usually invest capital in much larger quantities than the $10m-50m chunks allowed. Such frustrations are likely to be repeated in the case of Mainland China, although the risks of a sudden depreciation are currently low.

The CSRC and PBOC will experiment with the new QFII scheme for a couple of years, with the first few starting operations in 2003. The scheme should not threaten the capital account, as the entry and exit of foreign exchange will be controlled. It should prove a popular thing for the major institutions to experiment with, on the understanding that this is only a start, and the potential for liberalisation and growth in the market is there.

A link with Hong Kong: the qualified domestic institutional investor framework

The CSRC has also floated plans to allow Mainland investors into the Hong Kong stockmarket. The idea has been pushed by both the HKSAR government, which wishes to boost its own market, and institutional investors within the Mainland who wish to gain exposure to better-quality companies at lower P/E ratios. Many in the CSRC are backing the scheme since it would give Mainland financial institutions an opportunity to gain valuable experience in investment, trading and risk management in an international market. The proposal made in 2002 would allow a small number of authorised Mainland funds to invest in Hong Kong equities under a scheme similar to the QFII framework, the Qualified Domestic Institutional Investor (QDII). It was estimated that QDII could eventually facilitate the flow of $5bn-10bn into the HKEX. But opponents of QDII, who seem now to have the upper hand, argue that QDII would reduce demand for equities listed in the Mainland. One analyst writing in the *21st Century Economic Report*, a newspaper, claimed that it would in effect be "using the rice-soup money of

Mainland investors to support Hong Kong's shark's-fin meals". China's households have enormous stocks of savings, and given the right companies and regulation they would invest in both the Mainland and Hong Kong markets. Indeed, it seems only fair to allow Mainland investors access to the many decent companies listed in the HKSAR, especially if the government continues to send p-chips to Hong Kong and elsewhere abroad to list.

The future

On a visit to Shanghai in September 1999, municipal officials arranged a tour of the new Shanghai Stock Exchange building for General Secretary Jiang Zemin and his entourage. The hugely impressive ultra-modern structure stands in the centre of Lujiazui, Shanghai's new financial district in Pudong. With a square-shaped hole in its middle, it was designed to resemble an old Chinese coin. At one point in the tour, Xu Kuangdi, the mayor, explained to Jiang how well qualified the stock exchange staff were, highlighting the large number of accountants and lawyers among them. Jiang turned to a nearby female member of staff, a PA with little financial training, and asked her what she did. "I am a chartered accountant, Mr Chairman," the lady replied. Jiang then turned to a well-built male member of staff standing next to her, "And you?" "Oh, I'm a lawyer, Mr Chairman," said the man, having recently taken early retirement from the army. Jiang's entourage departed much impressed.

It is easy to be impressed by appearances. The size and the speed of the development of China's stockmarket certainly impresses many. While the rest of the world's markets were melting down in 2000, China entered the 21st century with the world's only bull market. It was by then, by some estimates at least, the largest stockmarket in Asia outside Japan. But as most who work in the industry – on both the business and government sides – readily admit, China's stockmarket is still extremely immature and does not yet hold comparison with markets in more developed economies or, if truth be told, with many in emerging markets. China's stockmarket is not especially large, its firms are overvalued and it has more than its fair share of regulatory problems. Indeed, by the end of 2002, with the market having lost over 30% of its value in the space of two years, and with little prospect of bull sentiment returning, it was easy to despair.

All developing country stockmarkets suffer from corruption and poor regulation, as indeed did Wall Street in the 1920s and Hong Kong only a few decades ago. But what makes China's problems especially tricky is that many of the institutions set up by the government actually foster that corruption and poor governance rather than act to limit and resolve it. Russia's stockmarket is perhaps just as speculative and has had its fair share of insider dealing and price manipulation. However, its path to maturity and better-quality regulation is much clearer than China's. As the preceding chapters have attempted to show, China's stockmarket needs much more than time if it is to mature and serve the economy as it should. Its problems are not simply a function of its small size and the limited instruments traded there. State shares, the subordination of the stockmarket to industrial policy, the political control of the regulator – these are all institutional problems that need solving before China's stockmarket can develop as it should. Until then it will remain an inefficient way to allocate capital and a corrupt place in which to trade. Fundamental institutional change must take place before this casino becomes a market in corporate control.

There is much cause for optimism. Significant improvements to regulation have taken place since 1997. The CSRC has been empowered and given a stronger mandate to investigate and punish securities-related crimes. Local governments and the PBOC have been sidelined from policy, making the policy process more rational and decisions easier to implement. The press and the courts are gradually getting involved in regulation. Disclosure standards have improved; people are now going to prison for faking their accounts. There have been moves to delist companies that do not deserve to be listed and to sell off state shares. A small number of private companies have been permitted to list. Foreign investors are slowly being allowed to enter. And the development of a market for control of listed companies in recent years is a hugely positive sign. It augurs a time when China's stockmarket will lose its mission to save the failed SOE sector, become a vehicle for privatisation and provide finance for the most dynamic parts of the economy. All these recent developments indicate a government that understands the challenges that it faces and which is willing to suffer some short-term pain for the right long-term gains.

APPENDICES

Appendix 1 Abbreviations

ADR	American depositary receipt
AMC	asset management company
CB	corporate bond
CCP	Chinese Communist Party
CDR	Chinese depository receipt
CEO	chief executive officer
CIRC	China Insurance Regulatory Commission
CITIC	China International Trust and Investment Corporation
CLA	Commission of Legislative Affairs (of the NPC)
CPPCC	China People's Political Consultative Conference
CRA	credit rating agency
CRS	contract responsibility system
CSRC	China Securities Regulatory Commission
CV	convertible bond
EPS	earnings per share
FDI	foreign direct investment
FEC	Finance and Economics Committee (of the NPC)
FIE	foreign-invested enterprise
GDP	gross domestic product
GEM	Growth Enterprise Market
HKEX	Hong Kong Stock Exchange
HKSAR	Hong Kong Special Administrative Region
ICBC	Industrial and Commercial Bank of China
IEAC	Issuance Examination and Approval Committee (of the CSRC)
IFC	International Finance Corporation
IPO	initial public offering
JVFMF	joint-venture fund management firm
JVSF	joint-venture securities firm
LP	legal person
M&A	mergers and acquisitions
MBI	main business income
MOF	Ministry of Finance
MOFTEC	Ministry of Foreign Trade and Economic Cooperation
MOPS	Ministry of Public Security
NASDAQ	National Association of Securities Dealers' Automated Quotations (of the United States)

NAV	net asset value
NBFI	non-bank financial institution
NETS	National Equity Trading System
NGO	non-governmental organisation
NPC	National People's Congress
NPL	non-performing loan
NSSF	National Social Security Fund
NYSE	New York Stock Exchange
OEF	open-ended fund
OTC	over-the-counter
P/E	price-earnings ratio
PBOC	People's Bank of China
PLA	People's Liberation Army
PRC	People's Republic of China
QDII	qualified domestic institutional investor
QFII	qualified foreign institutional investor
ROE	return on equity
SAFE	State Administration of Foreign Exchange
SCORES	State Commission for Restructuring the Economic System
SCSC	State Council Securities Commission
SDPC	State Development and Planning Commission (formerly known as the SPC)
SEC	Securities and Exchange Commission (of the United States)
SEEC	Stock Exchange Executive Council
SETC	State Economic and Trade Commission
SHGSE	Shanghai Stock Exchange
SHZSE	Shenzhen Stock Exchange
SIA	Securities Industry Association
SME	small and medium-sized enterprise
SOE	state-owned enterprise
SPC	State Planning Commission
STAQS	Securities Trading Automated Quotation System
STC	securities trading centre
T-bond	Treasury bond
TIC	Trust and investment company
WTO	World Trade Organisation

Appendix 2 **Chinese terms**

baozhuang   packaged. Used to describe a listed company whose accounts have been manipulated in order to qualify for a stockmarket listing

bu guifan   not well-ordered

buru duchang   literally worse than a casino (phrase used by economist Wu Jinglian in 2001 to describe China's stockmarket)

buwei   central government ministries and commissions. The term also refers to the administrative rank of these organs. A ministry (*buwei*) is one rank above a bureau (*ju*)

Caijing   finance and economics. The name of a fortnightly magazine published by the SEEC which has since 1998 uncovered a series of stockmarket scandals

chao gupiao   to "stir fry", or trade, shares

chouzi   raised capital

dahu   a wealthy individual investor. The phrase was used in the early 1990s when the stockmarket was new (now the term *zhuangjia*, see below, is more common)

danwei   work unit

faren gu   legal person (LP) shares

fazhi, jiangguan, zilu, guifan   rule of law, supervision, self-discipline, standardisation, a four-word phrase coined by Zhu Rongji in 1995 to describe the government's priorities for the stockmarket

gaige kaifang   reform and opening up coined by Deng Xiaoping to sum up his attitude to China's development

geren gu   individual share

guahu qiye   hang-on enterprises. Private firms that use close relations with SOEs to take advantage of the government's more favourable attitude to state firms

guanxi   connections, good relations

gufen youxian gongsi   limited liability shareholding company

gufenzhi   the shareholding system

gumin   investors

guojia gu   state shares

guoyou rongzi gongsi   a state-owned company (SOE)

gupiao   share

gupiao re   stockmarket fever

haiguipai   Chinese returnees from abroad (now occupying senior positions in government, especially in economic affairs)

hebing   merger

hong maozi   red hat. Used to describe private firms that registered as collectives in order to profit from the preferential treatment extended to state firms

hongqui gu   red-chips (companies)

jiaoyisuo   stock exchange

jingying   main business income (MBI)

jiti qiye   collective

ju   bureau. Also used as an administrative ranking for state organs operating at a rank one below a ministry or provincial government

kezhuan zhaiquan   convertible bond

minying   private

nanxun   Southern Tour. A phrase used in imperial times to describe the voyage of the emperor to the southern provinces and to describe Deng Xiaoping's trip to the coast in early 1992 to revive reform

paimai   auction

peigu   rights offerings

rengouzheng   application forms

rongzi   raising finance, a phrase used in a variety of ways; it can refer to the practice of a brokerage extending credit to its customers, and it can also refer to securities companies raising money from banks

shenpi   authorisation

shiyinglu   price-earnings ratio (P/E)

shougou   acquisition

shougou yaoyue   mandatory offer, or tender, the requirement that the purchaser of a firm, once a certain threshold ownership stake has been reached, must make an offer to the other shareholders for their shares

simu jijin   privately-raised funds

siyouhua   privatisation

tikuanji   loan-making machine. Used to describe listed companies, which have been good sources of loans for their controlling shareholders

touzi   to invest, investment

weituo   to entrust (when assets are entrusted to another party to manage)

xieyi shougou   agreed takeover

xishengpin   sacrificial objects, a politically incorrect way of referring to China's small investors

yigu duda   one-shareholder dictatorship, a politically incorrect way of referring to dominant LP shareholders who abuse their powers

yingye fei   business tax

yingyebu   business branch. Used to refer to the brokerage offices of securities firms

yinzhengtong   bank securities link; a newly invented system by which investors can use their bank accounts to trade shares

youxian zeren gongsi   limited responsibility company

zhaiquan   bond

zhengguanban   securities administration bureau (run between 1993 and 1998 by provincial governments, but since absorbed into the CSRC)

zhengquan jiaoyi zhongxin   securities trading centre

Zhongguo Zhengquan Jiandu Guanli Weiyuanhui   China Securities Regulatory Commission

Zhongyang Jinrong Gongwei   Financial Work Committee

zhuangjia   a word used in imperial times to denote a landlord but now used to describe investors who manipulate share prices on a professional basis

zhuguan bumen   chief administrative bureau

zichan chongzu   asset restructuring

zonghe   comprehensive; comprehensive securities companies have registered capital of over Rmb500m and can broker, underwrite and trade shares

zong jingli   president or general manager

Appendix 3 **Glossary**

American Depositary Receipt (ADR)   Tradable receipts that are issued by an American bank to represent a foreign company's securities that are held on deposit. The ADRs can then be traded in the United States just as if they were the shares of that foreign company, avoiding exchange-rate risks and allowing institutional investors (who are often prevented from trading in foreign securities) to gain exposure to these companies.

There are four different types of ADR, each involving its own regulatory standards and conferring different benefits.

- Level I: when a company issues a level-I ADR, it does not raise capital in the United States, but does list its shares on an OTC market. Its share price is published daily by the National Daily Quotation Bureau in the "pink sheets". The advantage of a level-I ADR is that an issuer can easily gauge investors' interest in its shares before considering a higher-level issue.
- Level II: again, when a company issues a level-II ADR it does not raise any capital but it does list its shares on a stock exchange or the NASDAQ. This offers greater visibility compared with level-I, but the company is required to comply with the SEC's standard disclosure requirements.
- Level III: companies which choose this most high-profile type of ADR are allowed to issue shares to raise capital and then make a public listing. Again, this requires full compliance.
- Rule 144A ADRs: only issued to and traded by institutional investors, and thus do not require review by the SEC.

Asian financial crisis   Triggered by attacks on the Thai baht in July 1997, various Asian countries underwent runs on their currencies, severe liquidity problems and terrible economic reversals during 1997–98. Although triggered by speculative currency attacks, the underlying weaknesses of these economies – over-investment, weak corporate governance at banks and firms, and huge exposure of companies to the US dollar – created ideal conditions for a crisis. Five years on, the countries that recovered best, like South Korea, did so by thoroughly restructuring their industrial sectors, forcing banks to write off bad loans, floating their currencies and eliminating the cosy relationships that had existed between the government, companies and banks.

A-shares   Individual shares issued and listed within Mainland China which are denominated in renminbi and are tradable on the two stock exchanges.

Asset management company (AMC)   Four AMCs were established in 1998 by the PBOC and MOF to restructure and sell off Rmb1.4trn worth of bad loans purchased from the four large state banks. Although the reported cash recovery rates are encouraging – some 20–30% – it is likely that this rate will fall as more difficult loans are tackled.

Asset management   A management service provided by investment professionals to rich clients, in which the manager is either paid a fee or takes a cut of the increase in value of the assets managed. In China asset management services are widely available but still poorly regulated.

Asset restructuring   A process through which a company's assets and liabilities are reorganised, with new assets being inserted into the company and old debts removed.

Bond   A fixed-income security. A bond pays its holder a fixed rate of return and does not, like equity, involve any ownership rights in the issuing entity. The capital is repaid at the bond's maturity.

Brokering   The business of providing trading facilities for securities. Brokerage branches are a common sight in China's urban centres and a large proportion of securities firms' income is derived from the brokering fees levied. As Internet usage increases, however, and the CSRC pushes for consolidation of the sector, brokerage revenues will fall as a proportion of income.

B-share   Individual shares issued and listed within the Mainland that are denominated in hard currency (US$ in Shanghai and HK$ in Shenzhen) and are tradable on the two stock exchanges.

China Securities Regulatory Commission (CSRC)   The CSRC is China's securities market regulator. Established at the end of 1992, it grew in strength during the 1990s, gaining its own local offices, regulatory powers from competing ministries such as the PBOC and a staff of more than 3,000 people. It is widely recognised as one of the most professional of China's organs at ministry level. It is not, however, a State Council member and derives its funds from fees levied on market participants rather than from the government budget.

Chinese depository receipt (CDR)   Similar to an ADR, but issued by a PRC bank which holds non-PRC shares on deposit. The CDR idea was proposed in 2001 as a way of allowing Mainland investors access to foreign companies' shares. However, it ran into opposition on the grounds that domestic capital should be conserved for Mainland companies. CDRs therefore remain on the drawing-board.

Closed-ended funds   A type of investment fund in which a fixed number of units are issued and then traded, like standard shares, on the market. Known in the UK as an investment fund, it is different from an open-ended fund since units are not bought or sold when investors buy or sell them.

Collective   A firm owned by a sub-provincial government organ. Collectives existed under Mao, but under Deng they boomed. During the 1980s the term "collective" was used by many private firms that wanted the legitimacy that a state-owner provided.

Contract responsibility system (CRS)   Introduced in the early 1980s, the CRS extended more responsibilities to SOE managers and gave them contracts in which their firm's tax contribution was specified. Once this was met, a manager was free to use additional revenues as he saw fit.

Convertible bond   A bond that can be converted into equity at a set date and price.

Corporate bond   A bond issued by a corporation.

Credit-rating agency (CRA)   An agency that offers formal assessments of other companies' creditworthiness and their capacity to meet debt repayments. In China CRAs are still linked to local governments and their ratings are not reliable. International CRAs like Moody's and Standard & Poors' are not yet allowed to operate in the Mainland.

Equity   The ownership interest of shareholders in a company. Equity can usually be traded and entitles the owner both to vote at the shareholders' meeting and to receive dividends. In China, whether a company's equity can be traded depends on a number of rules to do with the type of company and the type of shares it can issue. Under company law, limited liability companies are allowed to issue only capital contribution certificates, rather than shares, and these cannot be traded.

Finance and Economics Leading Group (FELG)   The party's leading policymaking body on economic and financial affairs. During the 1990s it consisted of Jiang Zemin, Li Peng and Zhu Rongji, as well as a small number of other senior leaders.

Financial Work Committee   A committee set up by the CCP's Central Committee in 1998 in order to oversee political work and senior appointments in the financial sector. It is reportedly headed by Wen Jiabao.

Foreign direct investment (FDI)   Investment from overseas involved in buying fixed assets and operating them. Although China has attracted prodigious amounts of FDI during the reform years (the total stock of FDI now stands at above $400bn), some analysts argue that this is a sign of weakness. By allowing the SOEs to monopolise official finance – the banks and stockmarket – Chinese entrepreneurs have been forced to seek foreign investment for their ventures.

Generally Agreed Accounting Principles (GAAP)   A standard set of accounting principles and rules used by a country.

Gross domestic product (GDP)   The total worth of all the goods and services produced in one country during one year. Normally GDP is measured at current prices. Sometimes, however, purchasing power parity (PPP) is used, a technique which attempts to erase the effect of the US$/local currency exchange rate. PPP measures of GDP are useful when studying incomes per head across different countries, but not when comparing countries themselves.

Growth Enterprise Market (GEM)   A market operated by the Hong Kong Stock Exchange for small- and medium-capitalisation (or mid-cap) companies mainly operating in the IT sector. It has become a popular place for Mainland p-chips to list and its success is undermining the case for Shenzhen to establish its own GEM.

H-shares   The individual shares of PRC-incorporated firms that trade in Hong Kong. The term is sometimes also used to describe PRC shares traded in other places overseas, for example in New York and London, though these shares have their own labels of N- and L-shares respectively.

Hong Kong Special Administrative Region (HKSAR)   Established in July 1997 at the handover of Hong Kong to Mainland control. The HKSAR's Basic Law guarantees the continuation of Hong Kong's political and economic institutions for 50 years.

Individual shares   Shares issued by PRC companies that can be listed, traded and owned by natural persons. The category consists of A-, B-, H- and N-shares.

Initial public offering (IPO)   A company's first offering of shares to the public.

International Accounting Standards (IAS)   A set of accounting standards issued by the International Accounting Standards Committee in an attempt to create an international best-practice standard.

Investment fund   A fund that issues shares to investors and uses the money raised to invest in a portfolio of securities. The term is often used just to refer to closed-ended funds, in contrast to the more common open-ended funds which in the United States are known as mutual funds. Most of China's 60-odd funds are closed-ended.

IPO lottery   The system used in China to choose which investors can subscribe to an IPO. Applicants place money in their share account and apply. The CSRC then chooses by lottery which accounts can go forward to buy shares at the IPO. During the 1990s the prices of IPO shares would rise up to 900% on the first day of trading, creating huge incentives to win the IPO lottery. Many investors illegally opened thousands of accounts each in order to increase the chances of winning. In 2002 the lottery system was altered, forcing those involved to own shares in the secondary market already.

IPO quota system   A quota organised by the State Planning Commission between 1993 and 1999 that set an annual issuance amount for shares. The quota was, however, frequently altered in order to manipulate investor sentiment and was formally abandoned in 2000. However, the SDPC still has considerable say in how many shares can be issued and in what firms can issue shares.

Issuance Examination and Approval Committee (IEAC)   A committee established within the CSRC that oversees share issuance applications and is made up of CSRC personnel, industry participants and academics. The IEAC has enjoyed de facto power over share issuance since 1998, and has also established a subcommittee that oversees applications for significant restructuring from listed companies.

Legal person (LP) shares   Shares issued by restructured SOEs to legal persons, which are either companies or social entities with independent legal status, that cannot be listed on the stock exchanges. Since 1998, a vibrant market in LP shares has developed, with an increasing number of deals being done on a one-to-one basis.

Mainland China   A term used to describe the state of China (or PRC) minus the special administrative regions of Hong Kong and Macao. These operate under the sovereignty of the PRC but maintain their own legal systems. Mainland China also excludes Taiwan and its surrounding islands, territories claimed by the PRC but which are in effect independent and run by the government based in Taipei.

Market capitalisation   A common way of measuring the size of a stockmarket. It involves multiplying the number of shares by the value of those shares. The United States' stockmarket had a market capitalisation of some $14trn at the end of 2001. If only tradable shares are included, China had a market capitalisation of $200bn, some 1.4% of the size of the United States', for the same period.

Market maker   A participant in the securities market who offers to buy and sell securities at its own published prices. Some markets, like NASDAQ, are run by market makers. However, the stockmarket in China is run on an auction basis in which bids for shares are matched by a centralised, bid-matching computer system.

Market socialism   A theory popularised by Deng Xiaoping that seeks to legitimise market reforms and continued CCP rule. One central tenet of the theory is that market development is necessary during the current "primary stage of communism", the logic appearing to be that China must industrialise in order to create a proletariat which will then lead the country into a truly Communist future.

Ministry of Finance (MOF)   The ministry responsible for collecting tax revenues, issuing T-bonds and managing the government's budget. The MOF also supervises the development of accounting standards, regulates accountants and organises asset appraisals at SOEs.

Ministry of Foreign Trade and Economic Co-operation (MOFTEC) The ministry responsible for all aspects of foreign trade and investment. MOFTEC was responsible for negotiating China's entry into the WTO and is now overseeing the implementation of the agreement.

Net Asset Value (NAV)   The NAV is calculated by subtracting a firm's liabilities from its assets. It is a useful measurement of a firm's net worth.

N-shares   Individual shares of PRC companies listed in New York.

Open-ended funds   A mutual fund which issues (and buys back) fund units when its customers buy (or sell) its units. By far the most popular form of investment fund in Western markets.

Over-the-counter (OTC)   A style of trading in which market makers offer to buy and sell securities at their own published prices. This was the style of trading in the first share markets in reform China in Shenyang and Shanghai in 1986, when share and bond trading was carried out over counters and prices were chalked up on blackboards.

P-chip   The name given to the shares of private Mainland companies which trade in Hong Kong and elsewhere. P-chips were a hot investment target in 2002 and will continue to be the leading light of Chinese stocks overseas. But they also entail risks, as the demise of Euro-Asia Agriculture, once a hot p-chip which underwent a CSRC investigation for accounting fraud, revealed.

Particular Transfer (PT)   A trading category invented in 1999 for companies with three years of continuous losses and/or serious problems in their operations or finances. Trading in PT companies is restricted and the managements and owners of these firms are encouraged to organise asset restructurings. In 2002 the CSRC announced plans to delist companies with three years' losses, a sign that the days of the PT category are numbered.

People's Bank of China (PBOC)   Established in 1948, the People's Bank became a central bank in 1983. It is responsible for setting interest rates and regulating the banking sector. It is a State Council member and takes its orders from the party leadership. During the 1990s the PBOC had regulatory responsibilities for securities companies, but now only partly regulates TICs and investment funds. Rumours in early 2003 suggested that its bank regulatory functions would be split off to form a new bank regulation commission.

People's Republic of China   The state established in October 1949 by the Chinese Communist Party.

Price-earnings ratio (P/E)   A company's share price divided by its reported (or anticipated) earnings per share. The P/E ratio is a simple way of assessing the value of a company's shares. In Japan P/Es have historically been high (above 50), due to the limited number of traded shares and investors' willingness to profit from capital gains rather than dividends. In Europe and the United States, in contrast, P/Es have usually moved between 10 and 15, though in the 1990s they rose to 20 and above. Mainland China is well known for its high P/E ratios of above 40 for much of the 1990s, because of the limited number of shares floated and the lack of other investment avenues.

Primary market   The market into which securities are sold when they are first issued. Since share prices in the 1990s rose by several hundred per cent on the first day of trading, the primary market was a very popular place in which to buy. The rules governing IPO prices have since been relaxed, leading to higher IPO prices and smaller mark-ups.

Proprietary trading   Trading securities on one's own account. China's securities firms are keen proprietary traders, although since 1998 only comprehensive firms, those with Rmb500m or more in registered capital, are allowed to engage in it.

Qualified Domestic Institutional Investor (QDII)   A scheme allowing PRC investors to remit capital out of China (avoiding the closed capital account and other restrictions) for the express purpose of trading securities overseas, particularly those listed in Hong Kong. The idea ran into opposition from those fearing that it would decrease the funds available for companies trading in the Mainland.

Qualified Foreign Institutional Investor (QFII)   A scheme allowing foreign investors to remit capital into China (avoiding a closed capital account and other restrictions) for the express purpose of trading Mainland securities. China is in the midst of implementing QFII, following Taiwan and many other emerging markets. It is a good way to absorb foreign portfolio capital while minimising the destabilising effects that it can have.

Receivables   Money owing to a company that has not yet been paid. A popular part of the financial statement for accountants who need to manipulate a firm's financial performance.

Red-chip   A company registered and listed in Hong Kong but with the majority of its operations in Mainland China. Red-chips like CITIC were popular in the early 1990s, and in the run-up to the handover of Hong Kong in 1997. However, most are now trading below their issue prices because of their failure to build up successful core businesses and a number of scandals.

Repurchase (repo) contract   A contract between two parties in which one uses securities as collateral to borrow cash. There is an agreement to reverse the trade at a future date (usually a few days later) at an agreed price. (In Western markets, repos are popular ways for banks and other financial institutions to cover their short-term liquidity needs.) Repo contracts between commercial banks and securities firms were extremely common during the 1990s, and allowed banks to make long-term loans for the purpose of share trading. A crackdown by central government in 1997 resulted in the commercial banks being thrown off the stock exchanges and banned from lending to securities firms.

Return on equity (ROE)   A key measure of company performance, the ROE relates a company's profit to the amount of equity/capital that was employed to earn that profit. It is therefore a measure of the efficiency with which a company uses its assets.

Rights offering   A share issue that allows existing shareholders to buy shares at a discount to the current market price. In the UK rights offerings are common – much more so than in the United States. In China rights offerings have also been immensely popular, and their number and size have had to be limited by the CSRC.

Sarbanes-Oxley Act   Legislation passed in the United States in July 2002 in the wake of several high-profile corporate scandals. It aims to improve corporate governance and financial accounting. It also extends the reach of American criminal law to the executives and auditors of foreign companies listed in the United States. Such extra-territorial legal powers clearly present a threat to the executives of Chinese companies listed in the United States.

Secondary market   After securities are sold initially into the primary market, they then usually trade freely in the secondary market.

Secondary offering   A share issue by a company after its IPO that is open to the public, in contrast to a rights offering.

Securities Exchange Commission (SEC)   Established in the United States in 1934, the SEC is a powerful, independent securities regulatory agency. Its effectiveness, recently called into question, lies in its ability to force companies issuing securities to make extensive disclosures. If proper disclosures are made, the SEEC cannot prevent the company from issuing shares. In many ways a model for the CSRC, the two commissions do have a significant number of differences, most notably the CSRC's lack of independence from the executive part of China's government and the CCP.

Securities Industry Association (SIA)   An industry grouping made up of China's securities firms and fund firms. The original aim of the SIA was to be a self-regulatory organisation, like America's National Association of Securities Dealers, with powers to discipline its own members. However, for a long time it was redundant since the government monopolised all the powers. That remains the case, but in recent months the CSRC has given the SIA new offices near its own headquarters in

Beijing's Finance Street and is using its staff to draft regulations and advise on policies. All senior appointments to the SIA are made by the CSRC. The current head, Zhuang Xinyi, was formerly head of the Shenzhen exchange.

Securities Law   Passed in 1998, after six years of drafting, the Securities Law provides the legislative basis for the issuance and trading of securities in reform China. It did not have much of an impact because State Council regulation on the stockmarket was already extensive and effective.

Securities trading centre (STC)   During the 1990s, denied the opportunity to establish their own stock exchanges, provincial governments established STCs instead. These centres provided trading facilities for securities listed in Shanghai and Shenzhen, but also (illegally) listed both national and local bonds, as well as shares issued by local companies. They were mostly closed down during 1998–99 on the orders of Zhu Rongji, who was concerned about their effect on the financial sector's stability.

Self-regulatory organisation (SRO)   A membership organisation that has the power to monitor, regulate and discipline its members. An SRO, like the New York Stock Exchange, may itself be regulated by a higher organ, such as the SEC. In theory, both the Shanghai and Shenzhen exchanges are SROs but since the 1997 takeover by the CSRC they have not been able to practise any of their SRO powers.

Shareholding reform   Beginning in the mid-1980s, many thousands of SOEs converted into companies limited by shares. By clarifying the property rights over their assets, as well as establishing clear divisions between their owners, the local administration, a board of directors and the management, the hope was that performance would be improved. Many large and medium-sized shareholding companies then sold off shares to the public; smaller ones were bought out by their employees or sold to private investors. The problem with the former group was that the government retained large ownership stakes and continued to interfere and/or badly regulate these firms. In the latter group, shareholdings appear to have become too dispersed for good governance practices to be feasible.

Short contracts   Selling shares today that one does not own to buy at some point in the future. Short-selling can be hugely profitable if the price of the securities one sells falls, allowing one to buy it at a lower price later. Conversely, it can be a very risky business if the price rises.

Soft budget constraint   A concept developed by Janos Kornai, an economist, to describe an apparently common characteristic of SOEs. Kornai argued that since these firms played an essential role in providing employment, the government would always provide them with funds and would not let them go bankrupt. Their budgets are therefore soft.

Spot trading   A market in which securities are purchased and settled.

Special Treatment (ST)   A special trading category created in 1998 for shares that have sustained two years of continuous losses. Although ST shares are subject to some trading restrictions, the most important thing is that the ST prefix warns investors to take extra care. However, because of the expectation that they will have new assets inserted into them, ST companies are subject to very high levels of speculation.

State Commission for Restructuring the Economic System (SCORES) Established as the think-tank of the premier, and then general secretary, Zhao Ziyang, the SCORES was at the heart of formulating market-oriented reform policies during the 1980s. Its influence began to fade, however, in 1989 after Zhao's sacking after the Tiananmen protests, and the subsequent less radical approach to enterprise reform taken by senior officials. During the 1990s many of the SCORES's powers were transferred to the SETC, Zhu Rongji's own think-tank, and in 1998 the commission was downgraded to become the Economic Restructuring Office of the State Council.

State Council   The executive part of China's government, the State Council is responsible for implementing legislation and governing the country. It prepares economic plans and the state budget, oversees government work throughout the country and is able to issue regulations with the force of law. It is currently made up of 29 ministries and commissions, and is led by the premier, a number of vice-premiers and state councillors and one secretary-general. It meets once a month and its standing committee meets twice each week.

State Council Securities Commission (SCSC)   A high-level organisation of government officials established in 1992 to provide co-ordination on stockmarket policy. Initially the CSRC served as its administrative office, but after 1997 the CSRC assumed most of the SCSC's policy-making powers and the commission was disbanded.

State Development Planning Commission (SDPC)   Formerly known as the State Planning Commission, this State Council member was at the heart of the plan economy but has retained influence in the reform era. Under the auspices of the five- and ten-year plans that it prepares, the SDPC determines national development goals, co-ordinates policies across industries, formulates pricing policies, co-ordinates regional development and plans agricultural trade and government investment. Many of its powers over enterprises have been assumed by the SETC, partly because Zhu Rongji wanted to bypass the commission's somewhat conservative instincts. Rumours in early 2003 suggested it would absorb the State Council's Development Research Centre and lose more of its planning functions.

State Economic and Trade Commission (SETC)   Established in May 1993 with the support of Zhu Rongji, the SETC is intimately involved in enterprise reform and trade policy. It oversees the implementation of policies in particular sectors and since 1998 has been implementing a three-year plan to rescue debt-ridden large- and medium-sized SOEs. Rumours in early 2003 suggested it would be broken up and absorbed by other bureaus.

State-owned enterprise (SOE)   An enterprise owned, in theory at least, in its entirety by the state on behalf of the people. In practice, however, an SOE usually has no real ownership rights: no one official or agency profits from its success, suffers from its failure or can sell the firm. This lack of real property rights forms the basis of criticisms of state ownership.

State shares   A type of shares issued by restructured SOEs which are allocated to administrative bureaus and which cannot be listed or traded. They represent the state's ownership stake and are managed by bureaus of the MOF. There have been two attempts by the government to reduce these holdings in 1999 and 2001, both of which triggered panic selling. The State Council appears to have decided to sell some of its state shares, but has not yet come up with a way to do so without harming the market.

Stock exchange   Traditionally the place where securities are bought and sold. With the computerisation of trading, however, stock exchanges are now more important for supplying centralised trading facilities and regulating trading. China's two stock exchanges were both established in December 1990, the Shenzhen one without authorisation from the central government. They are now managed by the CSRC.

Stock Exchange Executive Council (SEEC)   An organisation established in the late 1980s by a group of Chinese returnees from Wall Street, including Gao Xiqing (once a CSRC deputy chairman) and Wang Boming. After creating the initial plans for the two stock exchanges, the group was sidelined by the two local governments and retired to Beijing. Here the SEEC established a successful private company that provides financial consultancy and training services, runs a popular website (www.homeway. com.cn) and publishes Caijing magazine.

Stock index future   A contract for the future purchase of an index instrument. Buying an index future is useful if one owns shares and wants to hedge against the prices of those shares falling.

Stockmarket index   A statistical average of share prices used to represent the general state of prices. During the 1990s China had a series of indices created by the Shanghai and Shenzhen exchanges. The first national index was created in 2001.

Treasury bond (T-bond)   A bond issued by the MOF on behalf of the central government. Whereas in developed markets T-bonds of a wide variety of maturities (between three months and ten years) are issued, China currently only issues long-term T-bonds. Without an auction of short-term bonds, it is difficult to set the interest rate on market lines.

Treasury-bond future   A contract to buy a T-bond in the future at a price agreed in the present. The SHGSE began offering trading in T-bond futures in December 1992. However, owing to poor regulation and a trading scandal (which bankrupted Wanguo Securities, a leading securities company) in February 1995, the market was forced to close. Many in central government oppose the return of futures trading, although there are rumours that an index futures contract may soon be authorised.

Trust and investment company (TIC)   Established in the early 1980s by the central government and various local governments, TICs operated as fund-raising vehicles for government-sponsored projects. International TICs (ITICs) were permitted to raise money overseas. The sector as a whole is recognised now as the most dangerous part of the financial sector, since huge sums of money were stolen or diverted into a wide range of speculative investments, including real estate and share trading. The TICs are currently being sorted out by the PBOC with many, including most spectacularly Guangdong's ITIC, being closed down. Others are being restructured into trust companies.

Trustee   A person or company who is entrusted with property that belongs to another.

Underwriting   When a company or government issues shares or bonds, an investment bank usually underwrites the issue. This means that it prepares the issuance and commits to buy any securities not purchased by the market.

World Trade Organisation   A multilateral organisation established in 1994 at the end of the Uruguay round of the General Agreement on Tariffs and Trade (GATT) talks. The WTO is a small organisation which serves its constituent members and whose highest authority is the Ministerial Conference, held at least every two years. It promotes free trade on the basis that free trade is a force for creating economic prosperity for rich and poor alike.

Appendix 4 Chronology of events

1978

December   The third plenum of the 11th central committee of China's Communist Party. Deng Xiaoping launches free-market reforms and the "open-door" policy.

1980

February   Hu Yaobang becomes general secretary of the Communist Party.

September   Zhao Ziyang becomes premier.

1984

November   The first issuance of standardised shares by Feile, a collective enterprise, in Shanghai. A handful of other firms issue shares to their employees and the public.

October   The third plenum of the 12th central committee of the Communist Party urges a "deep transformation of the socialist superstructure". Industrial reform commences as the party approves "flexible economic arrangements of all kinds".

1986

August   The first formal trading in shares begins in Shenyang in Liaoning province at a small counter of a commercial bank.

September   Shanghai follows Shenyang and opens an OTC for share trading. The central government issues regulations on the corporate responsibility system. This remains the main thrust of SOE reform while shareholding experiments continue in a small number of locales.

November   A delegation from the New York Stock Exchange visits Deng Xiaoping. Deng presents his guests with a Feile share certificate. This signal of his approval of the stock market experiment boosts investors' confidence. Rumours later surface that the chairman of the NYSE has lost the certificate.

1987

January   A *People's Daily* editorial attacks bourgeois liberalisation. Hu Yaobang, apparently one of its main proponents, is removed and replaced as general secretary by Zhao Ziyang. Li Peng, a conservative with links with Zhou Enlai and Chen Yun, is later confirmed as Zhao's successor as premier.

March   The 13th NPC endorses continued trials with the shareholding system.

October   Zhao, speaking at the party's 13th congress, argues that China is in the primary stage of socialism, a stage where a little capitalism is necessary to industrialise the country.

1988

August   The politburo backs Deng and allows the liberalisation of commodity prices. Panic buying and inflation result. The decision leads to criticism of Zhao (despite his initial opposition to the move) while Deng escapes censure.

September   Returnees from Wall Street and several in the central government who want to establish a stockmarket meet and present their proposal to the party leadership. They are given the green light to work out the details of how such a market could operate.

1989

April–June   The Tiananmen Square protests. Tens of thousands of students and workers demonstrate in central Beijing and across China against corruption, inflation and human rights abuses by the government.

June   The violent suppression of the Tiananmen demonstrations leads to the removal of Zhao from his leadership posts. He is replaced as general secretary by the Shanghai party secretary, Jiang Zemin, a relative unknown. China braces itself for a return to conservative politics. The future of the stockmarket appears bleak.

1990

April   Shanghai receives the central government's go-ahead for its development of Pudong, the rural area in the east of the city. By the late 1990s an ultra-modern stock exchange nestles in the middle of Lujiazui, Pudong's financial district.

October   STAQS, a bond-trading platform run by the SEEC and the SCORES, begins operations. In 1992 STAQS lists a number of LP shares, but then is banned from doing so by the CSRC in 1993.

December   Shanghai and Shenzhen both establish stock exchanges. The former has permission from the central government, as part of its Pudong development. The latter does not.

1991

April Zhu Rongji moves to Beijing from Shanghai to become vice-premier. After attempts by Li to sideline him, Zhu is given responsibility for the economy. The PBOC authorises Shenzhen to open its stock exchange.

August The Securities Industry Association is established. It is quickly sidelined by the CSRC after its foundation in late 1992.

December The first B-share, a foreign-currency-denominated share, is issued by Shanghai Vacuum.

1992

January Deng begins his southern tour of Wuhan, Guangzhou, Shenzhen and Shanghai. Through his speeches in favour of growth, Deng reinvigorates the reform agenda and triggers a wave of investment and share issuance across the country. Officials seem set on rolling out the shareholding reforms countrywide.

June SHZSE-listed Champagne Industrial becomes the first to sue the regulatory authorities (the Shenzhen branch of the PBOC) for falsely disciplining the firm for financial irregularities.

July The NPC's Finance and Economics Committee begins drafting the Securities Law. The official media reports that over 10,000 SOEs have applied to convert into shareholding companies.

August The 8.10 riots in Shenzhen, triggered by a badly handled IPO, force the local authorities to call in the army. The central government rethinks stockmarket regulation.

October China Brilliance becomes the first Mainland company to be listed in New York. The listed vehicle is an offshore holding company. The central government establishes the SCSC and CSRC in response to the crisis in the stockmarket. The People's Bank, the former regulator, resists the move but is sidelined. Local governments lobby for and win continued influence. In his speech at the 14th party congress Jiang outlines the intention to build a socialist market economy.

November Li visits the SHGSE and states that "stockmarkets help the construction of socialism".

December The first financial futures instruments, T-bond futures, are offered for trading at the SHGSE.

1993

February For the first time, central-party organs designate "Deng Xiaoping thought" as official party and state ideology. The NETS, a trading network for LP shares, is established by the PBOC. New listings of LP shares are banned shortly after by the State Council because of fears that they will undermine public ownership.

May The CSRC issues its first comprehensive regulations on share issuance and trading. The State Council warns provincial governments that if they do not buy T-bonds then, their SOEs will be prevented from making public share issues.

July Qingdao Beer becomes the first "H-share", the first PRC-registered company to issue shares in Hong Kong. Zhu Rongji, newly installed as vice-premier with responsibility for the economy, institutes a wide-ranging programme of reforms designed to dampen inflation and claw back controls from local government. His 16-point austerity plan is the closest thing the government has produced yet to an economic reform strategy.

August The Zibo investment fund is the first local investment fund to receive a listing on a stock exchange.

November The CSRC announces a new scheme for IPO applications. Applicants will have to deposit money into share accounts, rather than queue on the street for applications forms. The IPO lottery system is created.

1994

January Lhasa opens the Tibet Shares Business Centre, linked up with the SHGSE and SHZSE. Mrs Xu sues Zhejiang International TIC for allowing her late husband to trade shares on credit.

February The CSRC rejects Shanghai Dazhong's plan to convert its LP shares into B-shares.

March Shenzhen's Baoan Industries takes seats on the board of Shanghai Yanzhong after successfully organising reform China's first hostile takeover. Because of the small amounts of shares that are traded, only a handful of hostile takeovers of listed companies have since occurred.

April The State Council places the supervision of futures markets under the SCSC and CSRC.

July China's Company Law comes into effect, creating two kinds of limited companies. Companies limited by shares have a high capital requirement and their shares can trade in public. Limited-liability companies can only have 3–49 owners who are issued with "capital contribution certificates" rather than shares. The "three big policies" are announced by the CSRC in an effort to restore investors' confidence. A slowdown in the rate of new share issuance, experiments with Sino-foreign investment funds and allowing foreign investors direct access to A-shares are all announced. After an initial surge in prices, the lack of action on the latter two policies sends prices tumbling.

November   The media report that 10m share accounts have been opened.

1995

February   The 327 T-bond futures scandal bankrupts Wanguo Securi-ties, reveals the SHGSE to be a weak self-regulator and leads to the closure of China's nascent futures market.

March   The CSRC's first chairman, Liu Hongru, is made scapegoat for the 327 scandal and replaced by Zhou Daojiong. Zhou is mandated to institute stricter controls. The NPC adopts the Law on the PBOC that lays down the legislative foundation for the new central bank. It is given powers over all financial institutions, but its jurisdiction over the stock-market is unclear.

July   The NPC passes the Commercial Bank Law, the first legislative statement of the division between commercial deposit-taking banks and securities firms. Commercial banks are not allowed to invest in shares, TICs or real estate and commercial banks must disclose their consider-able holdings in securities firms.

August   The entrepreneurial SHGSE president, Wei Wenyuan, "resigns" from his post at the exchange and is replaced by Yang Xiang-hai, who has worked within the Shanghai industrial planning bureau-cracy for many years. Morgan Stanley establishes China's first JVSF, China International Capital Corporation (CICC). The state-owned China Construction Bank and Morgan are the dominant shareholders. After internecine fighting between the American and Chinese sides (which the latter won), CICC becomes hugely successful.

October   Premier Li Peng is angered by the takeover of Beijing Light-bus by Isuzu and Itochu, two Japanese firms, through their purchase of Lightbus LP sales. Further sales of LP shares to foreigners are banned, a ban that is to last until 2002. Zhuang Xinyi, from the CSRC, takes over as president of the SHZSE. Expectations that he will be a Beijing stooge are quickly dispelled as he moves decisively to compete head on with the SHGSE.

December   Zhu Rongji visits the SHGSE, his first visit since moving to Beijing, and talks about the need for more regulation.

1996

February The CSRC gains the right to levy fees on stockmarket participants and thus gains a source of stable revenues.

April The CSRC signals the central government's ambition to expand the stockmarket in support of SOE reform. Large SOEs are encouraged to restructure into shareholding companies and issue stocks.

June The CSRC establishes the first qualification system for underwriters.

October The CSRC reiterates its ban on securities companies lending money to their customers to trade shares. Its initial investigations in Shanghai have suggested that the practice is common. The CSRC issues its first rules on securities firms trading shares on a proprietary basis.

November Regulators begin to worry as prices reach record highs on a daily basis and they spot huge speculative positions being built up. Government officials begin to suspect local government collusion in speculation.

December The *People's Daily* publishes an editorial entitled "A correct understanding of the current stockmarket". Supposedly edited by Zhu, the piece compares China's stockmarket with the New York market on the eve of the great crash of 1929. A 10% limit on the daily price movements of shares is instituted and a huge Rmb10bn share issuance quota for 1997 is announced to dampen speculation.

1997

February Guan Jinsheng, the CEO of Wanguo Securities, is found guilty of stealing public funds and sentenced to 17 years' imprisonment. He has since been released on medical parole. Deng Xiaoping dies, age 93. The government is ready to channel funds into the share market to prevent falls, but the market barely registers the news.

March Red-chip madness increases. GITIC Enterprises, a marble and real-estate business based in Guangdong province, makes its IPO in Hong Kong and attracts some $13bn in subscriptions. In the week the company holds the funds before it issues the shares it earns $8m in interest, more than its entire profits for 1996.

May Zhou Zhengqing replaces Zhou Daojiong as head of the CSRC. He has a depth of knowledge about the market and, as a secretary-general to the State Council, can fight the CSRC's corner better than either of his predecessors. After speculative trading and sharp prices return to scare the government, the CSRC bans SOEs and listed companies from trading shares. The ban is lifted only in September 1999, but during this period many SOEs continue to speculate via illegally-opened individual share accounts.

July   Britain's colony of Hong Kong is handed back to the Mainland and the Hong Kong Special Administrative Region is created. The CSRC orders the closure of 12 futures brokerages, with more closures to follow. A plan is also rolled out to reduce the number of futures brokerages from 14 to three. A number of Mainland securities companies are punished for using bank deposits, rumoured to be worth some $1bn, to trade shares. Commercial banks are banned from making repo trades on the stock exchanges and are forced to use the interbank for their bond trading needs. The Asian Financial Crisis erupts in Thailand. The H-share bubble in Hong Kong bursts soon after. China, secure behind its capital-account controls, is protected.

September   CSRC staffers Tu Guangshao and Gui Minjie arrive at the SHGSE and SHZSE to institute CSRC control. The two local governments are sidelined. The CCP's 15th congress amends the party's constitution so as to adopt "Marxism-Leninism, Mao Zedong Thought and Deng Xiaoping Theory" as its guiding doctrine.

October   A joint CCP and government financial work meeting announces that the CSRC will be empowered as China's securities regulator.

1998

March   Zhu Rongji becomes premier, having run economic policy from the post of vice-premier since 1993. He introduces an ambitious plan to resolve the SOE problem within three years, reorganise the government bureaucracy and sort out the financial system. The first standardised investment funds, Jintai and Kaiyuan, are issued. In order to boost take up of the funds, the CSRC allows them to subscribe to 5% of all new IPO shares, guaranteeing them profits. The policy is soon dropped, however, because of criticism from other market participants.

May   The PBOC formally hands over its regulatory powers in the stockmarket to the CSRC.

June   Shenyin Wanguo, Haitong and Guangfa securities companies resume proprietary trading after a one-year ban for borrowing funds from commercial banks during 1996–97.

July   The State Council orders an investigation into attempts by officials at Junan Securities to privatise the company.

December   The NPC passes the Securities Law with 135 votes in favour, no objections and three abstentions. President Jiang signs a declaration to make it law in July 1999.

1999

March   The constitution is amended to recognise private firms as an "important component" of the economy.

May   Three NATO missiles destroy China's embassy in Belgrade, Yugoslavia. The strike triggers anti-American protests in major Chinese cities.

June   28 securities companies issue a joint statement to assure their customers (and the CSRC) that they are not engaged in illegal activities. They protest too much. An article in the *People's Daily*, also rumoured to have been edited by Zhu Rongji, entitled "Standardise and strengthen confidence in China's stockmarket", talks up the market. A brief rally begins. The government appears to believe that rising stockmarkets will encourage consumers' confidence and thereby help in the battle against deflation. Zhu had visited Wall Street in April.

July   Vice-Premier Wen Jiabao states that the stockmarket is a prerequisite of the new socialist market economy. The CSRC establishes its first regional branch, in Guangzhou. The stock exchanges, on orders from the CSRC, establish the PT trading category for firms with three years' continuous losses.

August   The CSRC allows underwriters and their clients to set their own IPO prices. Previously IPO prices had been set administratively at a P/E ratio of 14–18.

September   SOEs and listed companies are again allowed to trade shares, but initially not in the primary market. They are additionally expected to hold their shares for at least six months. The CSRC announces its intention to establish a second board for high-tech companies. The plan is soon undermined by the collapse of the NASDAQ market in 2000 and has been on the back-burner ever since.

December   The first organised attempt to sell off state shares ends in failure as the prices are set too high and investor confidence is undermined. China signs a bilateral agreement with the United States to join the WTO. China makes deep concessions across a wide range of sectors, including retail banking. Concessions in the securities sector are, however, extremely limited.

2000

January   Yuxing, a Beijing-based software company, becomes the first Mainland firm to list on Hong Kong's new GEM after an extended quarrel with the CSRC about who can authorise the deal.

February   Zhou Xiaochuan, a Western-trained economist, becomes chairman of the CSRC. His mandate is to institute more market-oriented reforms. One of the founders of the CSRC, Gao Xiqing, is bought back into the CSRC (having resigned in 1995) to head up policy development. The CSRC and PBOC allow a small number of securities firms to borrow funds from banks using their shareholdings as collateral.

March   At his press conference at the end of the plenary session of the NPC, Zhu remarks that China's stockmarket has developed quickly, achieved much, but is still not well-ordered.

April   The CSRC issues regulations that require anyone applying to buy IPO shares to have a minimum holding of Rmb10,000 ($1,200) worth of A-shares. Owing to technical problems, however, the scheme has to be postponed until 2002. Sina becomes the first Chinese Internet portal to list on the NASDAQ.

May   The European Union signs an agreement with China allowing it to join the WTO. The central government unveils the "Develop the West" programme in which large public works programmes are used to develop China's poor central and western provinces. Political considerations about growing inequality are paramount. Economists are sceptical about the efficacy of the scheme. To discourage speculators making easy money in the IPO market, the CSRC introduces rules that requires any applicants to buy IPO shares to already be share owners.

August   Sales of LP shares begin as rumours start circulating to the effect that the CSRC will soon allow LP shares to list and trade freely. By the end of the year an active auction market for these shares has sprung up.

December   Caijing magazine breaks a story about investment fund managers conspiring to manipulate share prices. The CSRC is forced to investigate and the reputation of fund managers takes a dive.

2001

January   The CSRC begins formal investigations into the Zhongke Chuangye and Yian Keji share manipulation scams.

February   The CSRC opens up the B-share market to those domestic investors who already have foreign-currency bank accounts. From June 2001 bank accounts can be opened for B-share purchases. B-share prices increase rapidly but after June the rally falters as a merger with the A-share market appears unlikely. The CSRC releases rules on delisting loss-making companies.

April   PT Shanghai Narcissus becomes the first company to be delisted. Its shares are later transferred to an OTC market run by securities firms and the SHZSE.

July   An attempt to sell off companies' state shares at the same time as their IPOs and secondary offerings begins. The move triggers a fall in prices that lasts into 2002. A huge public backlash ensues.

September   The CSRC begins its investigation into Yinguangxia, a notorious *baozhuang* firm, and its accountants Zhongtianqin, for securities fraud. The first open-ended mutual fund, Hua'an's Chuangxin Fund, is issued, to huge demand. A handful of other open-ended funds follow, but subscribers' numbers are thin.

October   Zhu calls fraudulent accounting a "malignant tumour" on China's nascent market economy.

November   The CSRC and MOF announce that the stamp tax levied on share trading is being reduced to 0.2%.

December   The CSRC announces that firms applying for a listing in 2002 will need to have their accounts audited by both domestic and international accountancy firms. China's accountants lobby hard and succeed in severely watering down the rule.

2002

January   A frustrated Zhang Jinghua, director of the CSRC's fund department, writes an open letter to the investment fund companies, criticising them for illegally oversubscribing to Shenzhen Expressway's IPO. The CSRC rules that securities firms, subject to receiving a licence, are allowed to establish asset-management and venture-capital subsidiaries.

February   New rules allow the trading of certificate T-bonds. Previously, individuals were not permitted to trade the certificate T-bonds that they purchased.

March   The NPC criticises the CSRC for "listing unqualified companies, [and for failing to stop] the falsification of financial statements by listed companies, insider trading of listed companies with their controlling shareholders, excessive speculation and manipulation". The CSRC allows IT companies and others to apply for brokerage licences. Previously only securities firms had been permitted to apply. Bank of China International establishes BOCI (China), a JVSF. This is the first JVSF established since China joined the WTO. All companies involved in the deal have Mainland parentage. BNP Paribas, a French bank, becomes the first foreign firm to gain permission to establish a JVSF. The CSRC and MOF announce the cancellation of their scheme to sell-off state shares.

May   Chengdu Fortune Science and Technology becomes the first company to successfully restructure, book a profit and leave the PT category. The CSRC partially liberalises brokerage fees with the aim of reviving the depressed share market and encouraging the consolidation of China's 100-plus securities firms.

June Seven defendants in the Zhongke Chuangye case are put on trial in Beijing for share price manipulation. This is China's first criminal case involving the stockmarket. The case is adjourned to allow the judges time to consider the case. The CSRC releases detailed rules on how JVFMFS and JVSFS will operate. The Hong Kong and New York stock exchanges suspend trading in the shares of China Brilliance, the first PRC company to list in the United States, after its CEO, Yang Rong, is investigated for corruption in Shenyang.

July Bank of China lists its Hong Kong operations in Hong Kong. Other Mainland banks look on enviously.

August The CSRC closes down Anshan Securities, the first brokerage to receive such severe treatment.

October The CSRC issues its first set of comprehensive rules on acquisitions of listed companies, providing the framework for an already vibrant acquisition market.

November Days before the CCP's 16th congress, the CSRC announces the imminent introduction of the QFII scheme that will allow foreign investors access to A-shares. It is a huge step forward, although the high entry barriers and P/E ratios mean that many foreign firms meet the news with a yawn. Hu Jintao becomes general secretary. Vice-Premier Wen Jiabao, who has been responsible for financial reform under Zhu since 1998, takes the no. 3 position in the politburo and is widely tipped to become premier in March 2003. The party work report supports the strengthening of the institutions of state asset management, a signal that privatisation is being resisted. Three former senior officials at SHGSE-listed Zhengzhou Baiwen are given suspended jail terms for making false disclosures about their firm's profitability. This is reform China's first successful criminal prosecution of a stockmarket-related crime.

December CITIC Securities becomes the Mainland's first securities firm to go public, raising Rmb1.8bn ($220m) by issuing 400m shares.

2003

January CSRC chairman Zhou Xiaochuan is transferred to the top post at the central bank, the PBOC. Shang Fulin, fresh from leading the Agricultural Bank of China, takes up the CSRC chairmanship. Zhou's most influential deputy chairman, Gao Xiqing, leaves too, destination unknown. Both men had attracted vitriolic criticism for the market price falls that had accompanied their attempts at reform. China's stockmarket hits a three-and-a-half year low and then rallies a little.

Appendix 5 **Recommended reading**

Economic and corporate reform

Huang, Yasheng, *Inflation & Investment Controls in China: The Political Economy of Centre-Local Relations During the Reform Era*, New York, Cambridge University Press, 1996.
A ground-breaking study of how disputes between central and local government influenced a series of investment booms in the late 1980s and early 1990s. Huang shows how the central government uses the nomenklatura system of political appointments to control economic development.

Naughton, B., *Growing out of the Plan: Chinese Economic Reform, 1978–1993*, Cambridge, Cambridge University Press, 1995.
By far the best study of the economic reforms of the 1980s. Naughton argues the key to this phase of growth was stabilising the amount of money flowing to and regulation of the state sector, and letting non-state firms grow outside the plan.

Nolan, P., *China and the Global Business Revolution*, Basingstoke, Palgrave, 2001.
A colossal work that assesses the prospects for China's conglomerate class of enterprises by benchmarking them against their global competitors. Nolan covers nine industries in enormous detail and argues that the current conglomerate strategy is doomed to failure.

Steinfeld, E., *Forging Reform in China: The Fate of State-Owned Industry*, Cambridge, Cambridge University Press, 1998.
Built on in-depth case studies of three steel-making SOEs, Steinfeld shows how industrial restructuring is destined to fail until real privatisation is allowed. Excellent on explaining why state ownership does not work.

Tenev, S. and Zhang, Chunlin, *Corporate Governance and Enterprise Reform in China: Building the Institutions of Modern Markets*, World Bank and IFC, Washington, DC, 2002.
Partly based on a survey by the Shanghai Stock Exchange and partly on World Bank research, this study provides an up-to-date and detailed

account of the state of SOE reform. It argues that corporate governance cannot be improved until state-owned firms are privatised.

Financial reform

Green, S., *Equity Politics: The Development of China's Stock Market, 1984–2002*, London, Routledge, forthcoming.
Based on the author's PhD thesis this book examines in detail the politics involved in the creation and development of the stockmarket. While it had tremendous difficulties controlling development before 1997, since then the central government has proven extremely adept at doing so, for the benefit of the market.

Hertz, E., *The Trading Crowd: An Ethnography of the Shanghai Stockmarket*, Cambridge, Cambridge University Press, 1998.
A fascinating account of the Shanghai stockmarket's developments during 1992 by an ethnographer. Immersing herself in the investment fervour, Hertz argues that a new cultural phenomenon in reform China was created in 1992 as the share market grew out of the reach of the state.

Lardy, N., *China's Unfinished Economic Revolution*, Washington, DC, Brookings Institution, 1998.
Essential reading on recent efforts at industrial and financial reform. Lardy is critical of the way banks have been used to subsidise loss-making state-owned firms, and less than optimistic about the future.

Tsai, K., *Back-Alley Banking: Private Entrepreneurs in China*, Ithaca, NY, Cornell University Press, 2002.
An original and excellent study of informal finance in the reform era. Based on her extensive fieldwork, Tsai examines community associations, pawnbrokers and small private banks to show the extent to which they funded the huge private sector.

Foreign investment and trade

Huang, Yasheng, *Selling China: The Institutional Foundation of Foreign Direct Investment During the Reform Era*, Cambridge, Cambridge University Press, 2002.
A detailed and provocative book that argues that huge inflows of foreign direct investment are a sign of China's economic weakness, rather than strength. A financial system that fails to supply funds to the

dynamic parts of the economy – the private sector – has meant that entrepreneurs have had to sell equity in their firms to foreigners.

Lardy, N., *Integrating China into the Global Economy*, Washington, DC, Brookings Institution, 2002.
Lardy argues that China has undergone radical and extensive reforms to its trade and investment policies over the past two decades, a trend which WTO entry continues. He is optimistic about the prospects for implementation and counsels developed countries not to use non-tariff measures to protect their markets from China's exports.

Studwell, J., *The China Dream: The Elusive Quest for the Greatest Untapped Market on Earth*, London, Profile Books, 2001.
An entertaining, if damning, review of the pitfalls of foreign investment in China, the so-called "Vietnam war of American business". If foreign investors have not been involved in processing for export, they have had irrationally high expectations of the size of the market and their profits.

Politics

Baum, R., *Burying Mao: Chinese Politics in the Age of Deng Xiaoping*, Princeton, NJ, Princeton, University Press, 1994.
Baum provides a blow-by-blow account of China's politics in the 1980s, showing how Deng Xiaoping steered a remarkable course between conservatives and radical reformist senior officials. Researched to the highest of academic standards and also immensely readable.

Fewsmith, J., *China since Tiananmen: The Politics of Transition*, Cambridge, Cambridge University Press, 2001.
The best review of China's elite politics in the 1990s: detailed, informed and opinionated. Fewsmith is especially good on the shifting intellectual debates that provide a backdrop to national politics, from a vibrant cosmopolitanism in the 1980s to a brittle nationalism in the 1990s.

Lam, Willy Wo-Lap, *The Era of Jiang Zemin*, Singapore, Prentice Hall, 1999.
An entertaining review of Jiang Zemin's climb up the greasy pole of Zhongnanhai politics. Includes accounts of his many friends and enemies, as well as plenty of Lam's speciality, anecdotes of cadre power games.

Magazines

English-language sources on continuing developments in the sector include *Business China,* published fortnightly by the Economist Intelligence Unit in Hong Kong (www.eiu.com) and the *South China Morning Post* (www.scmp.com).

Caijing magazine is an invaluable source in Chinese (www.caijing.com.cn) , as is *Xin Caifu* (New Fortune), another excellent popular magazine (www.p5w.net).

Appendix 6 Useful website addresses

Established in late 1996 by the Stock Exchange Executive Council, Hexun (www.homeway.com.cn) was the first securities-dedicated website and remains the most authoritative source for financial news and analysis. It was quickly followed by other high-quality sites, such as www.stockstar.com.cn, www.kangxi.com.cn, www.gotrade.com and www.genius.com.cn.

Major securities companies

Company	Website
Yinhe (Galaxy)	www.chinastock.com.cn
Shenyin Wanguo	www.sw2000.com.cn
Guotai Junan	www.gtja.com
Hailong	www.htsec.com
Guotong (Communications)	www.newone.com.cn
Zhongxin (CITIC)	www.citics.com.cn
Guoxin	www.guosen.com
Beijing	www.bsc.com.cn
Huaxia (China)	www.csc.com.cn
Guangdong	www.gds.com.cn
Dapeng	www.chinaeagler.com
Nanfang (Southern)	www.sostock.com.cn
Huatai	www.htsc.com.cn
Lianhe (United)	www.lhzq.com
Xiangcai	www.xcsc.com.cn
Guangfa	www.gf.com.cn

Source: www.p5w.net

Investment management companies, year-end 2001

Company	Website
Boshi	www.boshi.com.cn
Changsheng	www.changshengfunds.com
Dacheng	www.dcfund.com
Fuguo (Fullgoal)	www.fullgoal.com.cn
Guotai	www.gtfund.com
Hefeng	www.hefeng.com
Hua'an	www.huaan.com.cn
Huaxia (China Asset)	www.chinaamc.com, www.chinafunds.com
Jinshi (Harvest)	www.harvestfund.com.cn
Nanfang (Southern)	www.southernfund.com
Penghua	www.phfund.com.cn
Rongtong	www.rtfund.com
Yifangda	www.efunds.com.cn
Yinhua	www.yhfunds.com.cn

Sources: CSRC; author

Appendix 7 **References**

Numerous newspapers and other media sources, in both English and Chinese, were consulted for this book. They include: *Business China*, *The China Daily*, *China Law and Practice*, *China Online*, Foreign Broadcast Information Service, *Financial Times*, Hong Kong Associated Free Press, *International Herald Tribune*, *Jingji Ribao* (Economic Daily), *Nanfang Zhoumo* (Southern Weekend), *South China Morning Post*, *Shangshi Gongsi* (Listed Company), *Shanghai Zhengquan Bao* (Shanghai Securities News), *Zhengquan Shichang Zhoukan* (Securities Weekly) and *Zhongguo Zhengquan Qihuo* (China Securities and Futures). CSRC, as well as Shanghai & Shenzhen stock exchange annual reports, were useful sources of data. Research reports published by Chinese securities firms Changjiang, Guotai Junan, Haitong, Huaxia and Shenyin Wanguo, as well as by China's Securities Industry Association (SIA), were also essential.

Select bibliography

An Zhaohong, "PT Gongsi de Chongzu Shixian (The Practice of PT Company Restructuring)", in *Changjiang Zhengquan 2001 Nian Yanjiu Nianbao*, Beijing, 2001, pp. 330–337.

Bao Jingxuan, "Lun Woguo Zhengquan Jinguan Yu Zilu Tizhi Jiqi Wanshan (China's Securities Regulation and the Improvement of the Self-Discipline System)", *Fasheng Yanjiu*, No. 3, 1999, pp. 60–73.

Baum, R., *Burying Mao: Chinese Politics in the Age of Deng Xiaoping*, Princeton, NJ, Princeton University Press, 1994.

Cai Wenhai, "Private Securities Litigation in China: Of Prominence and Problems", *Columbia Journal of Asian Law*, Vol. 13, No. 1, 1999, pp. 135–51.

Cao Jianwen, *Zhongguo Gushi (The Chinese Stock Market)*, Beijing, Zhonghai Gongshang Lianhe Chubanshe, Beijing, 2000.

Chen Gong, *Zhongguo Zhengquan Fagui Zonghui (A Collection of China Securities Laws and Regulations)*, Beijing, Zhongguo Renmin Daxue, 1997.

Chen Xiangshui, "Shangshi Gongsi Guquan Jiegou (Listed company share structures)", *Zhengquan Shichang Daobao*, No. 4., 2000, pp. 34–41.

Chen Xiangyong and Huang Xueli, "Woguo Shangshi Gongsi Weituo Licai de Shizheng Fenxi (A Detailed Analysis of Listed Companies Using Asset Management Services)", in *Guotai Junan Zhengquan Yanjiusuo 2001 Nianbao*, Beijing, 2001, pp. 25–40.

Chen Yu, "Chonggou Woguo Zhengquan Shichang Jianguan Tizhi De Sikao (Thinking About Reorganising China's Securities Market Supervision System)", *Jingji Tizhi Gaige*, No. 3, 1998, pp. 114–117.

Chen Zhenrong, "Zhongguo Shangshi Gongsi zai Haiwai Shangshi (Domestically-listed Companies Listing Abroad)," *Ziben Shichang*, May 2002, pp. 49–53.

Chun, B., "A Brief Comparison of the Chinese and US Securities Regulations Governing Corporate Take-Overs", *Columbia Journal of Asian Law*, Vol. 12, No. 1, 1998, pp. 99–121.

Claessens, S., Djankov, S. and Klingebiel, D., "Stock markets in transitional economies", in *Financial Transition in Europe and Central Asia: Challenges of the New Decade*, Bokros, L. (ed.), Washington, DC, 2001, pp. 109–137.

Cui Huixia, "Zhengfu Jianguan Yu Zhengquan Shichang Yunzuo (Government Supervision and Securities Markets Supervision)", *Jingji Lilun yu Jingji Guanli*, No. 4, 1996, pp. 41–6.

Davis, L. and North, D., *Institutional Change and American Economic Growth*, Cambridge, Cambridge University Press, 1971.

Dong Shaoping, *Zhongguo Gushi Zhengce Yu Chaogu (Chinese Stock Market Policy and Speculation)*, Beijing, Jingji Guanli Chubanshe, 1997.

Dongfanggaosheng, "Zhongguo Goubingchao (China's Wave of M&A)", *Ziben Shichang*, No. 2, 2000, pp. 34–41.

Fewsmith, J., *China since Tiananmen: The Politics of Transition*, Cambridge, Cambridge University Press, 2001.

Fu Xiaomin, *Zhengquan Touzi Jijin (Securities Investment Funds)*, Beijing, Falu Chubanshe, 2000.

Girardin, E., *Banking Sector Reform and Credit Control in China*, Paris, OECD, 1997.

Green, S. and Wall, D., *The Challenges of Chinese Capital Market Liberalisation*, Report commissioned by the OECD, 2001.

Gregory, N., Tenev, S. and Wagel, D., *China's Emerging Private Enterprises: Prospects for the New Century*, Washington, International Finance Corporation, 2000.

Gu Mingde, "Zhongguo Zhengquan Shichang De Feidie Yu Zhentong (The Leaps and Throes of China's Stock Market)", *Caijing Yanjiu*, No. 10, pp. 3–11, 1993.

Guo Feng, *Zhongguo Zhengquan Jianguan Yu Lifa (China's Securities Supervision and Legislation)*, Beijing, Falu Chubanshe, 1999.

Hannan, K., *Industrial Change in China: Economic Restructuring & Conflicting Interests*, London, Routledge, 1998.

He Wei, "Zhengquan Guanli Tizhi Moshi Tantao (An Examination of the Style of the Securities Management System)", *Zhejiang Jinrong*, No. 3, pp. 18–20, 1998.

Hertz, E., *The Trading Crowd: An Ethnography of the Shanghai Stock Market*, Cambridge, Cambridge University Press, 1998.

Heytens, P. and Karacadag, C., *An Attempt to Profile the Finances of China's Enterprise Sector*, IMF Working Paper, Washington, DC, 2001.

Ho, K., *Demystifying China's QFII*, JP Morgan Securities (Asia Pacific), Hong Kong, December 2002.

Holz, C., "Economic Reforms and State Sector Bankruptcy in China", *The China Quarterly*, No. 166, 2001, pp. 342–67.

Hong Weilu, *Zhengquan Jianguan: Lilun Yu Shixian (Securities Regulation: Theory and Practice)*, Shanghai, Shanghai Caijing Daxue Chubanshe, 2000.

Hou Jixiong, "Shangshi Gongsi Shiji Suodeshuifu Yanjiu Ji Shou Suodeshuizhi Gaige de Yingxiang Fenxi (Research on the Tax Burden of Listed Companies and the Impact Upon Them of Tax Reform)", *Guotai Junan Jiguo Touzizhe*, March 2002, pp. 7-13.

Hu Bin, "2001 Nian Shangshi Gongsi Xianjinliu Fenxi (An Analysis of Listed Company Cash Flows)", *Huaxia Caijing Zhengquan Fenxi*, June 2002, pp. 38-45.

Hu Jizhi, *Zhongguo Gushi De Yanjin Yu Zhidu Bianqian (Institutional Change and Progress in China's Stock Market)*, Beijing, Jingji Kexue Chubanshe, 1999.

Hu Yebi, *China's Capital Market*, Hong Kong, Chinese University Press, 1993.

Hua Wannian, *Zhongguo Gushi: Zhengce Shi (China's Share Market: Policy Market)*, Beijing, Zhongguo Duiwai Fanxuan Chuban Gongsi, 1999.

Huang Yasheng, *Inflation & Investment Controls in China: The Political Economy of Centre-Local Relations During the Reform Era*, New York, Cambridge University Press, 1996.

Huang Yuncheng and Gao Xiaozhen (eds), *Zhongguo Zhengquan Shichang (The Chinese Securities Market)*, Wuhan, Hubei Renmin Chubanshe, 1999d.

Jefferson, G., Rawski, T., Li Wang and Yuxin Zheng, "Ownership, productivity change and financial performance in Chinese industry", *Journal of Comparative Economics*, No. 28, 2000, pp. 786-813.

Jiang Xiaowei, "Guanyu Zhengquanfa Shichang Jianguan De Tansuo (An Exploratory Study of Supervision of the Securities Markets)", *Zhongguo Renmin Daxue Xuebao*, No. 4, 1999, pp. 19-24.

Jin Dehuai, *Dangdai Zhongguo Zhengquan Shichang (The Contemporary Chinese Securities Market)*, Shanghai, Shanghai Caijing Daxue Chubanshe, 1999.

Kumar, A. et al., *China's Non-Bank Financial Institutions: Trust and Investment Companies*, Washington DC, World Bank, 1997.

Kumar, A. et al., *China's Emerging Capital Markets*, Hong Kong, FT Financial Publishing Asia Pacific, 1997.

Lardy, N., *China's Unfinished Economic Revolution*, Washington, DC, Brookings Institution, 1998.

Lardy, N., *The Challenge of Bank Restructuring in China*, CLSA Emerging Markets, 2000.

Lardy, N., *Integrating China into the Global Economy*, Washington, DC, Brookings Institution, 2002.

Li Jiange, "Zhongguo Qiye Gaige He Gupiao Shichang Fazhan (The Reform of Enterprises and the Development of the Stock Market in China)", *Gaige*, No. 6, 1996, pp. 9-15.

Li Zhangjiang, *Zhongguo Zhengquan Shichang Lishi Yu Fazhan (The History and Development of China's Securities Market)*, Beijing, Zhongguo Wuzhi Chubanshe, 1998.

Lieberthal, K. and Oksenberg, M., *Policy Making in China: Leaders, Structure & Processes*, Princeton, Princeton University Press, 1988.

Liu, G. and Pei, S., *The Class of Shareholdings and its Impacts on Corporate Performance*, Working Paper, Brunel University, 2002.

Liu Jia, "Shei Zhiyue Le Qiye Zhaiquan? (Who Restricts Enterprise Debt?)", *Ziben Shichang*, August 2000, pp. 26-29.

Liu Jin and Nan An, *Zhongguo Gushi Neimu, 1984–1997* (*The Inside Story of China's Stock Market, 1984–1997*), Beijing, Bingqi Gongye Chubanshe, 1997.

Naughton, B., *Growing out of the Plan: Chinese Economic Reform, 1978–1993*, Cambridge, Cambridge University Press, 1995.

Neoh, A., *The Chinese Domestic Capital Markets at the Dawn of the New Millennium*, Beijing, Beijing University (mimeo), 2000.

Nolan, P., *China and the Global Business Revolution*, Basingstoke, Palgrave, 2001.

OECD, *Reforming China's Enterprises*, Paris, OECD, 2000.

Qian Yingyi and Xu Chenggang, "Why China's Economic Reform Differ: The M-Form Hierarchy and Entry/Expansion of the Non-State Sector", *Economics of Transition*, Vol. 1, No. 2, 1993, pp. 135–70.

Qin Xiaoqing, "Jinliangnian Guanyu Gufenzhi Wenti Guandian Zongshu (A Summary of the Issues of the Share-Holding System in the Last Two Years)", *Gaige*, No. 3, 1991, pp. 59–65.

Ren Zhengde, *Zhongguo Zhengquan Daquan* (*A Comprehensive Handbook to Chinese Securities*), Beijing, Xinhua Chubanshe, 1996.

Saich, T., *Governance and Politics of China*, Basingstoke, Palgrave, 2001.

Steinfeld, E., *Forging Reform in China: The Fate of State-Owned Industry*, Cambridge, Cambridge University Press, 1998.

Studwell, J., *The China Dream: The Elusive Quest for the Greatest Untapped Market on Earth*, London, Profile Books, 2002.

Tang Dingzhong, "B-gu Gongsi Baogao Kuaiji Lirun Jingneiwai Chayi-xianzhuang yu Chengyin (Explaining the Difference in Profitability in the Domestic and Foreign Accounts of B-share Companies)", in *Guotai Junan Zhengquan Yanjiusuo 2001 Nianjian*, Beijing, 2001, pp. 39–46.

Teweles, S., *The Stock Market*, New York, John Wiley & Sons, 1998.

Tenev, S. and Zhang, C., *Corporate Governance and Enterprise Reform in China: Building the Institutions of Modern Markets*, Washington, DC, World Bank and IFC, 2002.

Tung, R., "Possible Developments of Mainland China's Private Enterprises", *Issues & Studies*, Vol. 133, No. 6, 1997, pp. 61–6.

Vogel, S., *Free Markets, More Rules: Regulatory Reform in Advanced Industrial Countries*, Ithaca, Cornell University Press, 1996.

Wall, D., *Collective Investment Schemes & Their Relevance to the Development of Capital Markets in China*, London, Royal Institute of International Affairs (mimeo), 1995.

Walter, C. and Howie, F., *'To Get Rich Is Glorious!' China's Stock Markets in the 1980s and 1990s*, Chippenham, Palgrave, 2001.

Wang Aijian, "Jiuwu De Qiwoguo Zhengquan Shichang Fazhan Fangxiang (The Developing Trend of China's Securities Markets During the Ninth Five Year Plan)", *Caimao Janjiu*, No. 2, 1996, pp. 32–7.

Wang Lianzhou and Li Cheng, *Fengfeng Yuyu Zhengquanfa* (*The Trials and Hardships of the Securities Law*), Shanghai, Sanlian Shudian, 2000.

Wang Xiyi, *Shenzhen Gushi De Jueqi Yu Yunzuo* (*The Rise and Operations of the Shenzhen Stock Market*), Shenzhen, Zhongguo Jinrong Chubanshe, 1992.

Wang Zuzhi, "Zhengquanfa De Chutai Shi Dang Wuzhiji (The Implementation of the Securities Law Is a Burning Issue)", *Xiandai Faxue*, No. 1, 1996c, p. 90.

Wei Gang and Zheng Xia, "Woguo Shangshi Gongsi Bu Fenpei Xianxiang De Shizheng Fenxi (An Analysis of Chinese Listed Companies' Non-Allocation of Dividends)", *Zhengquan Shichang Daoban*, No. 5, 1998, pp. 27-9.

Wei Xingyun, "Shangshi Gongsi Gupiao Jiage yu Yingli Zhijian Guanxi de Shizheng Yanjiu (A Detailed Research on the Relationship Between Listed Company Profits and Share Prices)", *Guotai Junan Zhengquan Tonxun*, December 2001, pp. 3-12.

Wen Zhongyu, *Zhengquan Changwai Jiaoyi De Lilun Yu Shiwu (The Theory and Practice of Off-Exchange Securities Trading)*, Beijing, Renmin Daxue Chubanshe, 1998.

World Bank, *China: The Emerging Capital Market, Volume I*, Washington, DC, World Bank, 1995.

World Bank, *China 2020. Old Age Security: Pension Reform in China*, Washington DC, World Bank, 1997.

Wu Jinglian, *Wu Jinglian: Shinian Fenyun Jiang Gushi (Wu Jinglian: Ten Years of Talking About the Stock Market)*, Shanghai, Shanghai Yuandong Chuanbanshe, 2001.

Wu Xiaoqiu (ed.), *Jianli Gongzheng De Shichang Chengxu Yu Touzizhe Liyi Baohu (Establishing a Just Market Order and Protecting the Rights of Investors)*, Beijing, Zhongguo Renmin Daxue, 1999.

Xia Mei, J.H. Lin *et al.*, *The Re-emerging Securities Market in China*, Westport, CN, Quorum Books, 1992.

Xia T., "The Shanghai Exchange Scandal and Chinese Bond Law", *Columbia Journal of Asian Law*, No. 10, 1996, pp. 281-303.

Xiao Lijian, 1990-1999 Nian Zhongguo Shenhu Gushi Jiaohushu He Gupiao Jiaoyi Qingkuang Huibian (A Review of the Index and Trading Situation of the Shenzhen and Shanghai Stock Markets 1990-1999), Shenzhen, Shenzhen Stock Exchange, 2000.

Xiao Yu, *Zhongguo Guozhai Shichang: Fazhan, Bijiao Yu Qianzhan (China's Treasury Bond Market: Development, Comparison and the Future)*, Beijing, Shehui Kexue Wenkuan Chubanshe, 2000.

Xu Cheng K., "The Micro-Structure of the Chinese Stock Market", *Issues and Studies*, Vol. 11, 2000, pp. 79-97.

Xu Ping, "Gaobie Qiongminyuan (Goodbye Qiongminyuan)", *Caijing*, No. 5, 1999, pp. 37-8.

Xu Xiaofeng, "Cong Caizheng Jinrong Zhengce Jaiodu Tan Wanshan Difang Zhengquan Shichang (On the Perfection of Local Stock Markets from the Perspective of Public Finance)", *Fudan Xuebao*, No. 5, 1990, pp. 12-15.

Yang Chengchang and Yang Dali, "Woguo Zhengquan Jiaoyi Yinhuashui De Gaige Silu (Thoughts About Reforming China's Securities Stamp Tax)", *Zhengquanye*, No. 3, 2001, pp. 24-9.

Yao, C., *Stock Markets and Futures Markets in the People's Republic of China*, Oxford, Oxford University Press, 1998.

You, J., *China's Enterprise Reform: Changing State/Society Relations after Mao*, London, Routledge, 1998.

Yuan Dong, "Zhongguo Gupiao Shichang De Jianguan Banfa (The Supervisory Method of China's Securities Market)", *Zhongguo Jingji Wenti*, No. 5, 1997, pp. 25–30.

Zhang Ling, "Guifanhua Shi Zhengquan Shichang Lishi Fazhan De Biran (The Standardisation of the Securities Markets Is an Inevitable Historical Development)", *Touzi yu Zhengquan*, No. 6, 1997, pp. 53–5.

Zhang Yilei and Thomas, W., "Operational Mechanisms and Characteristics of China's Primary and Secondary Stock Markets", *Journal of Asian Business*, Vol. 15, No. 1, 1999, pp. 49–65.

Zhang Yujun, *Zhongguo Zhengquan Shichang Fazhan De Zhidu Fenxi (An Institutional Analysis of the Development of the Chinese Securities Market)*, Beijing, Jingji Kexue Chubanshe, 1998.

Zhang Yujun (ed.), *Shenzhen Zhengquan Jiaoyisuo Disanjie Huiyuan Yanjiu Chengguo Pingxuan (A Selection of the Research Results of the Shenzhen Stock Exchange's Third Members Meeting)*, Shenzhen, Zhongguo Jinrong Chubanshe, 2000.

Zhang Yurun, "Lun Woguo Zhengquan Jiandu Tizhi De Gaige (A Discussion of the Reform of China's Securities Supervision Structure)", *Hebei Faxue*, No. 2, 1999, pp. 33–5.

Zhao Haikuan, "Jianlun Zhengquan Jiaoyisuo (A Short Discussion of Securities Markets)", *Jinrong Yanjiu*, No. 3, 1987, pp. 37–9.

Zhao Xiaoping *et al.*, *Zhongguo Gushi: Dakuorang, Dajishu (China's Stock Market: Large Expansion, Large Opportunity)*, Beijing, Zhongguo Caizheng Jingji Chubanshe, 1998.

Zhao Yipin, "Woguo Qiye Faxing Gupiao De Ruogan Falu Wenti (Some Legal Problems to Do with Chinese Enterprises Issuing Shares)", *Jinrong Yanjiu*, No. 2, 1985, pp. 29–32.

Zhen Yan, "Cong Hongguangan Kan Xinxi Pilu Bushi De Mushi Zeren (Lessons from the Hongguang Case)", *Zhengquan Shichang*, No. 1, 1999, pp. 24–30.

Zheng Zhong and Chen, Kexiong, *Zhongguo Di Yi Gu: Shenyin Shinian Fengyunlu (China's First Share: A Record of Ten Years of Rapid Change at Shenyin)*, Shanghai, Xueshu Chubanshe, 1994.

Zhou Xiaochuan and Zhu, Li, "China's Banking System: Current Status, Perspectives on Reform", *Journal of Comparative Economics*, Vol. 11, 1987, pp. 399–409.

Zhou Zhenqing, *Zhengquan Zhishi Duben (A Reader of Securities Knowledge)*, Beijing, Zhongguo Jinrong Chubanshe, 1998.

Zhou Zongan, "Zhongguo Zhengquan Jianguan Cunzai De Wenti (The Current Problems of China's Securities Market Regulation)", *Touzi yu Zhengquan*, January 2000, pp. 14–18.

Zhu Baoxian, "Xianjin Fenhong Qianxi (A Brief Analysis of Cash Dividends)", *Ziben Shichang*, January 2002, pp. 59–61.

Zhu Caosheng, "Maike Shangshi, Jieguan Chengxie Yu Shangshi Gongsi Kuisun (Buying Listed Shell Companies and Loss-Making Listed Companies)", *Touzi yu Zhengquan*, No. 5, 2001, pp. 89–94.

Zou Yang, "Dangqian Gupiao Shichangzhong De Zhengfu Ganyu (Governmental Interference in Today's Stock Market)", *Caijing Wenti Yanjiu*, No. 6, 1997, pp. 73–6.

Index